150 Amazing Mandalas
Coloring Book
For Adults

LILY LOVELACE

To my Family

Hello!

I'm _LiLy Lovelace_, full-time wedding photographer.
I love to color and drawing mandalas: they help me both develop creativity and cultivate spirituality.

Welcome to the Magic World of Mandalas,
I'm sure you'll enjoy it!

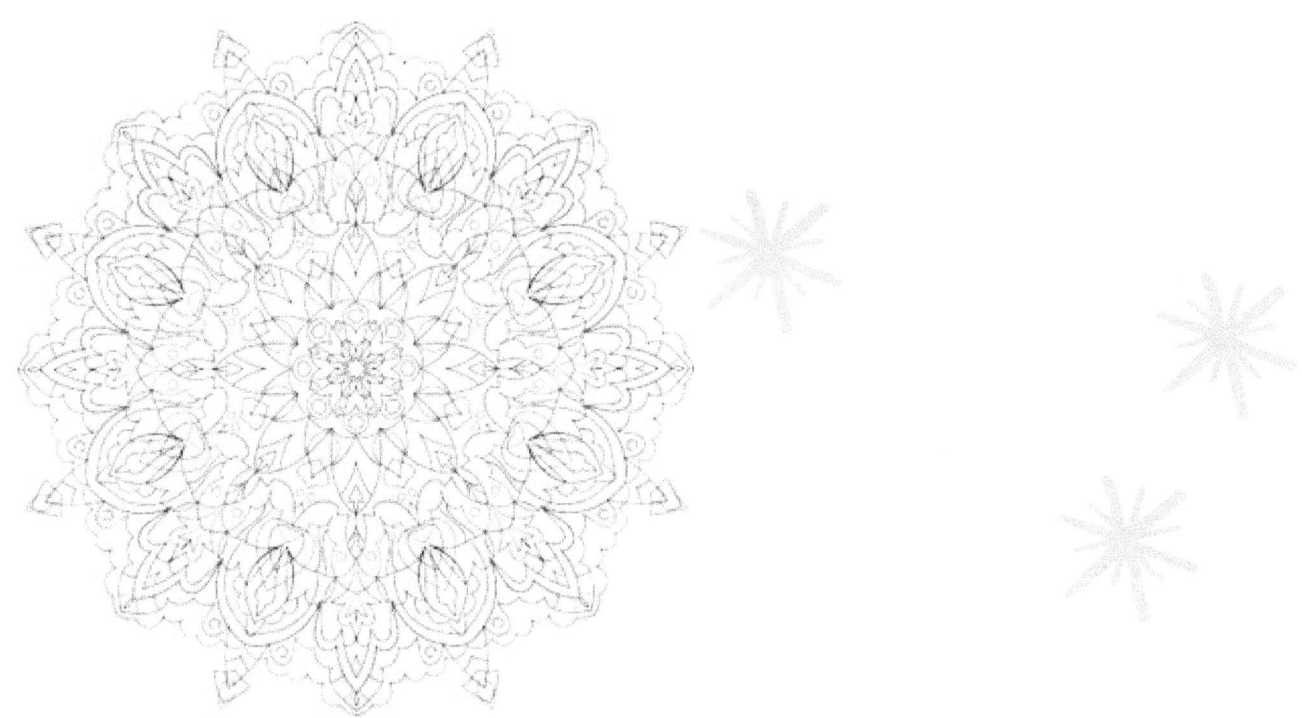

This Book Belongs To:

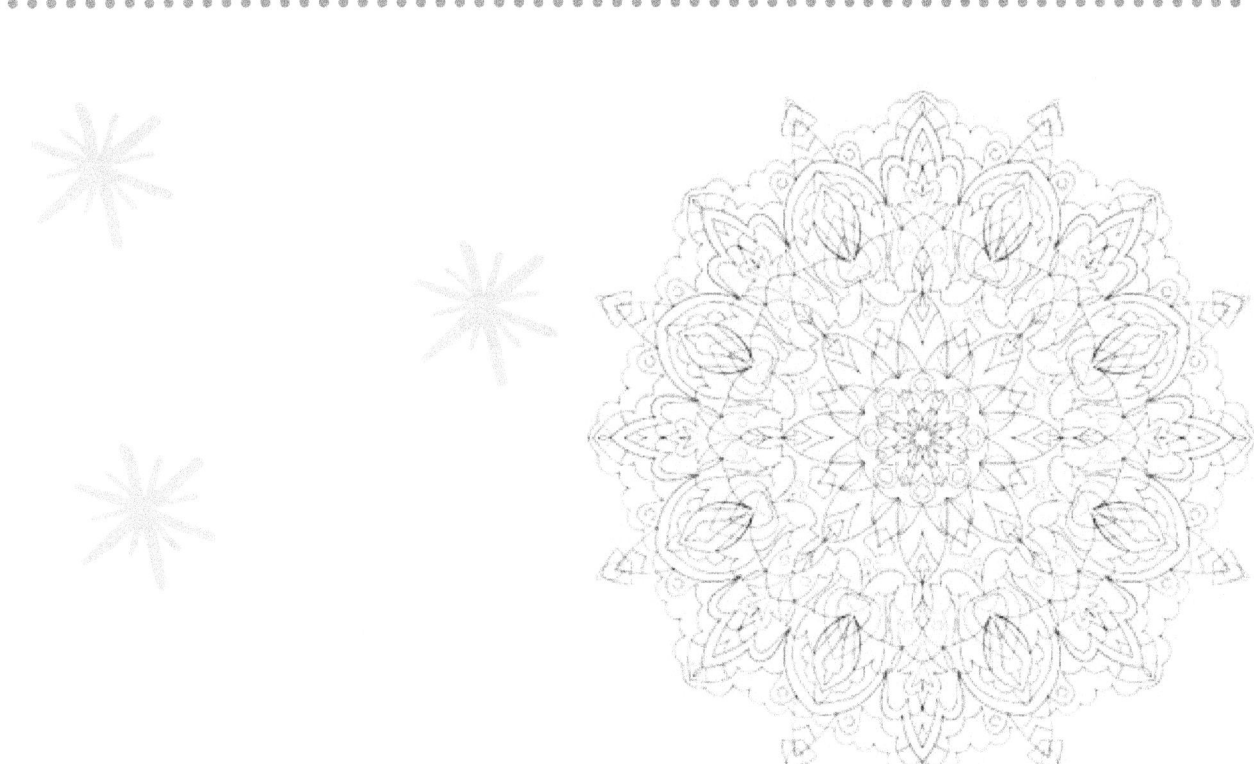

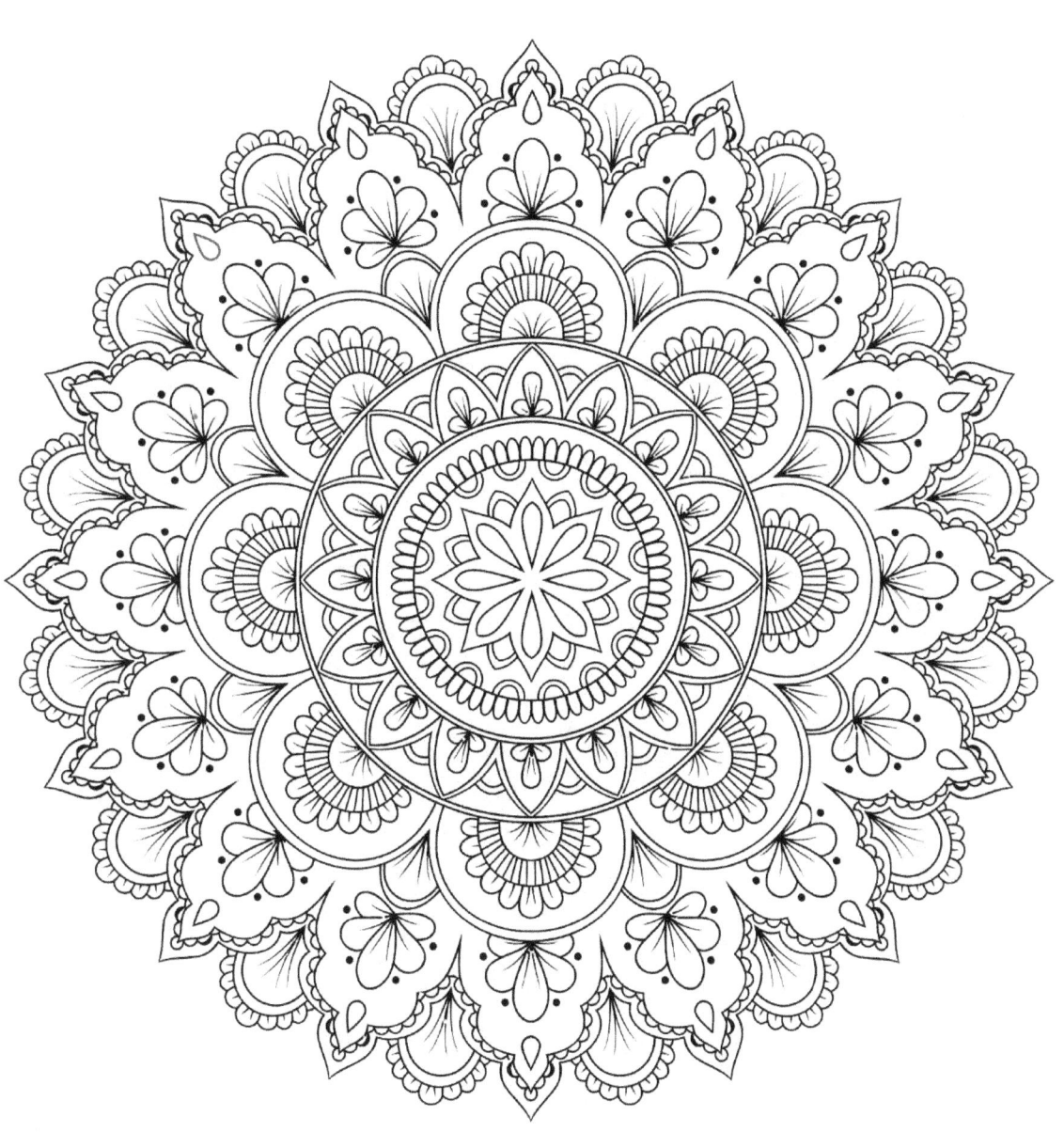

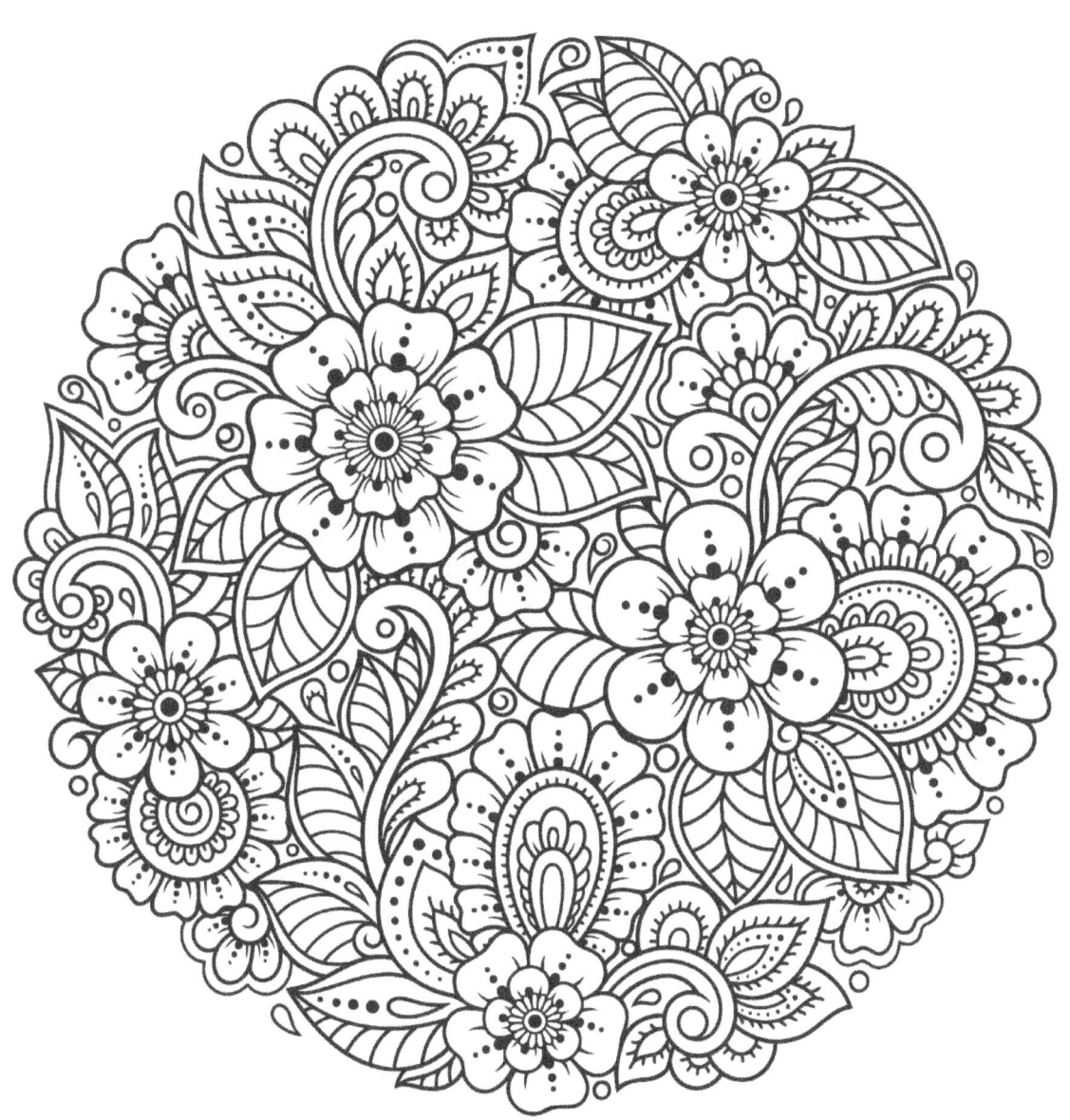

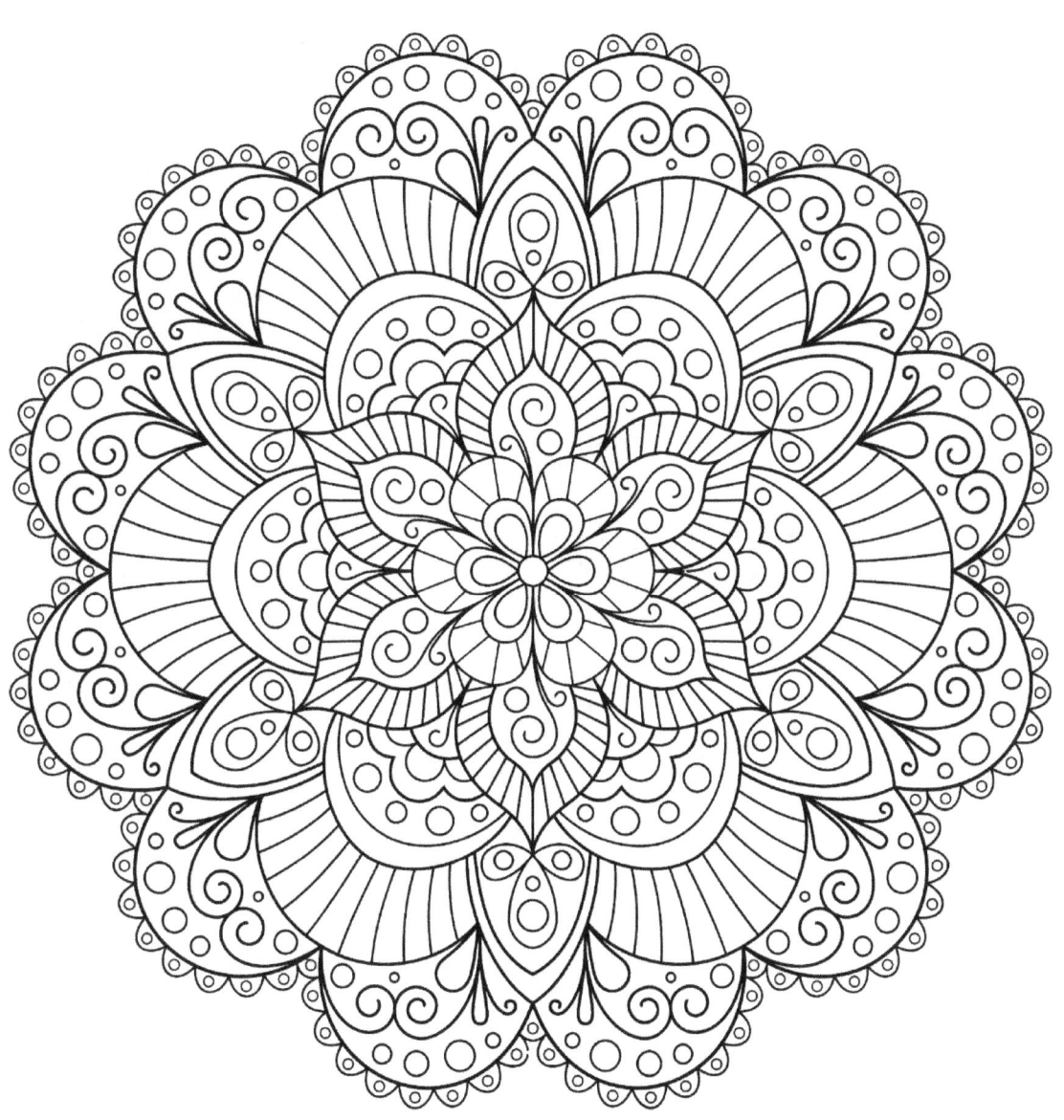

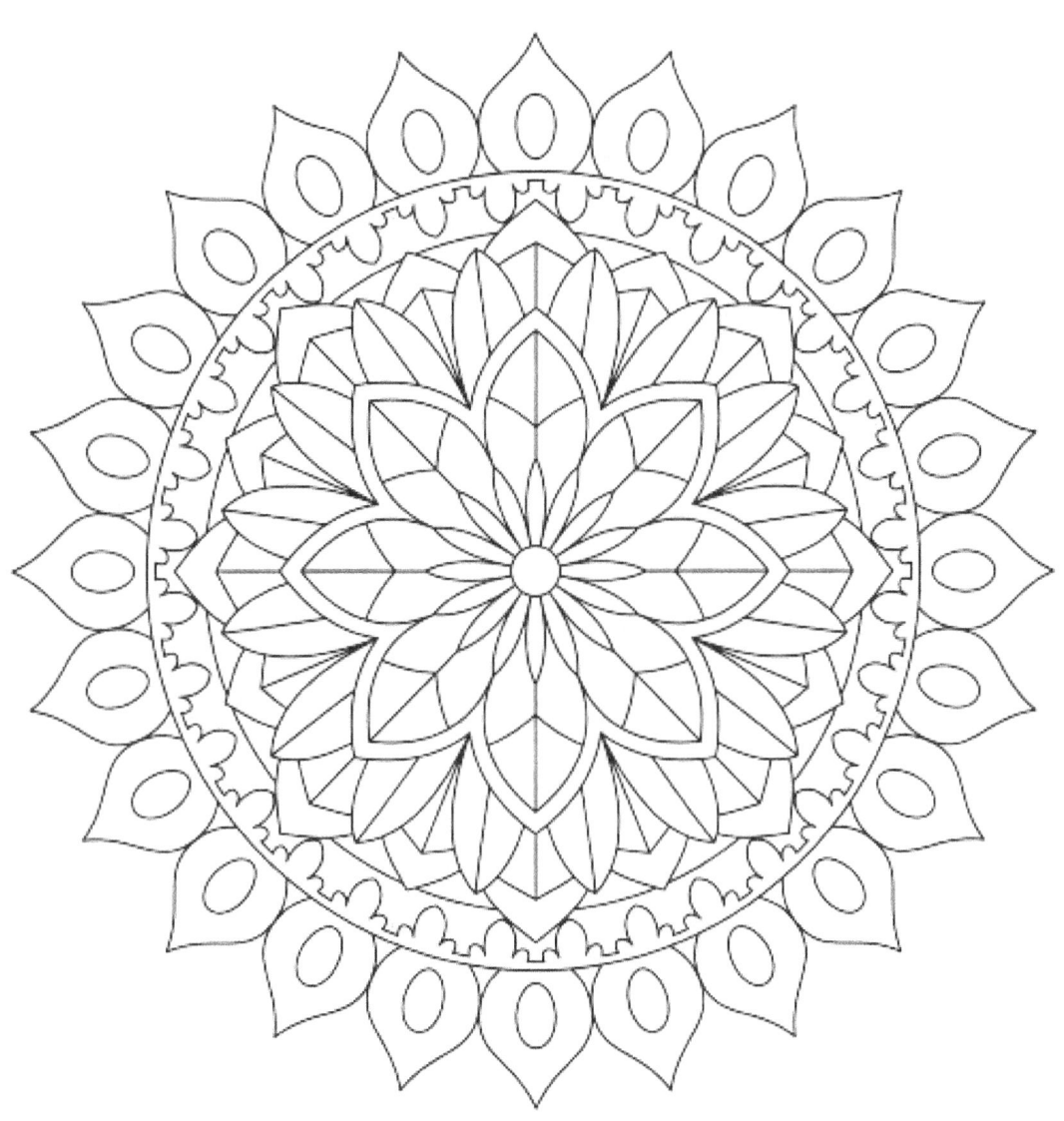

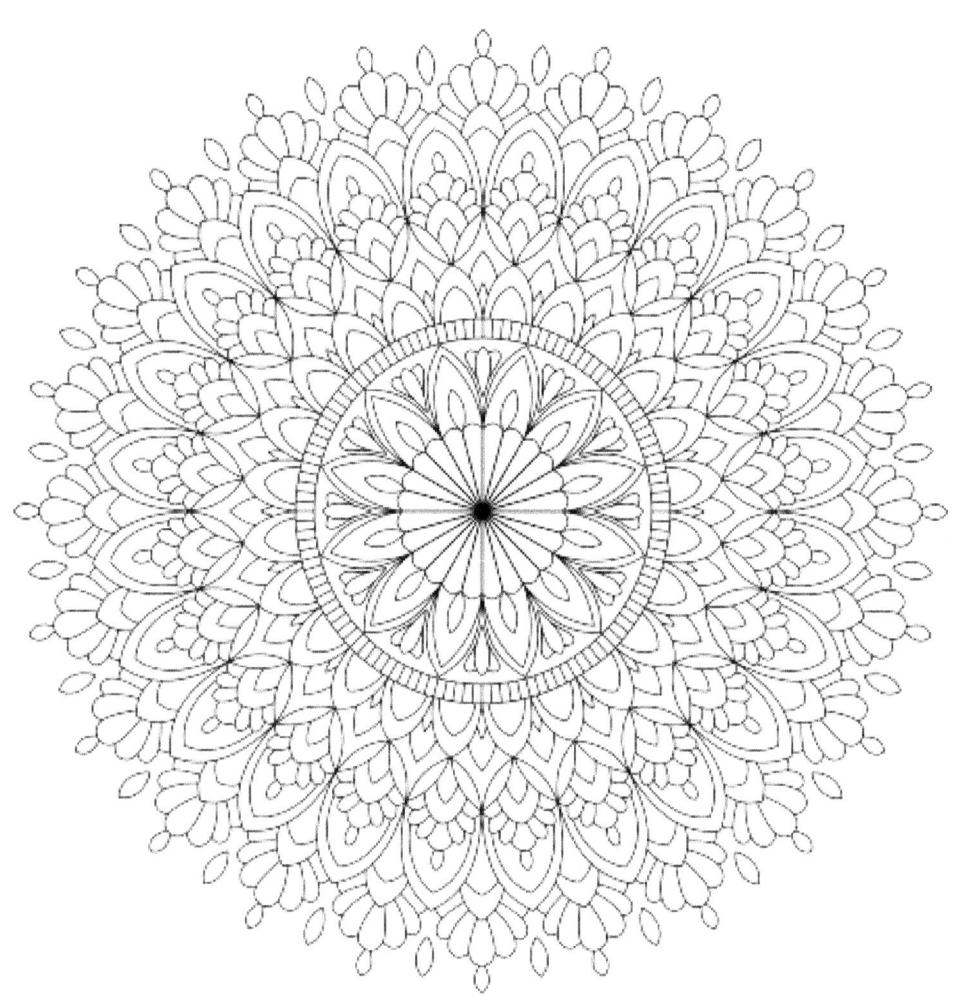

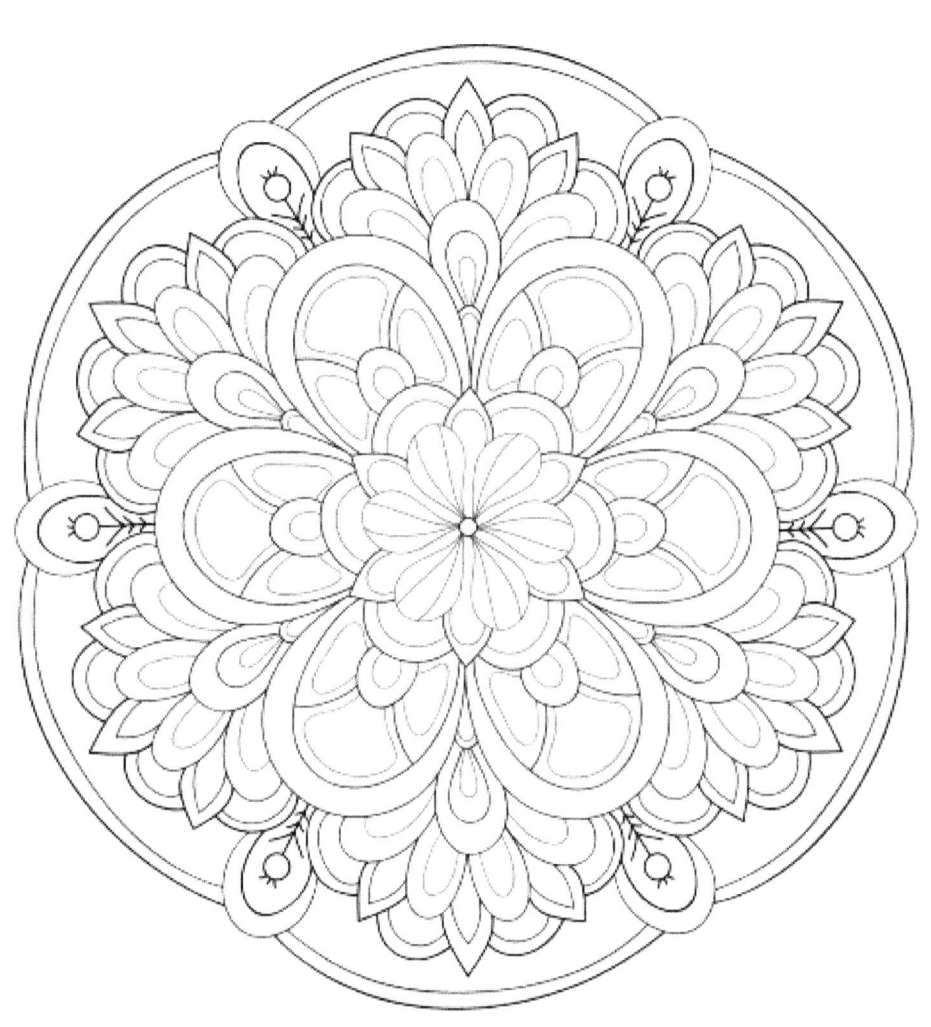

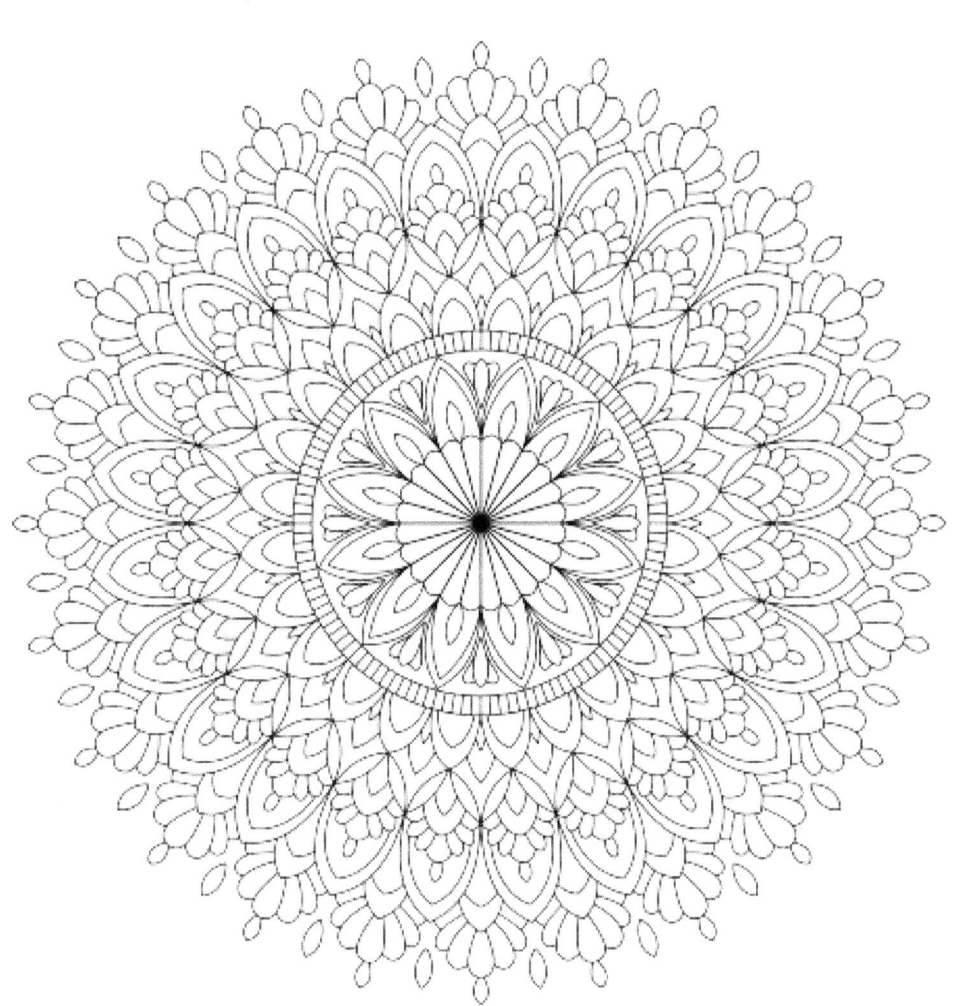

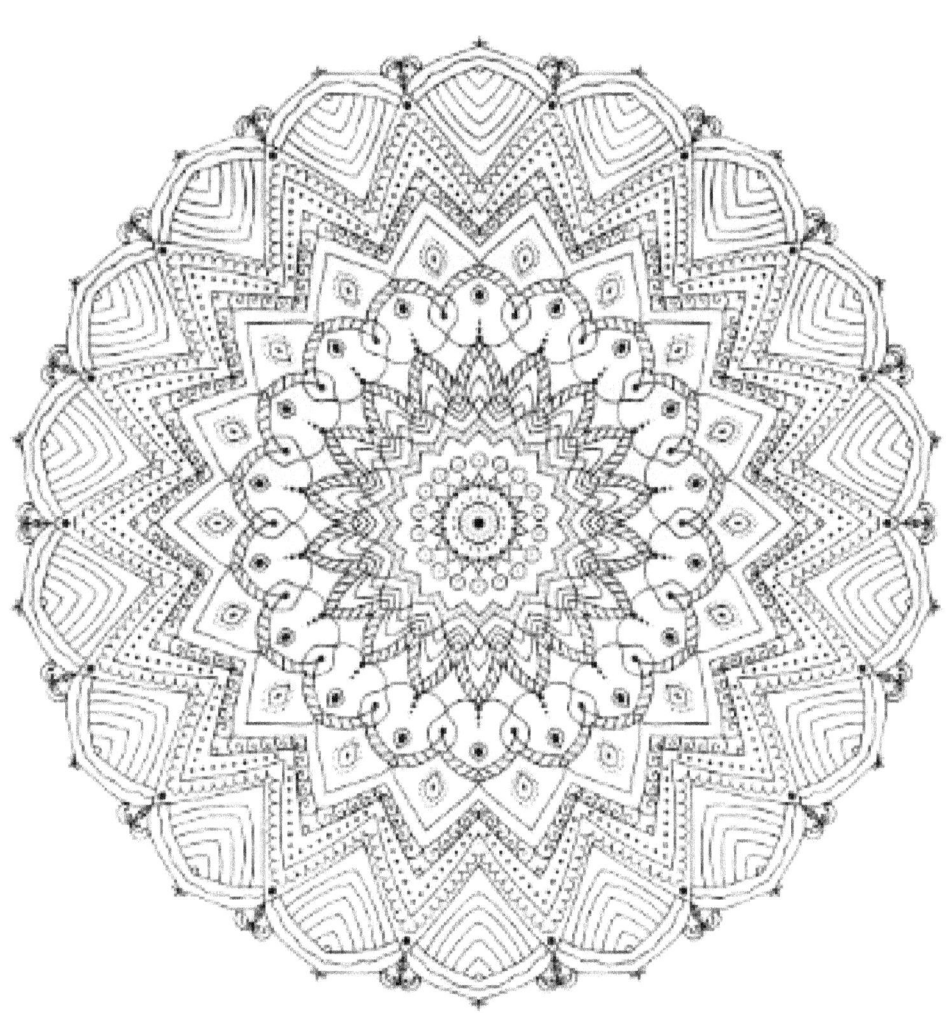

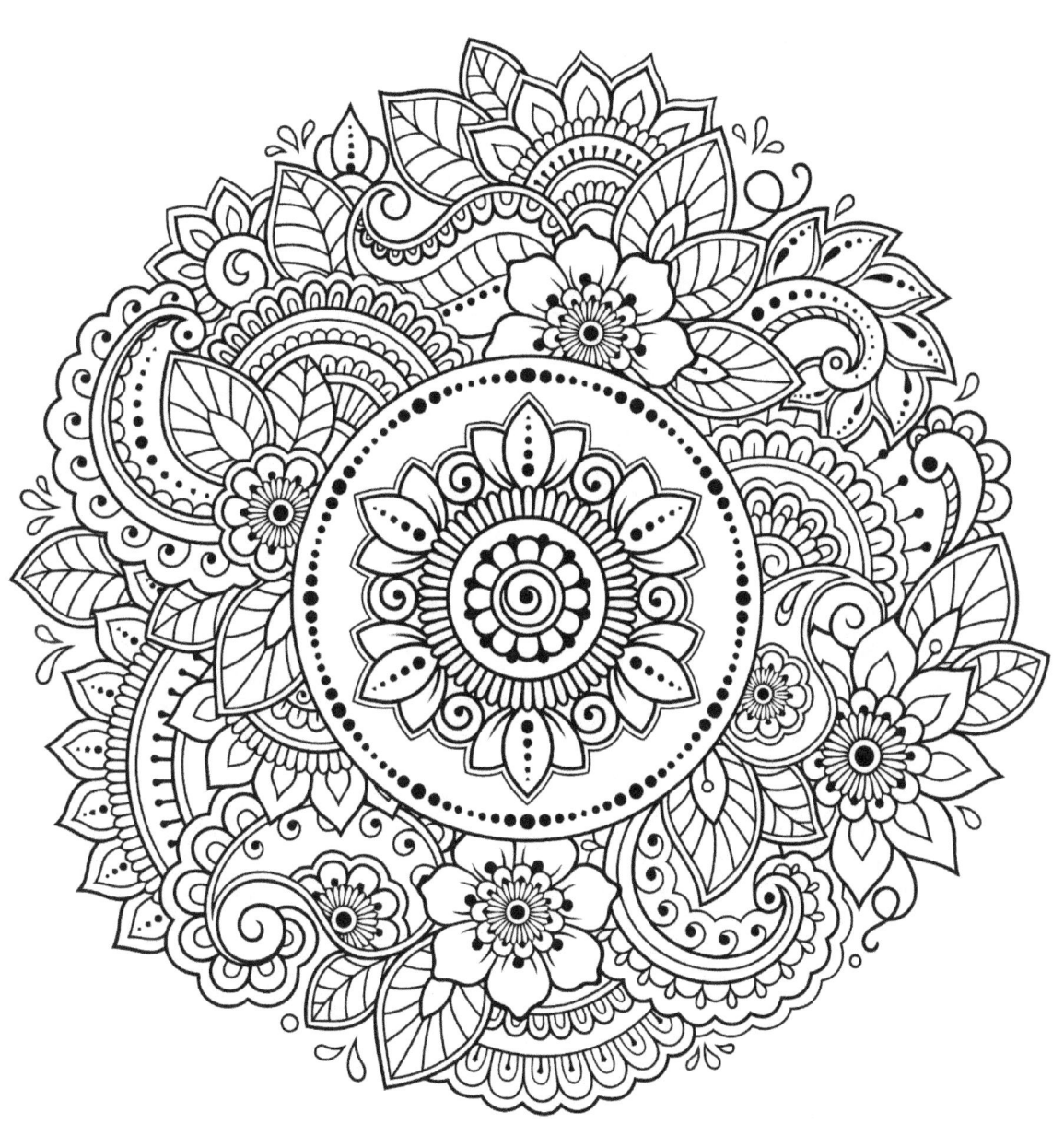

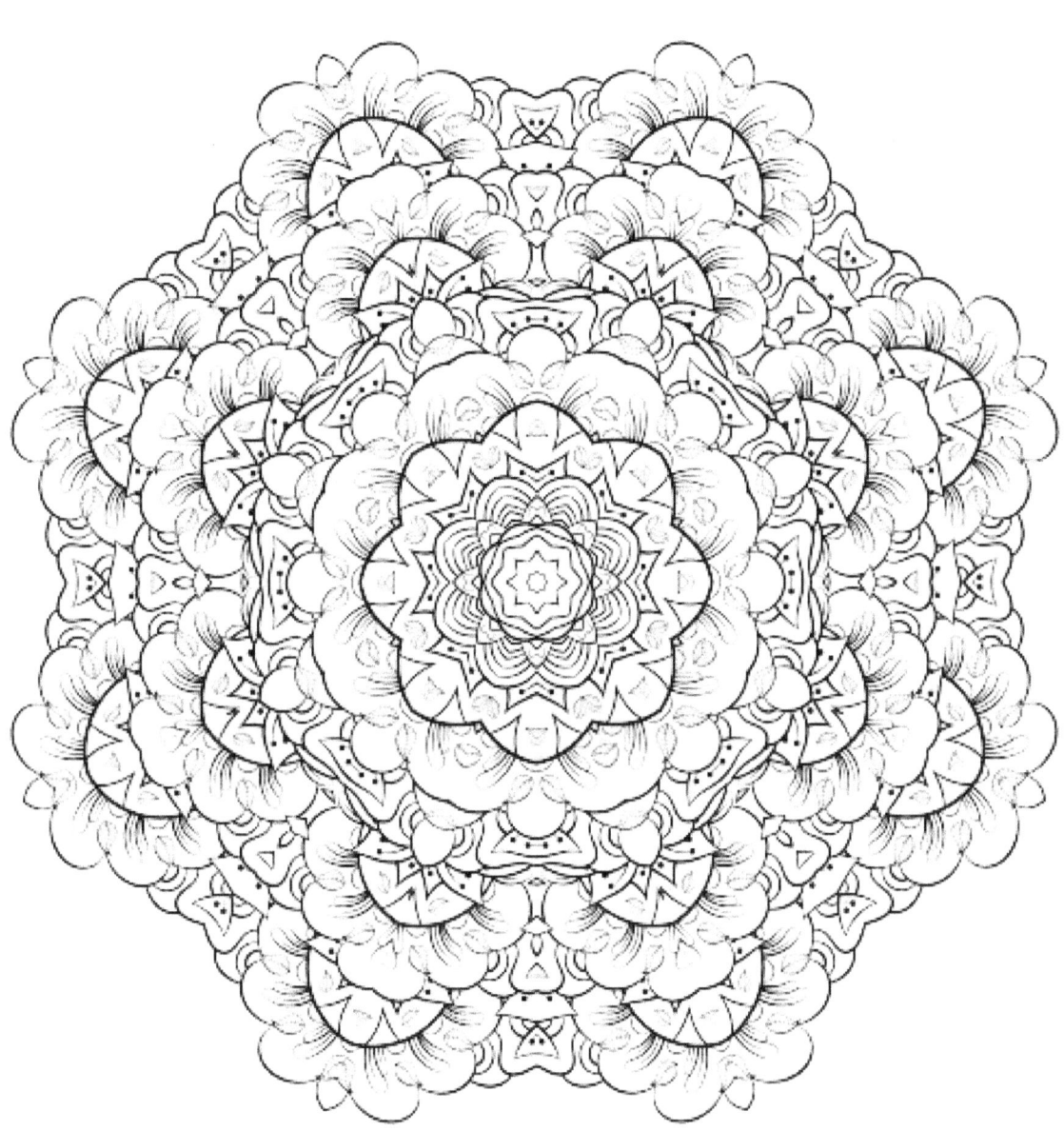

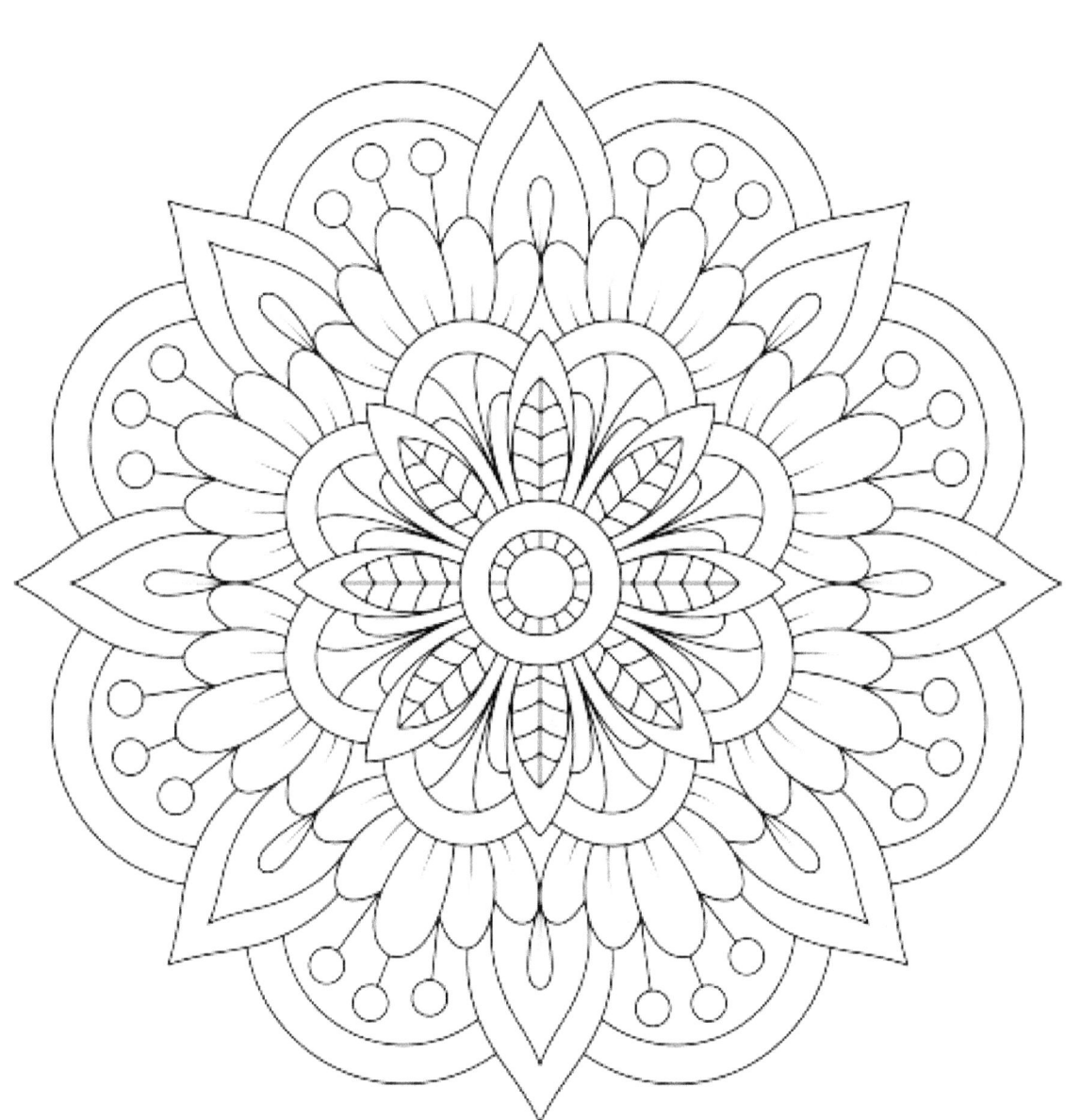

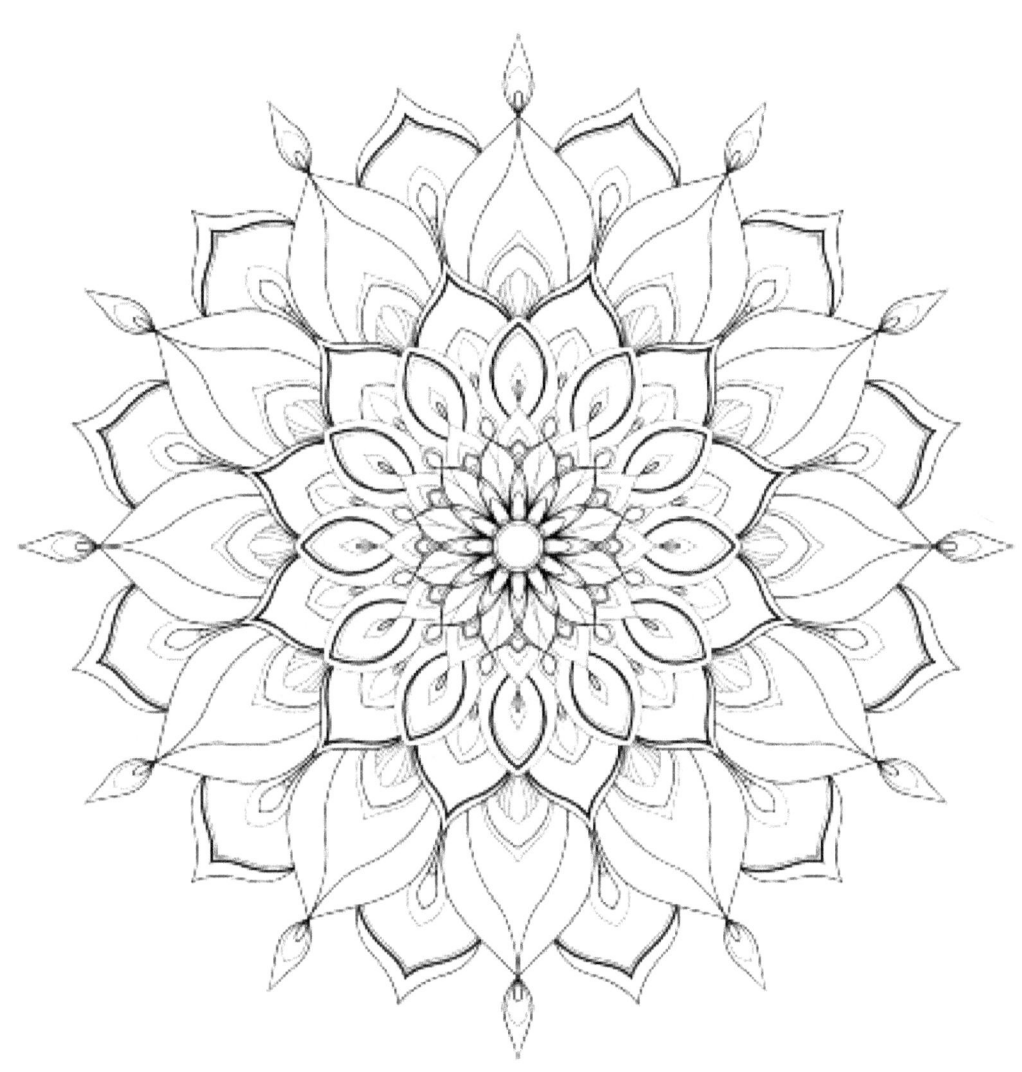

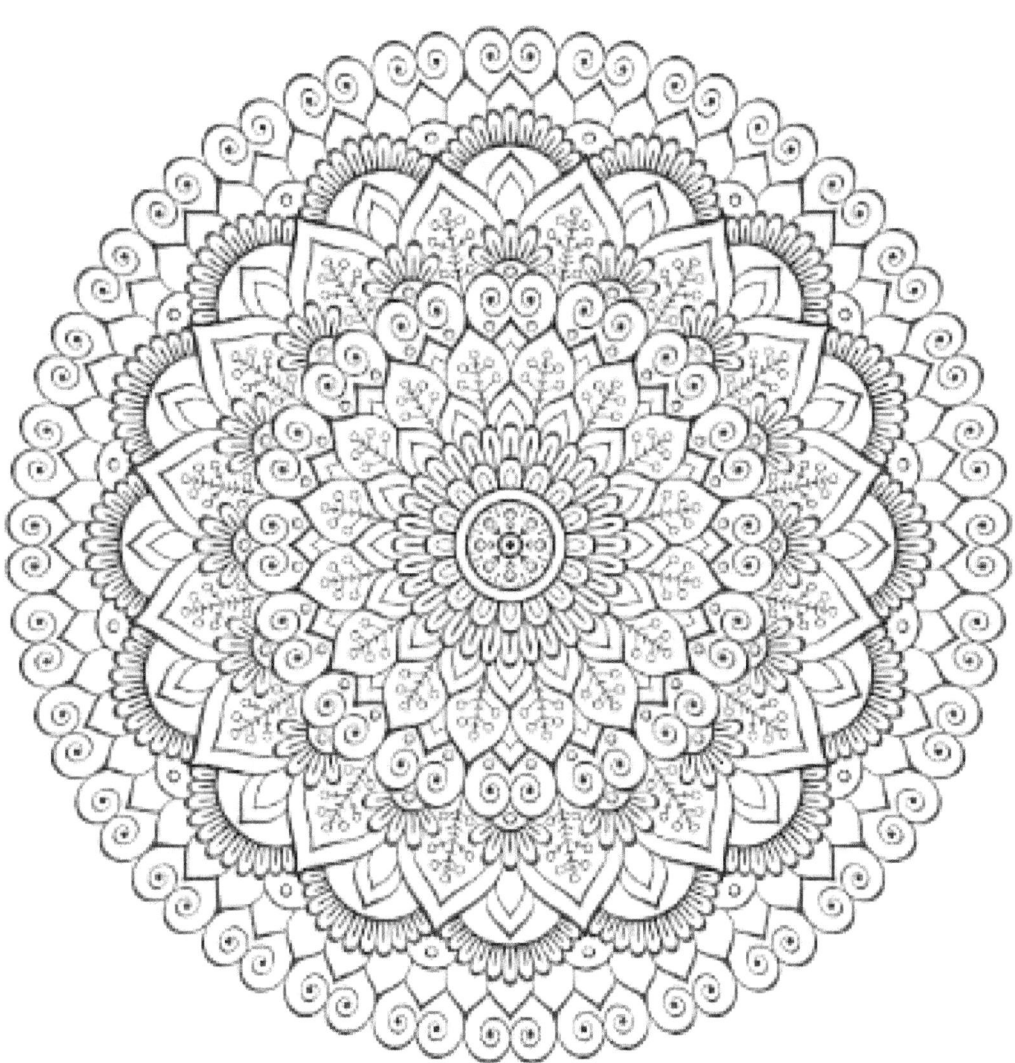

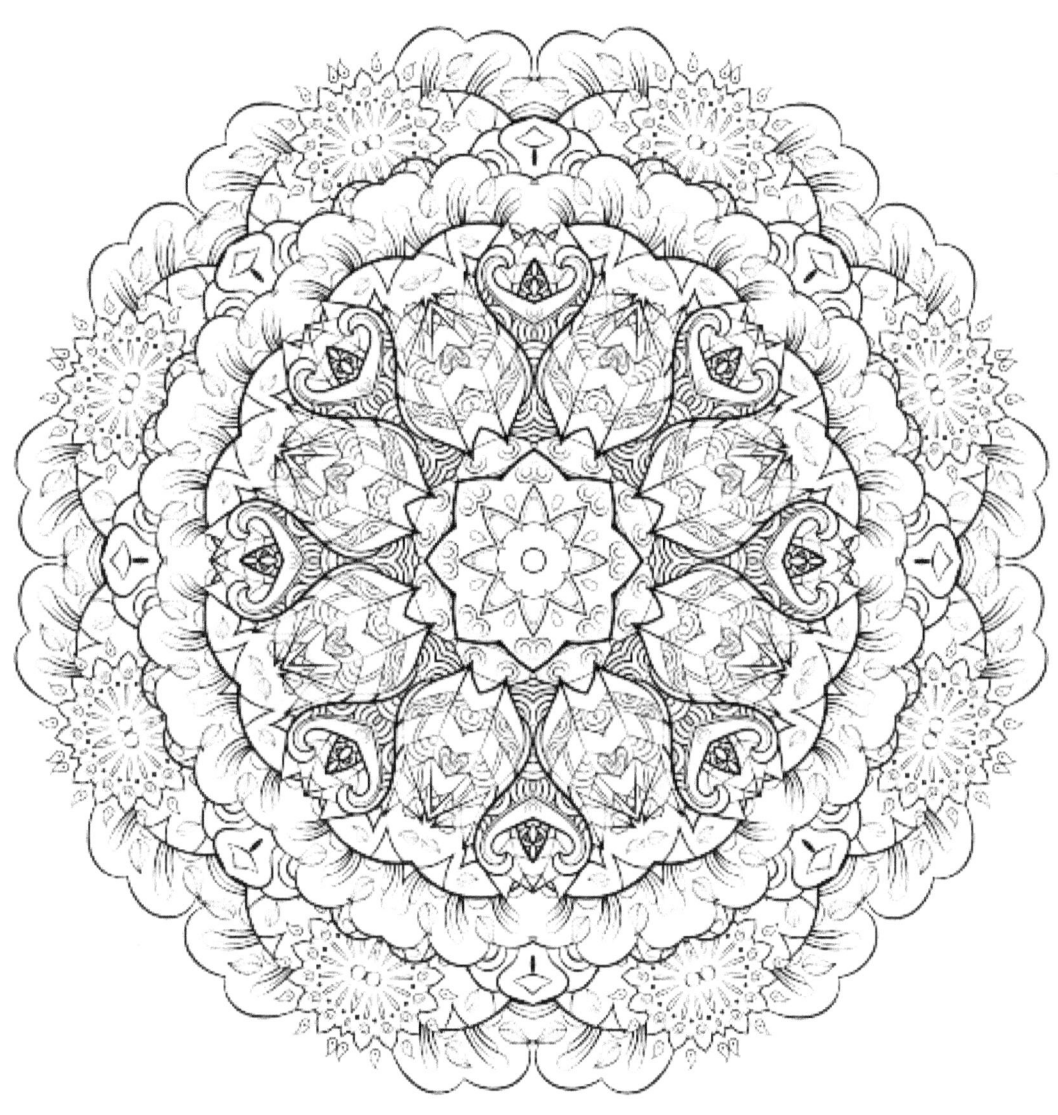

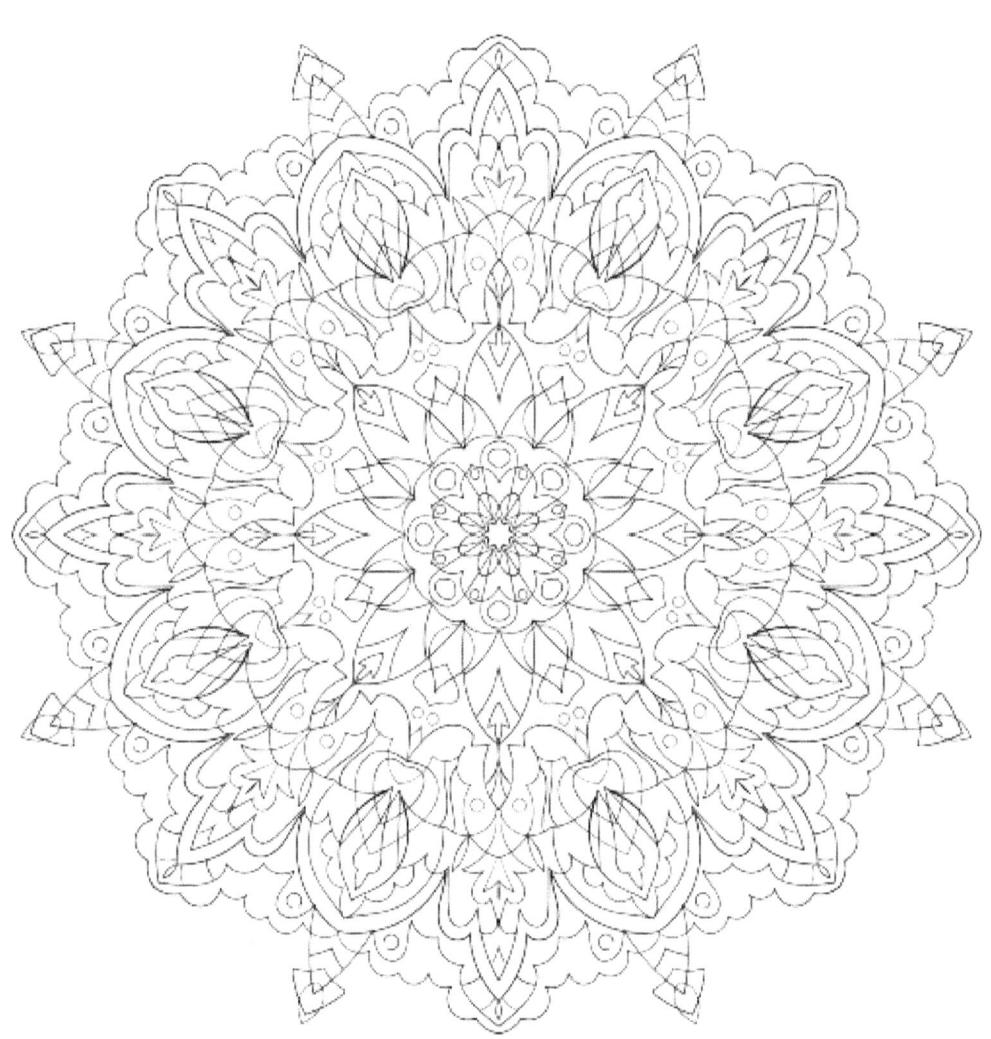

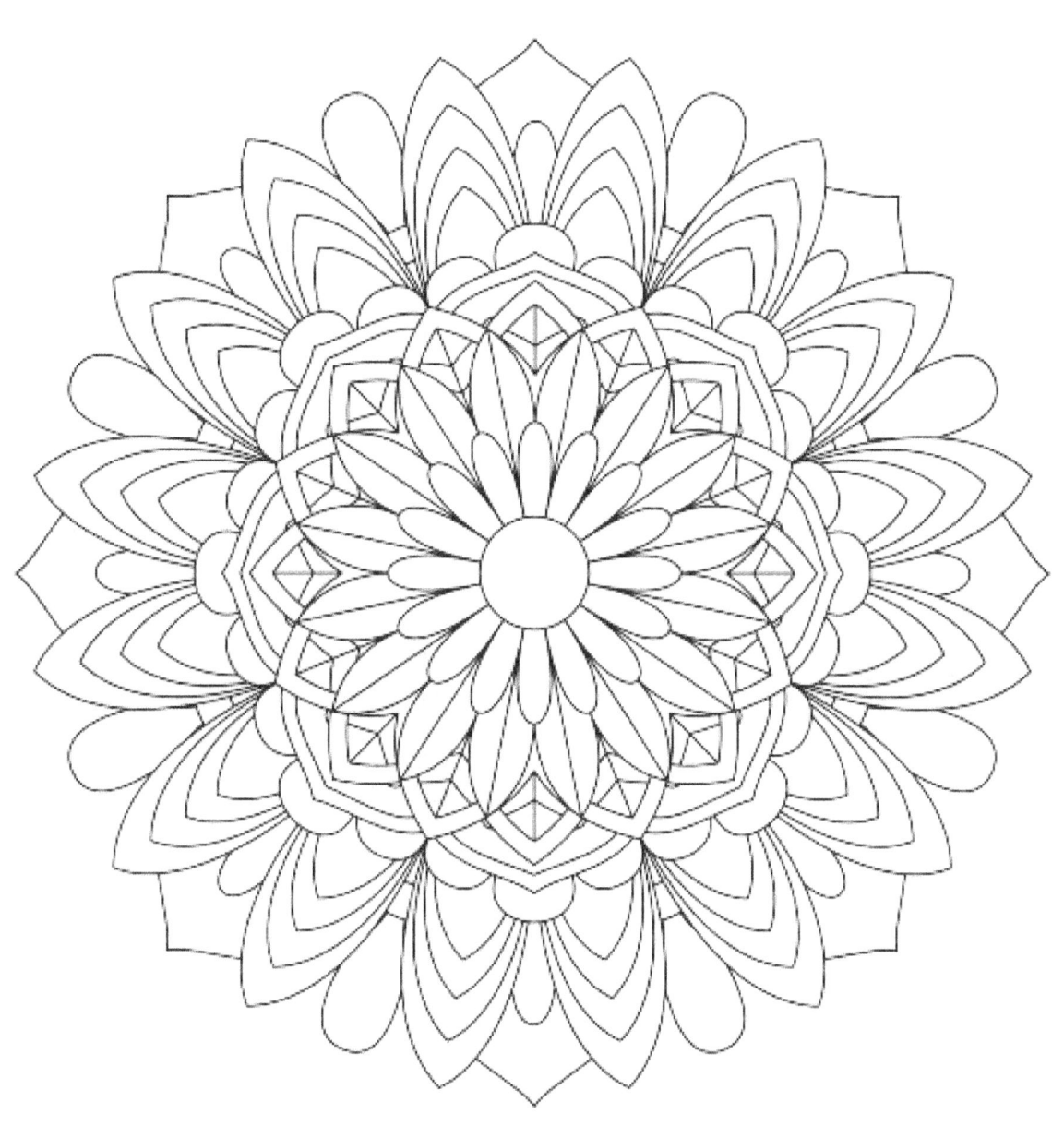

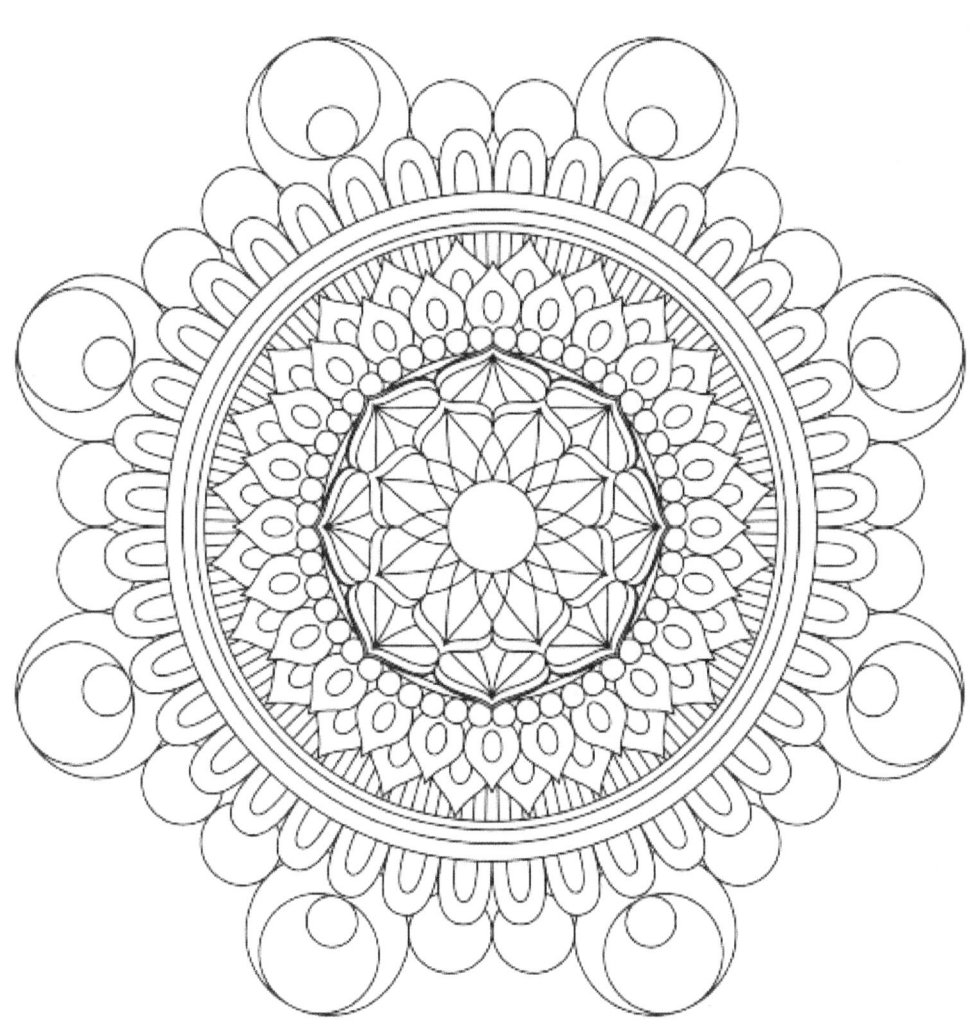

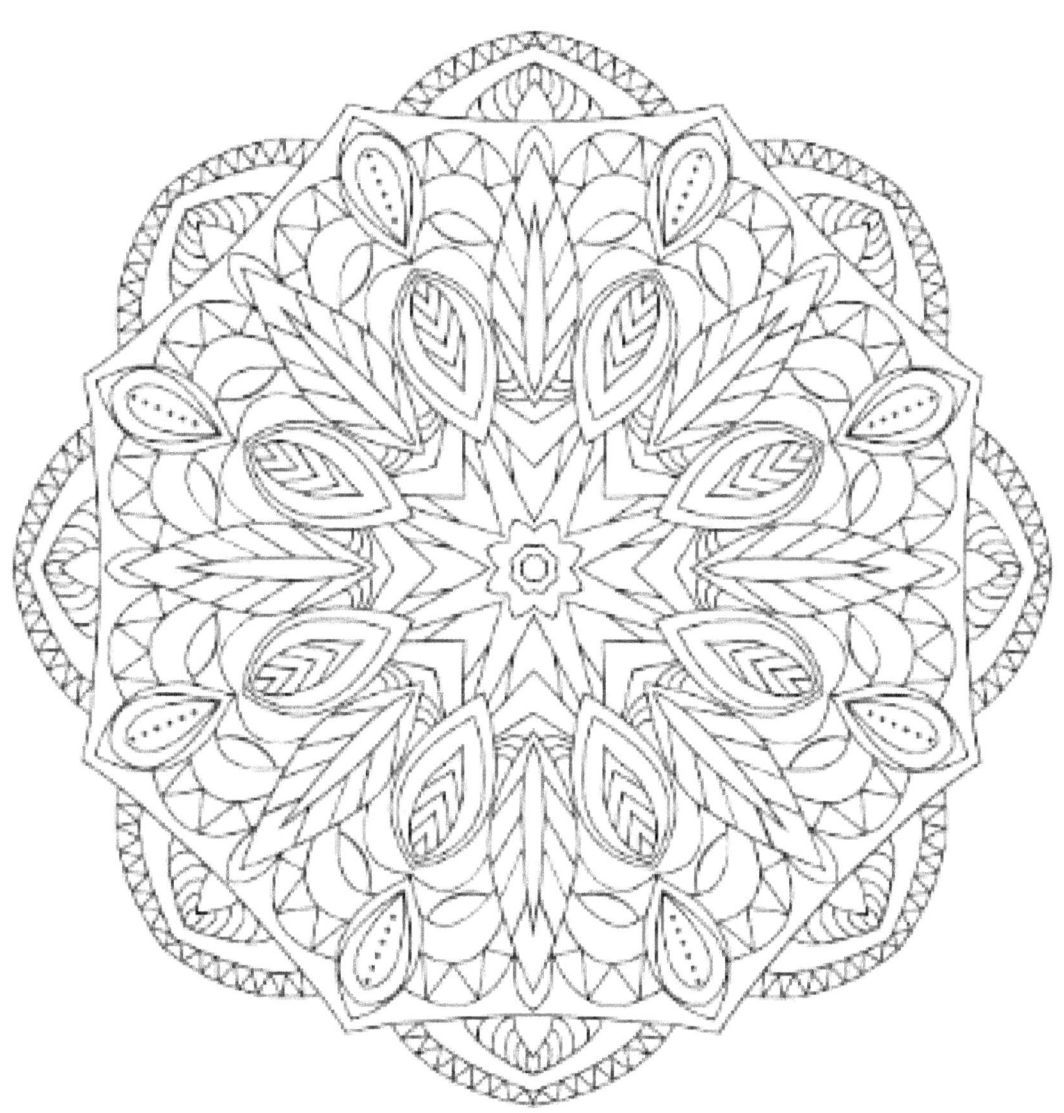

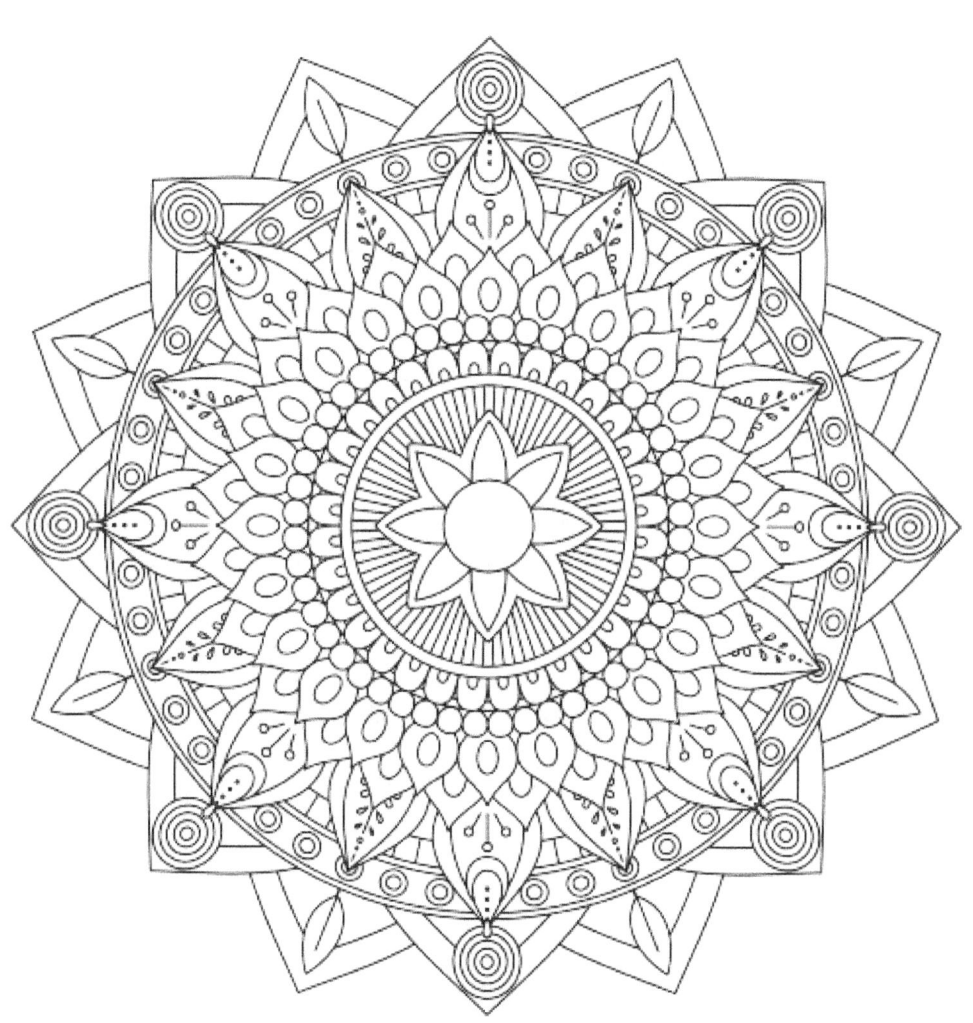

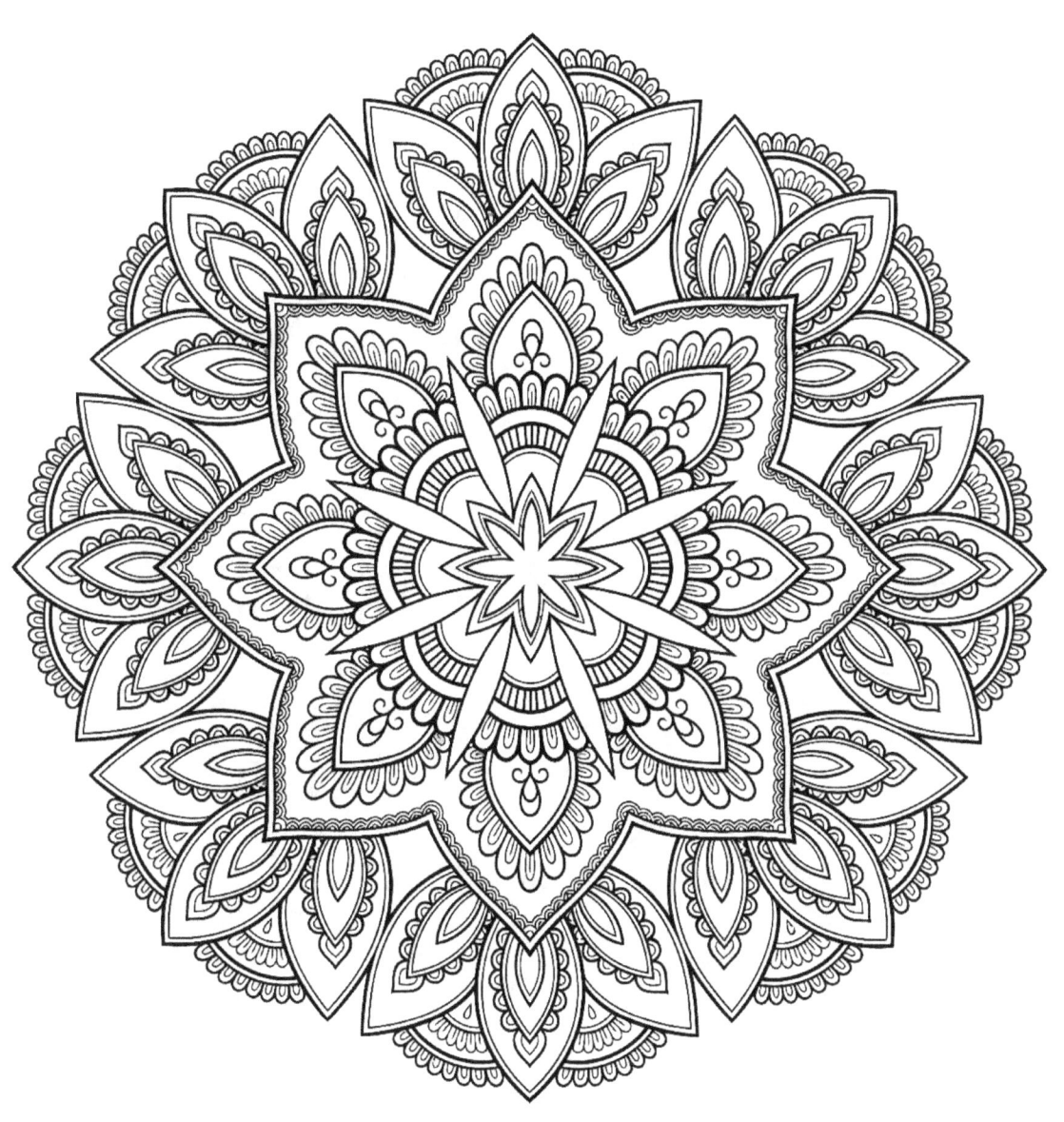

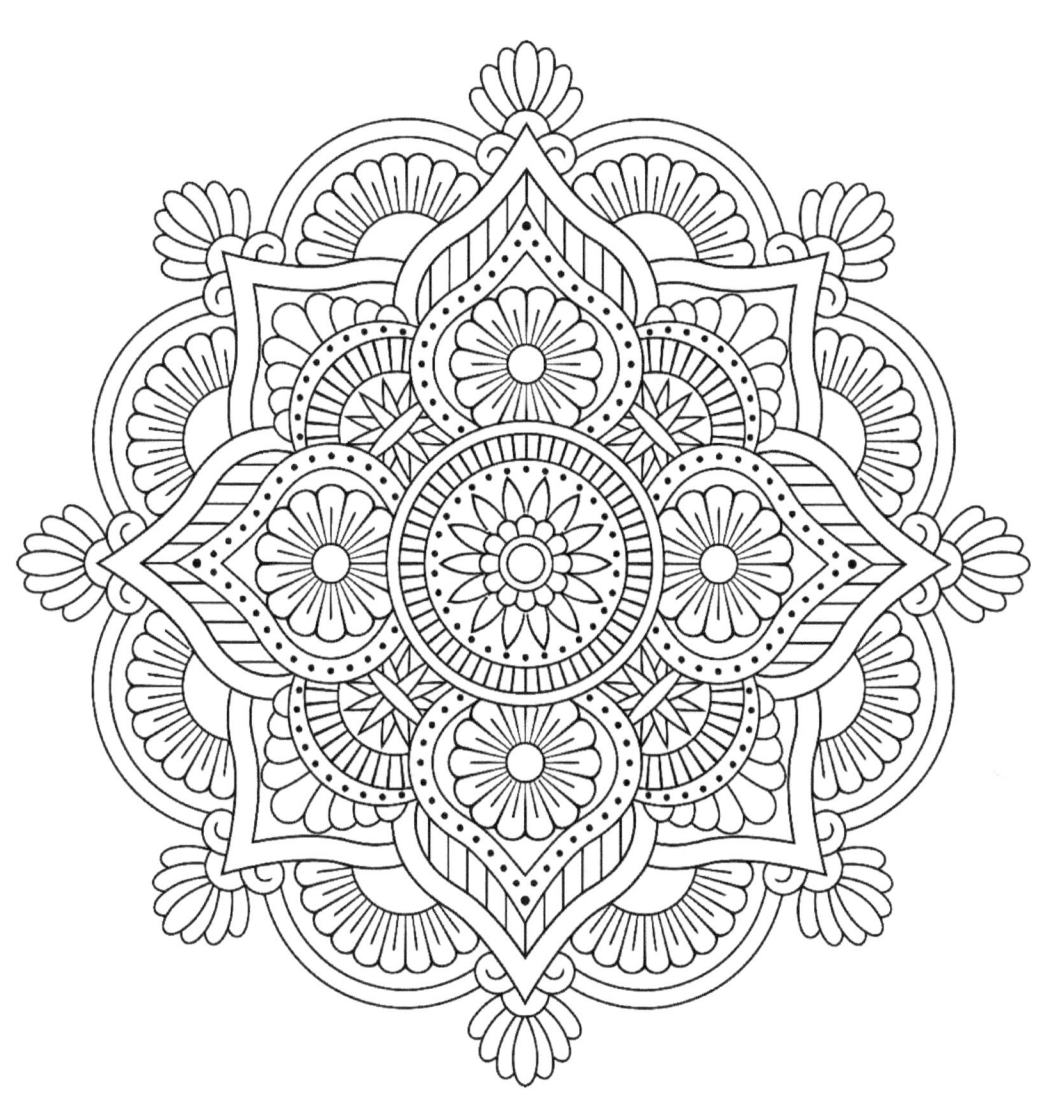

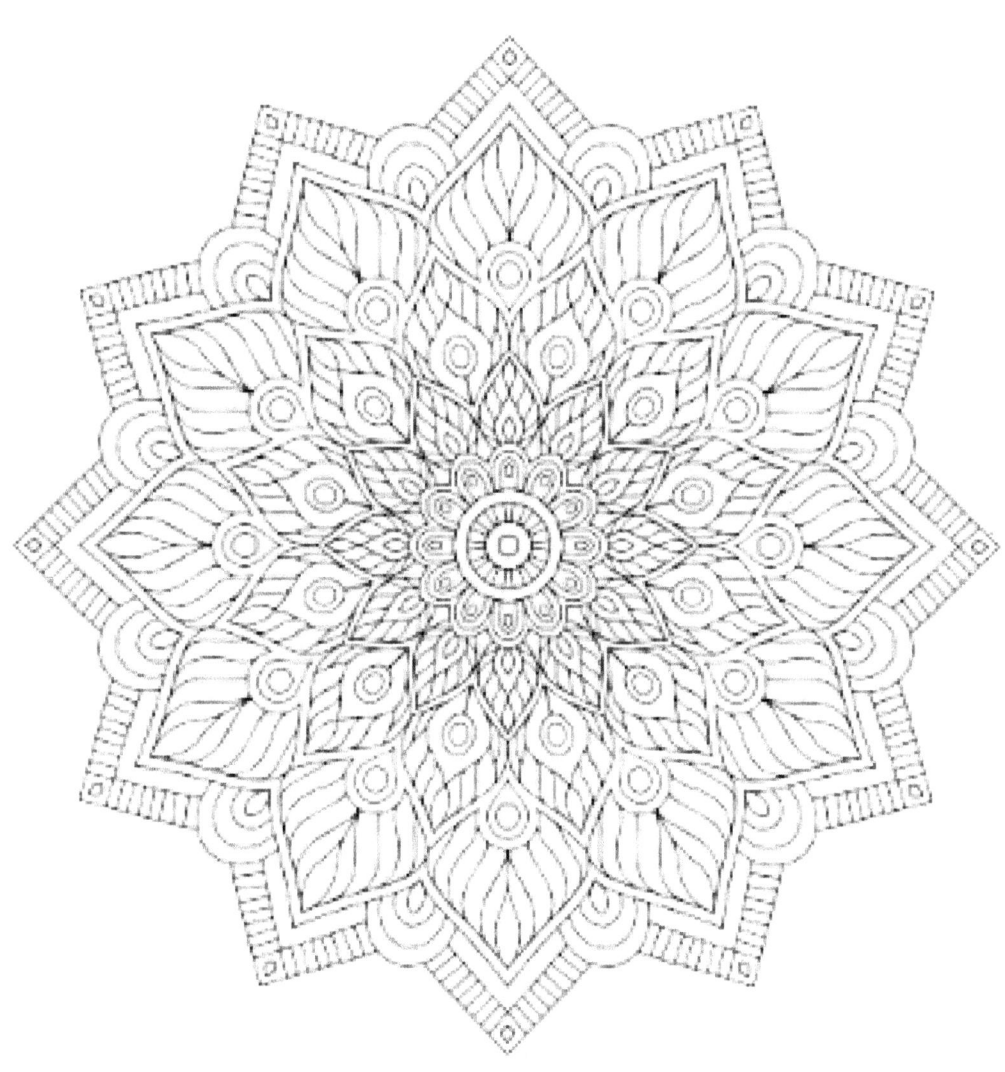

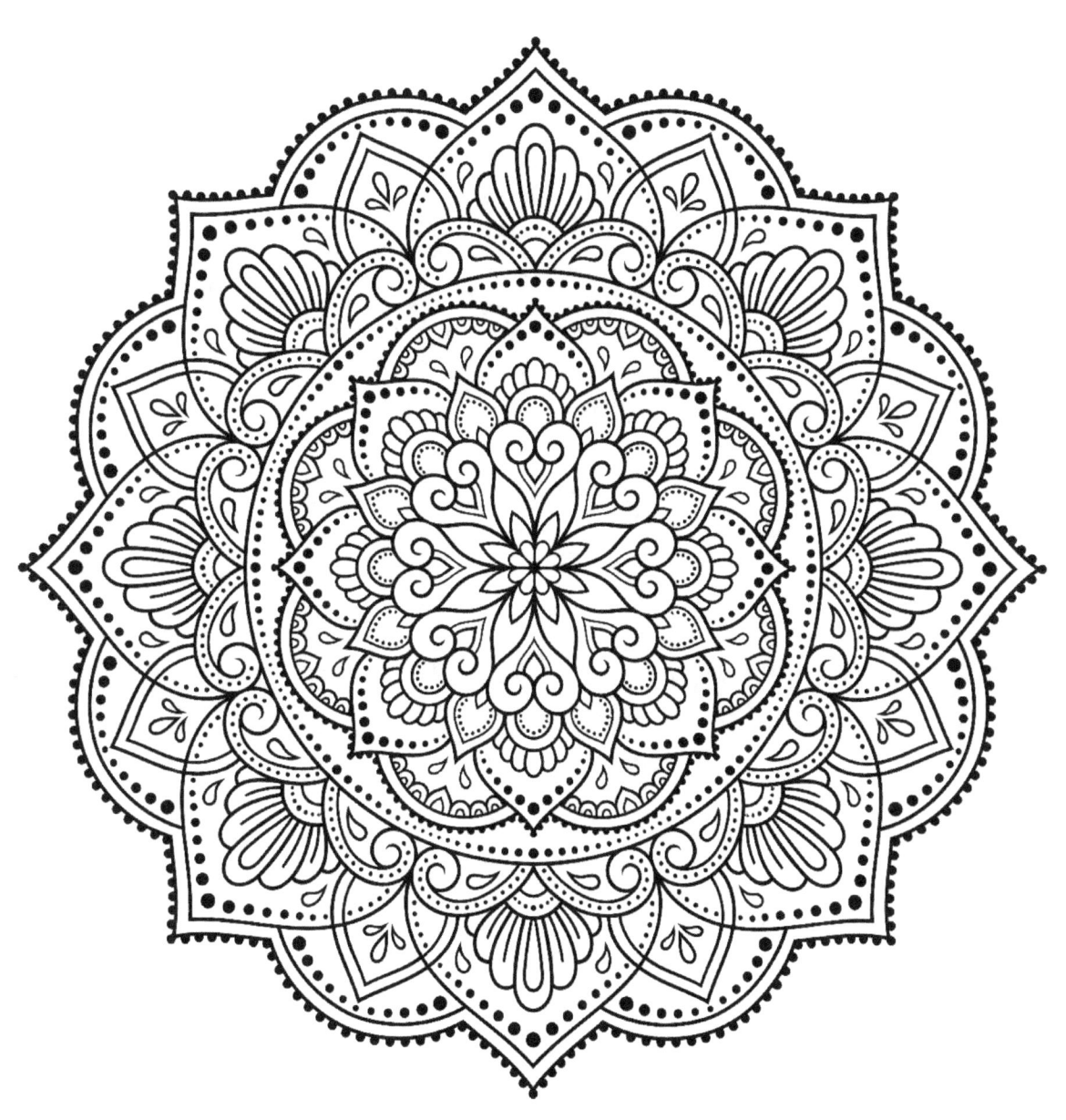

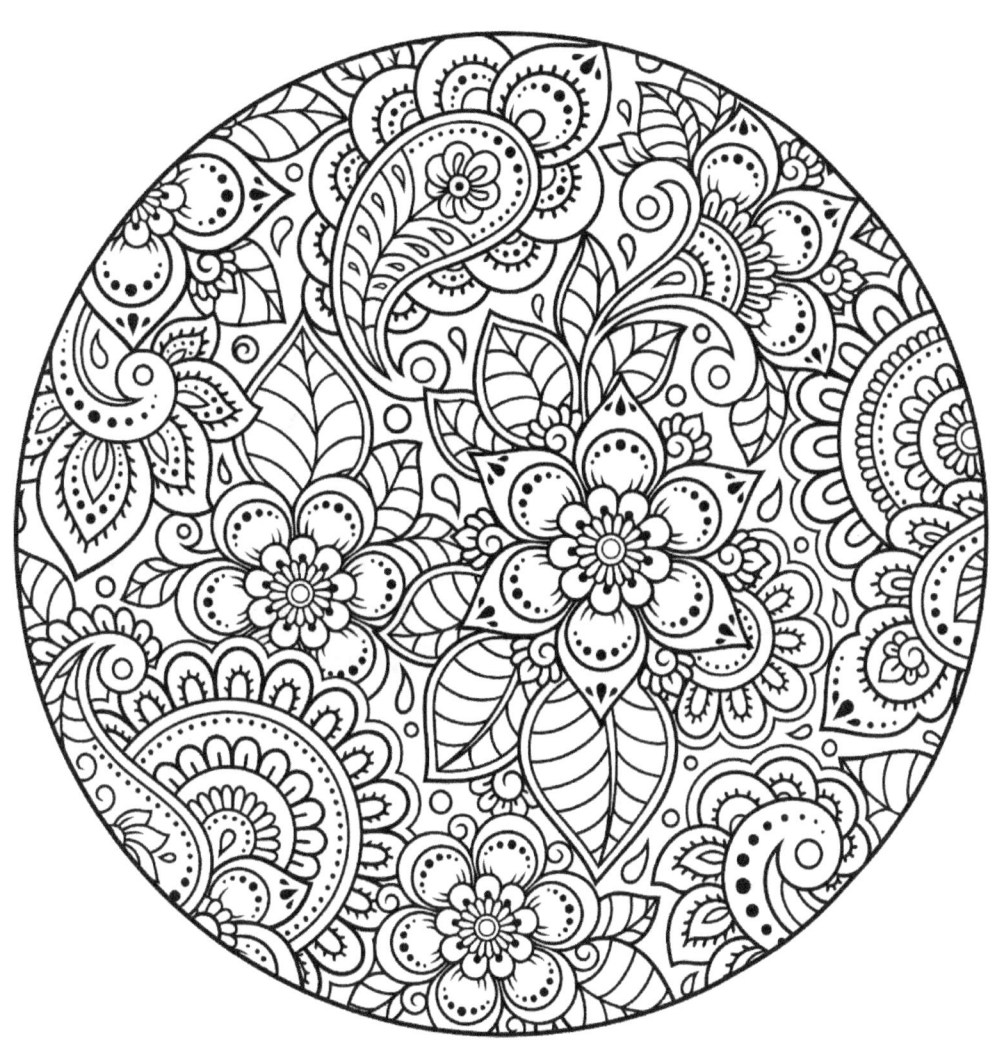

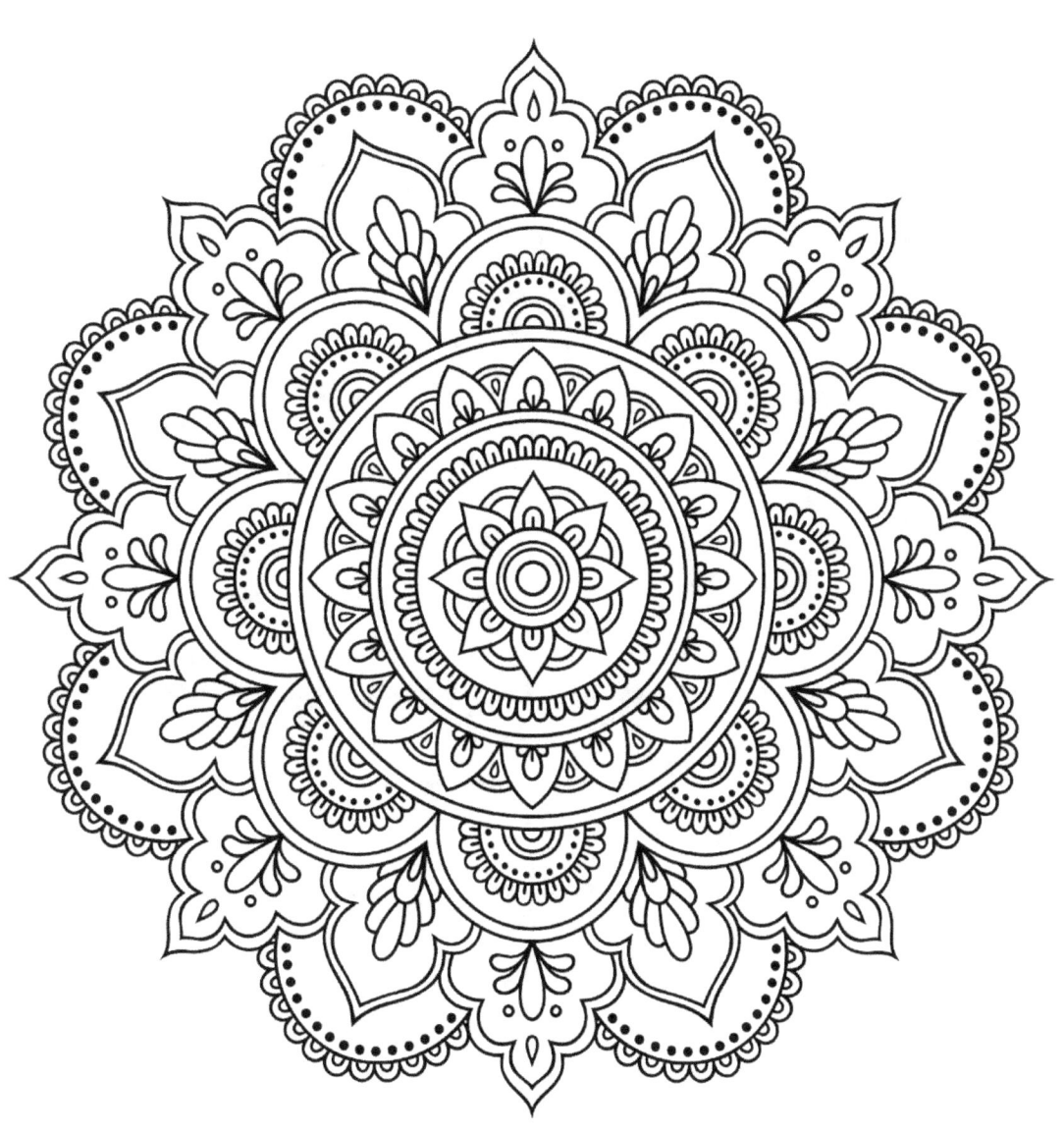

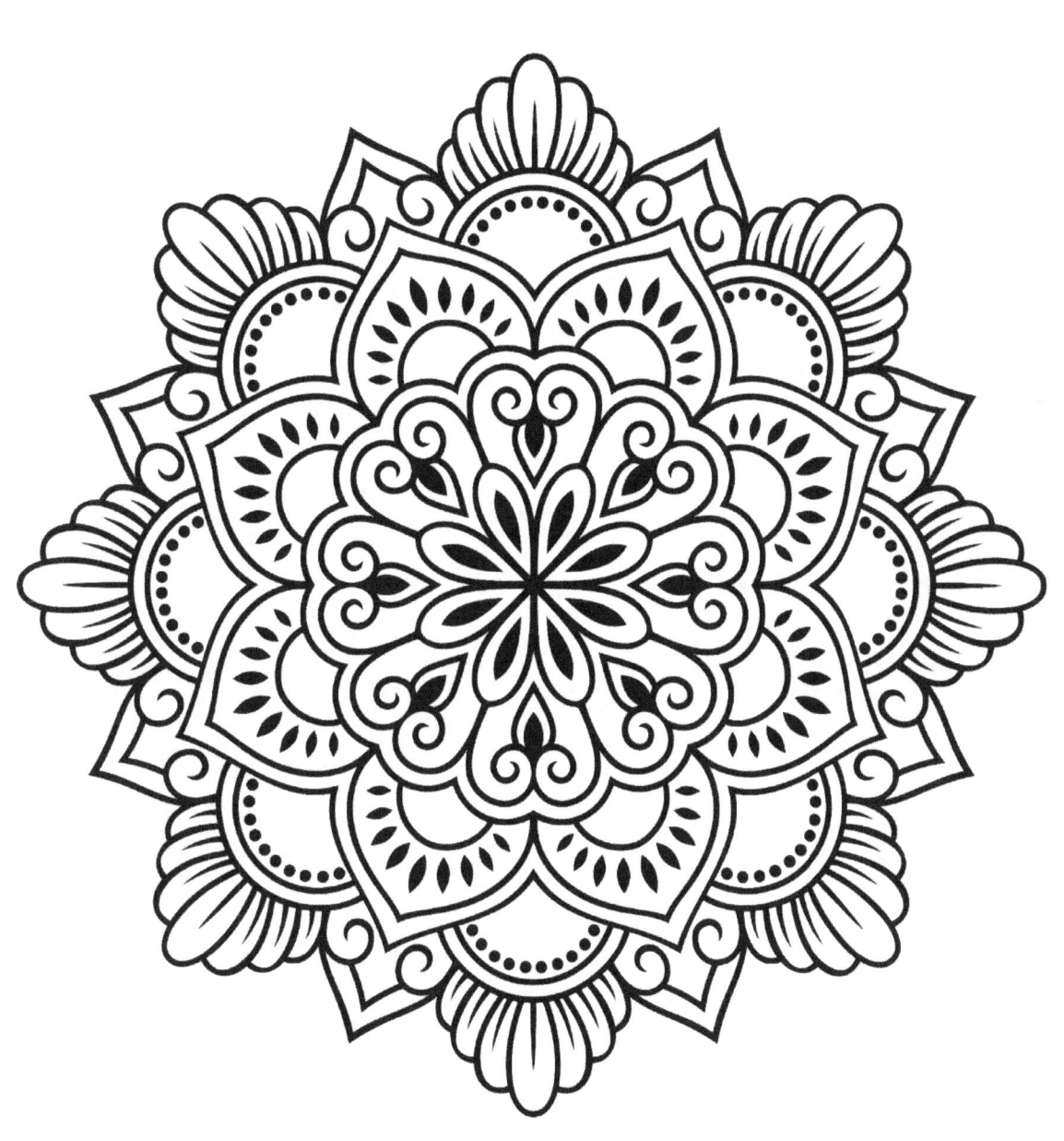

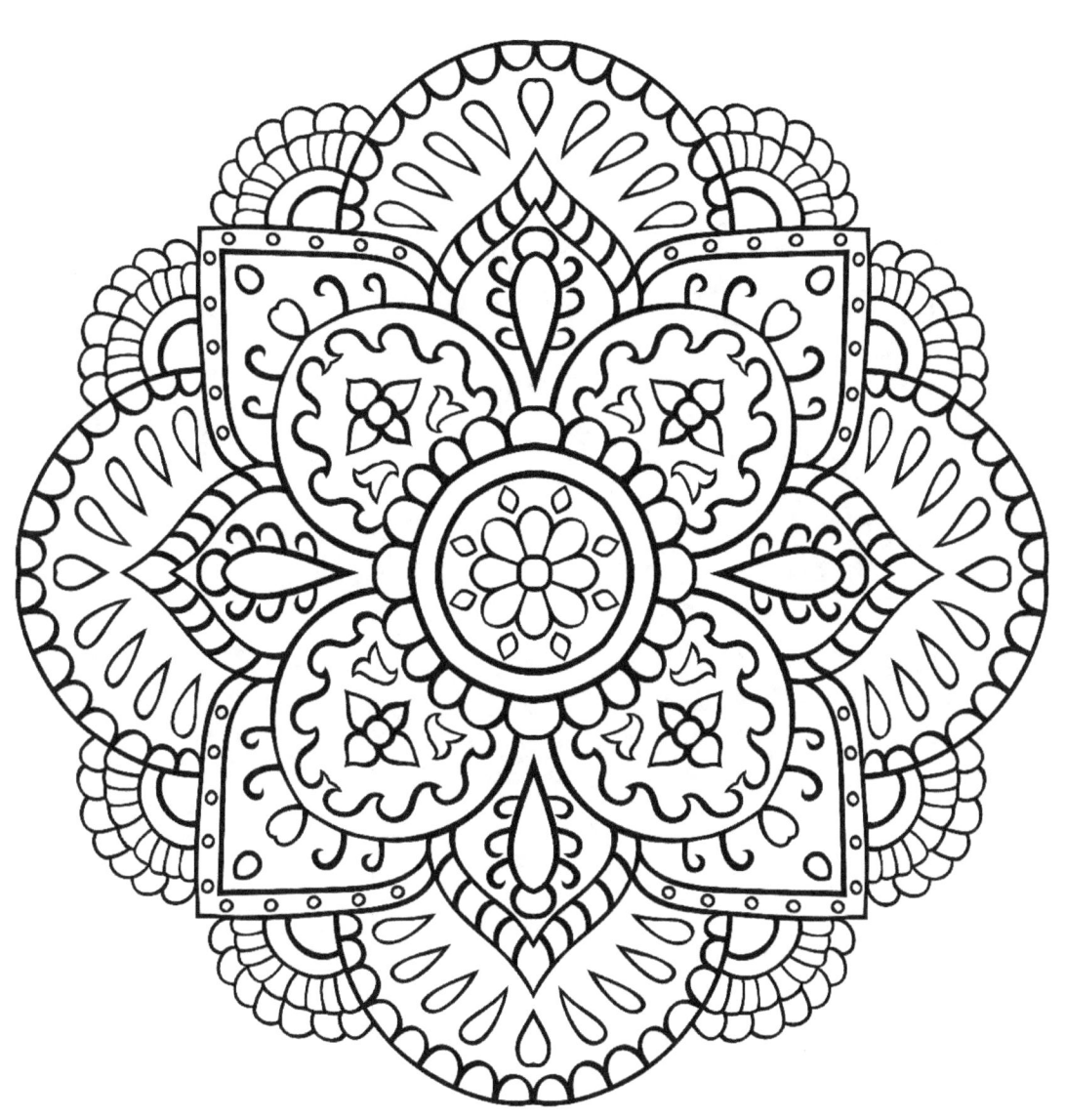

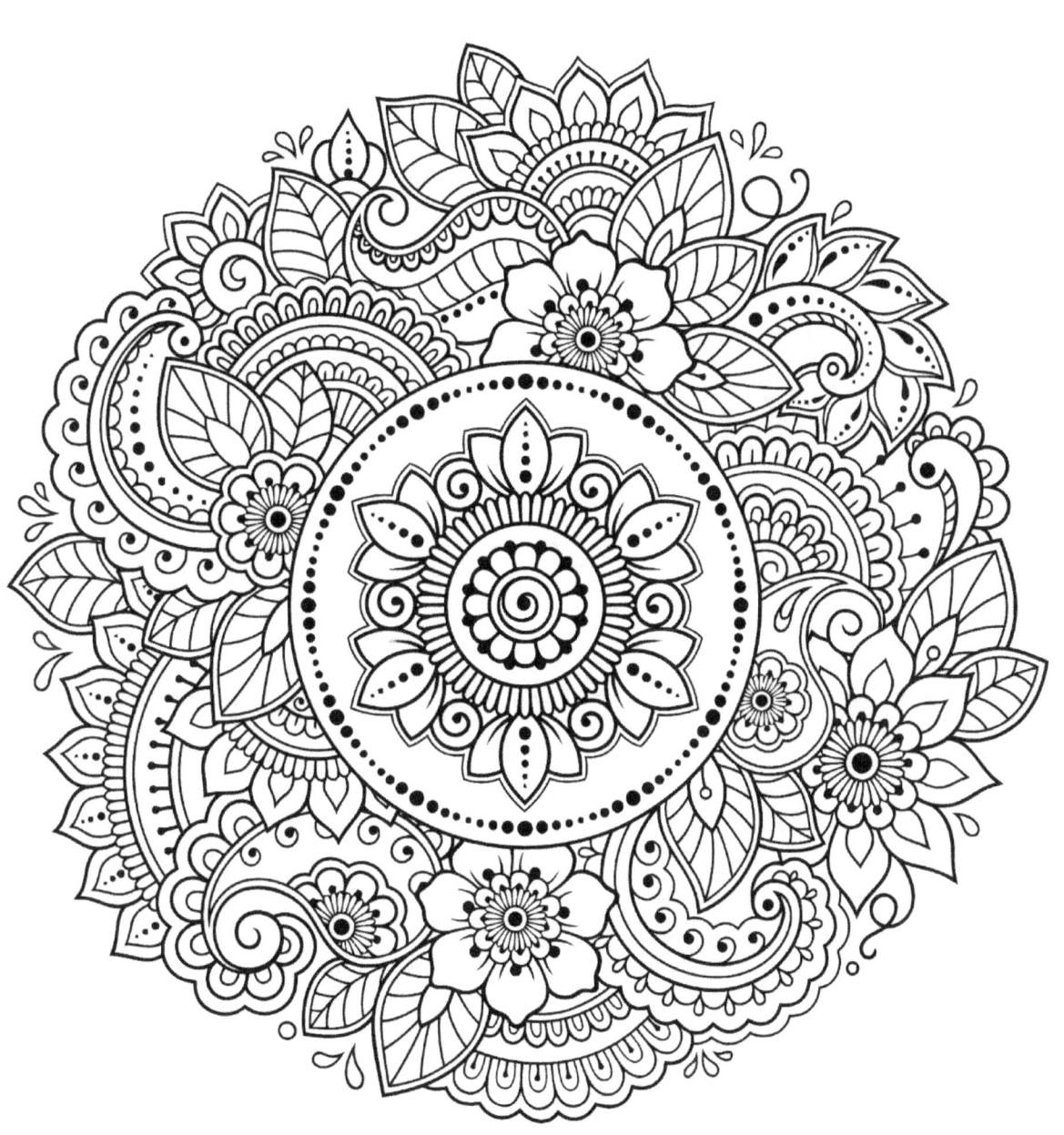

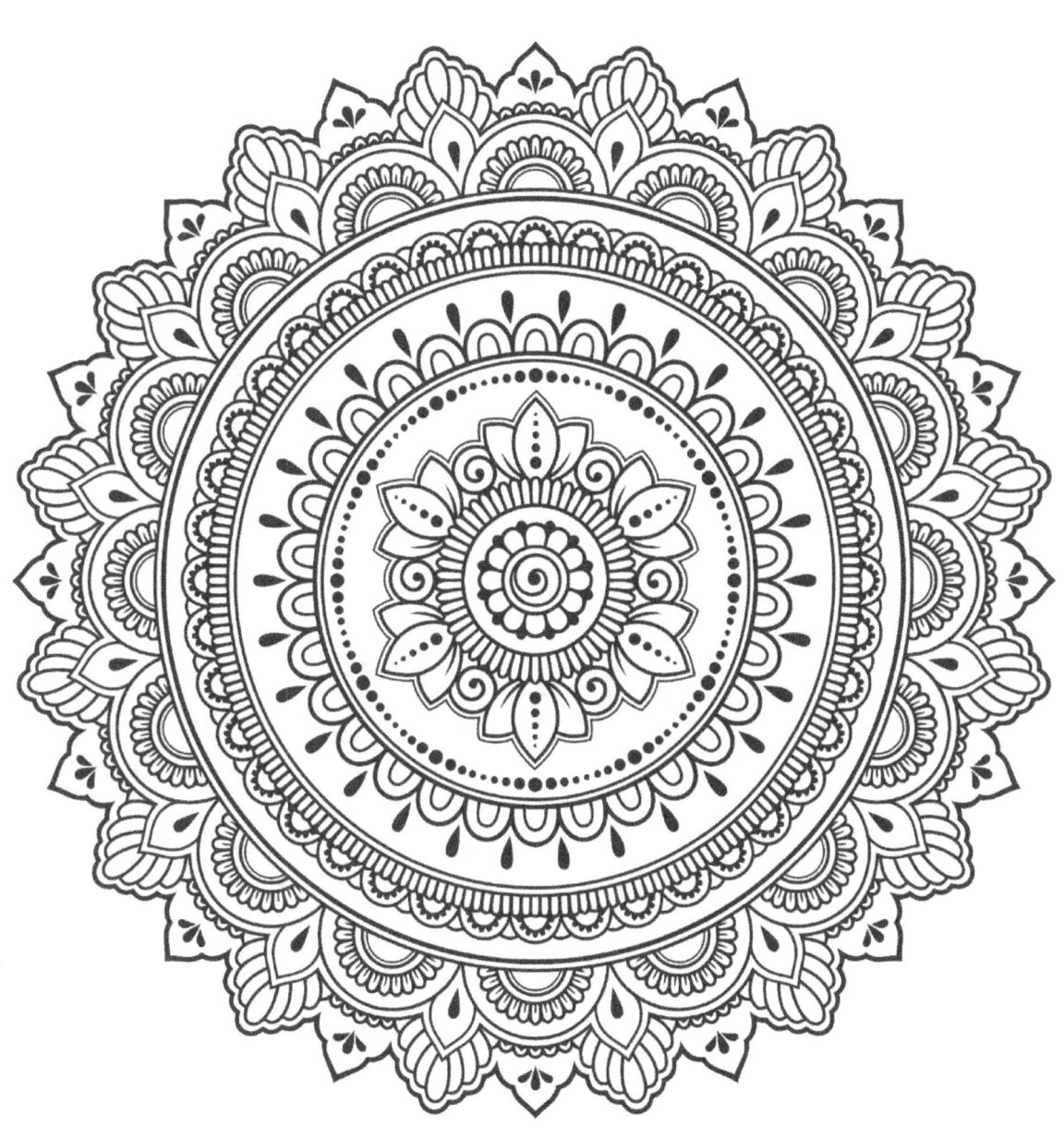

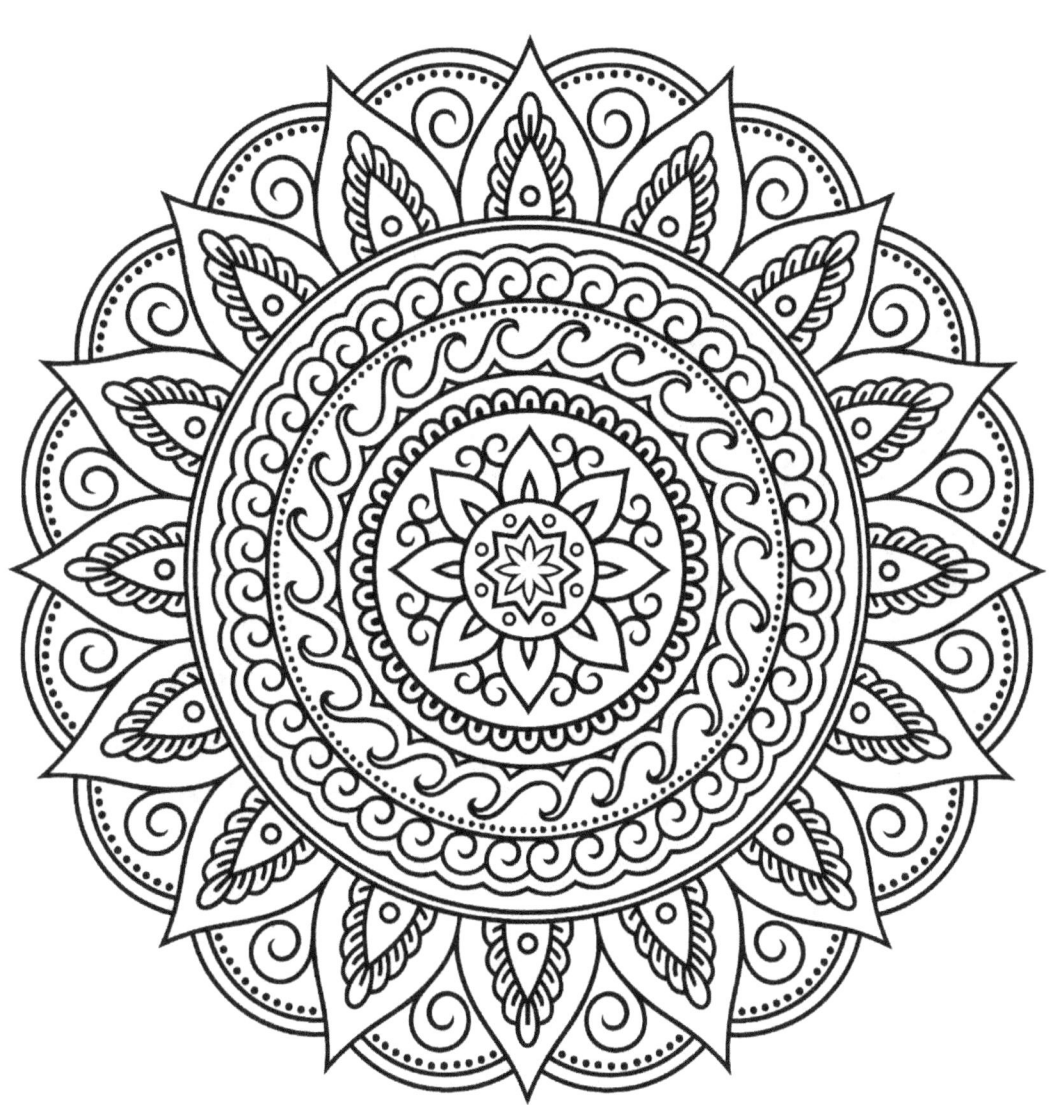

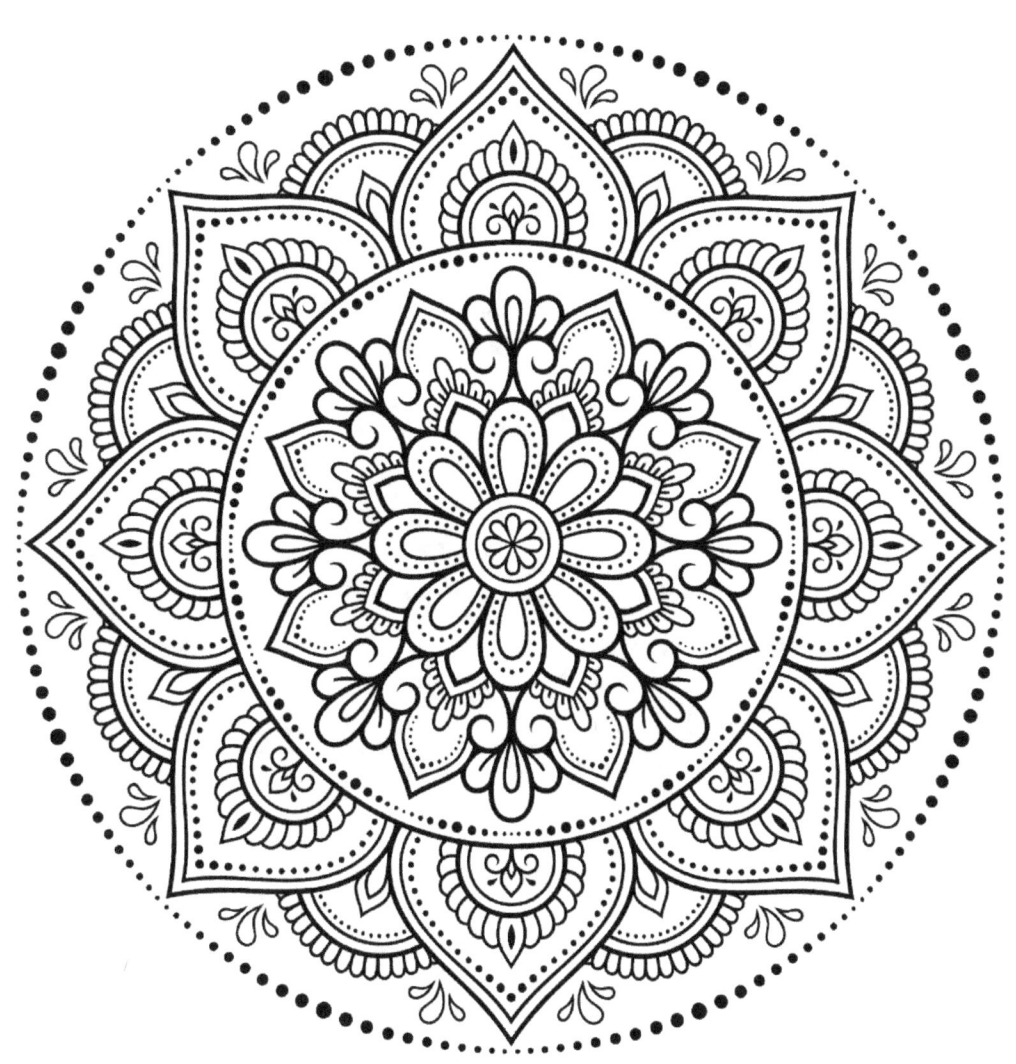

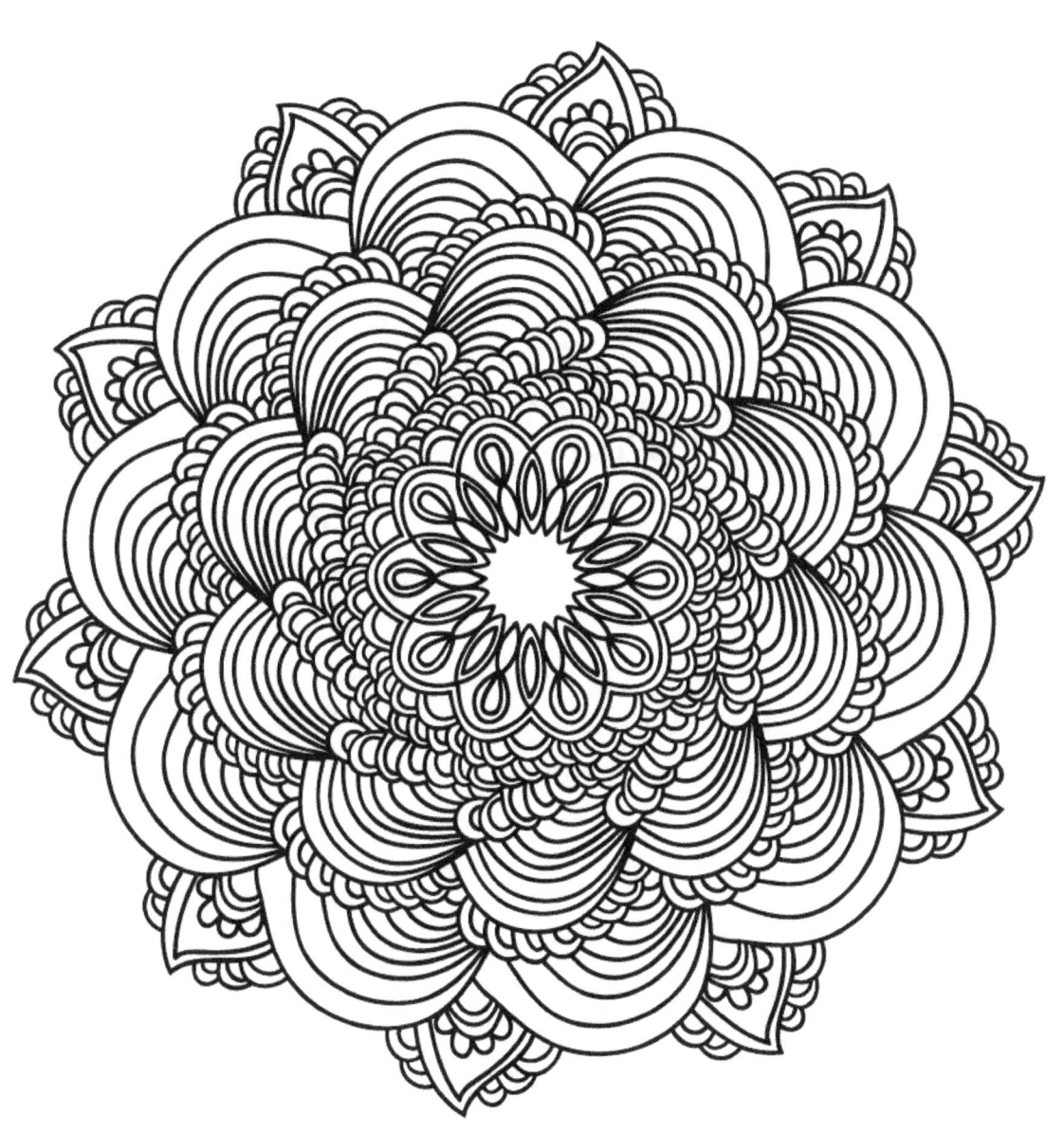

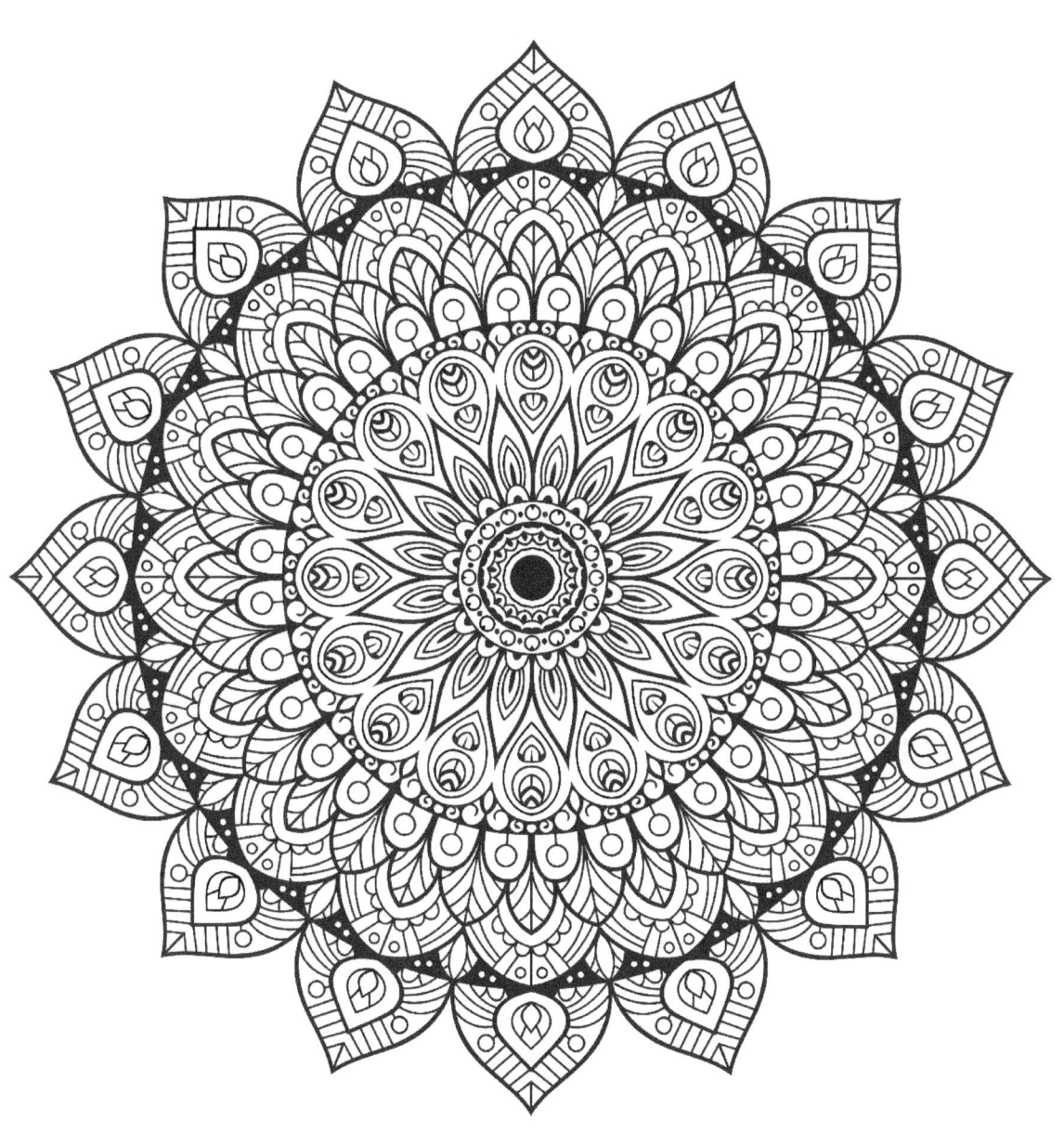

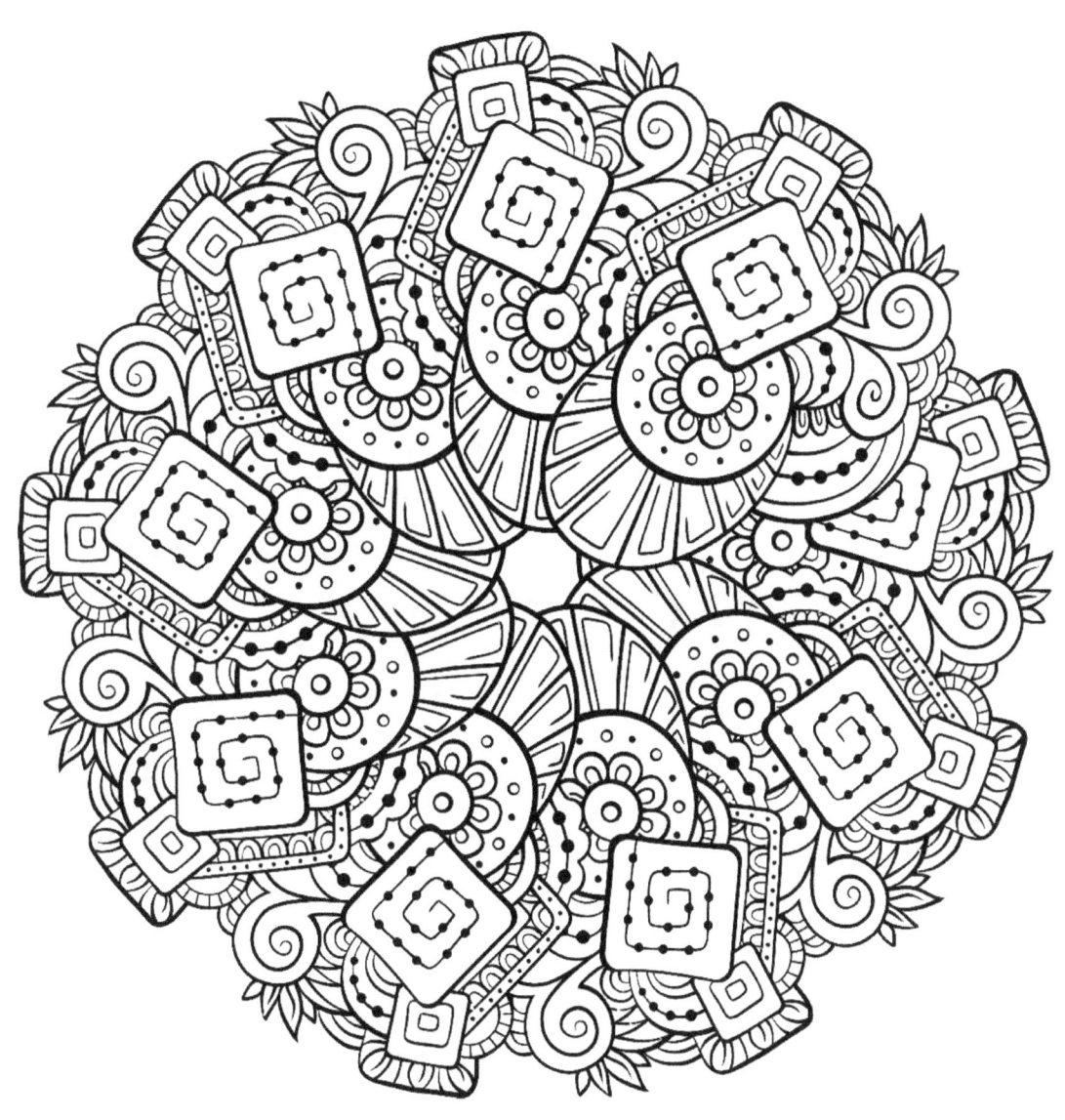

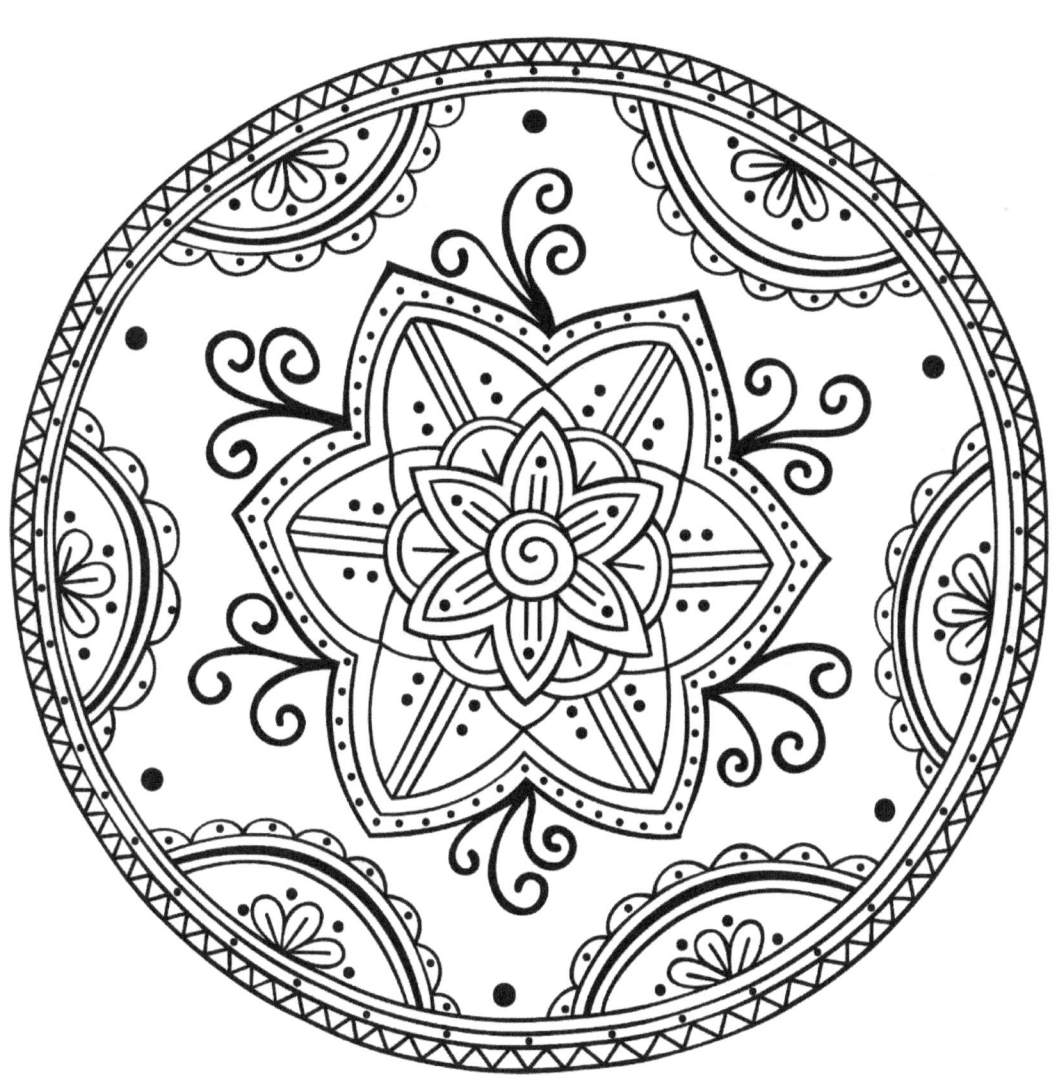

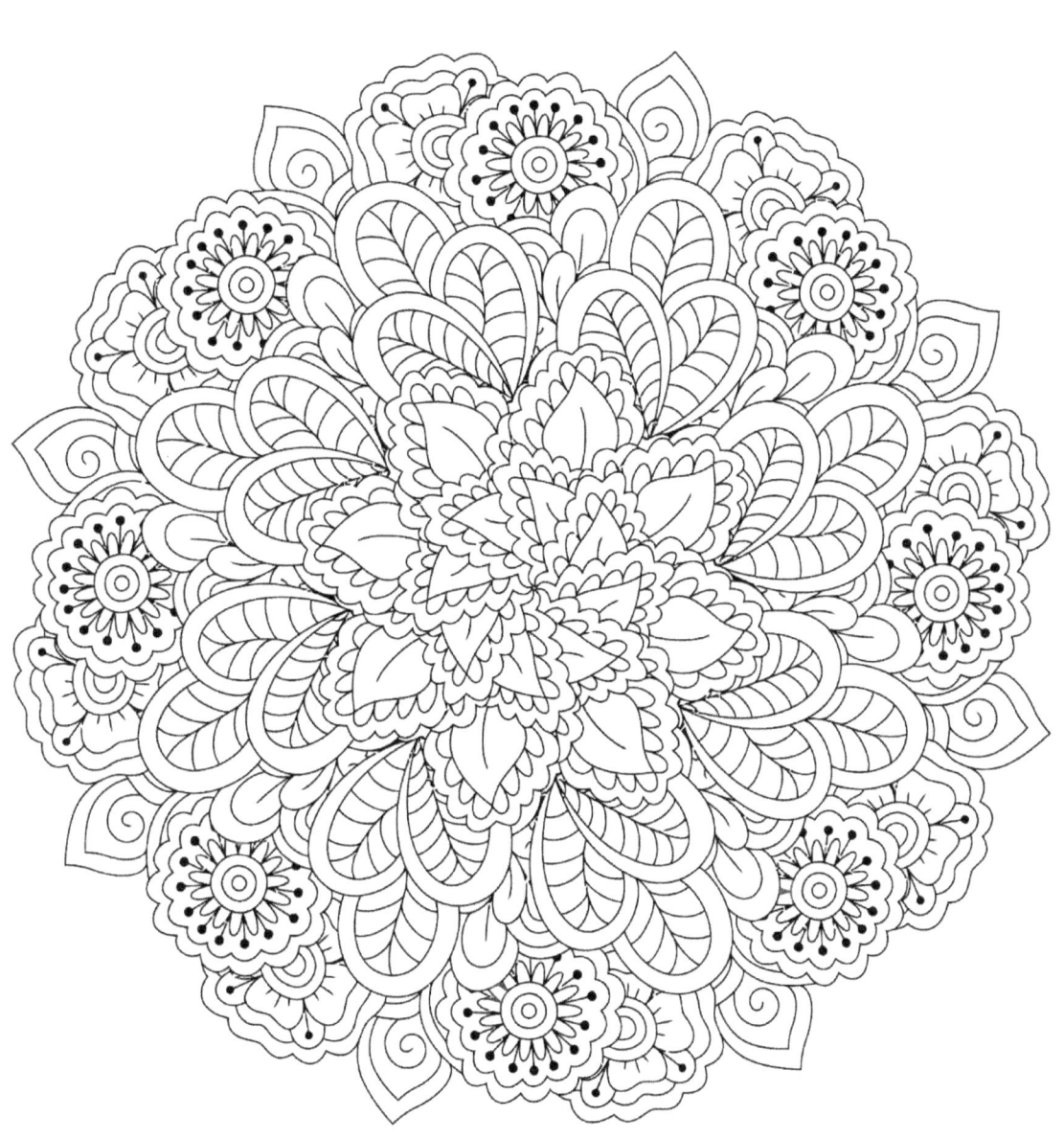

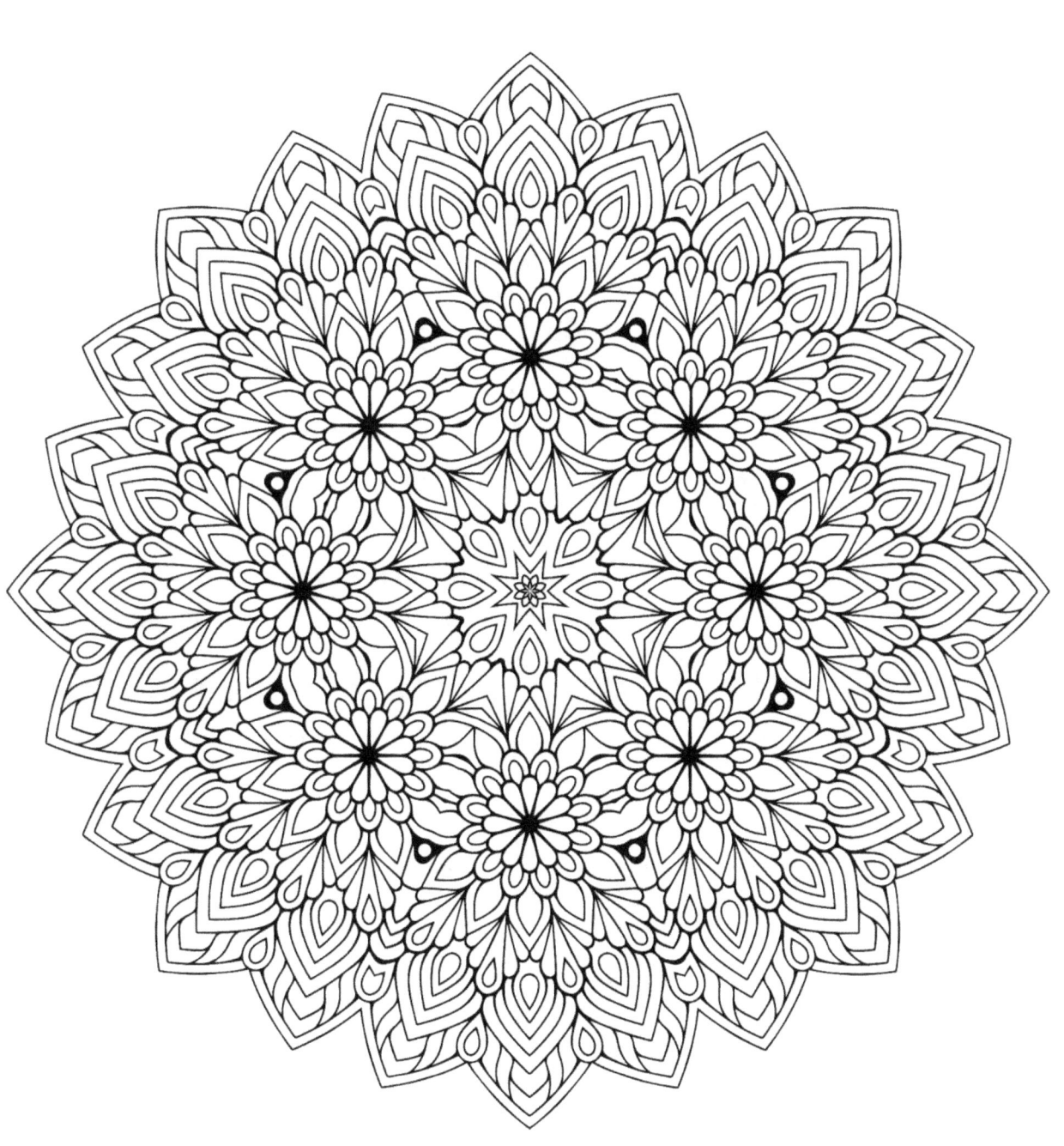

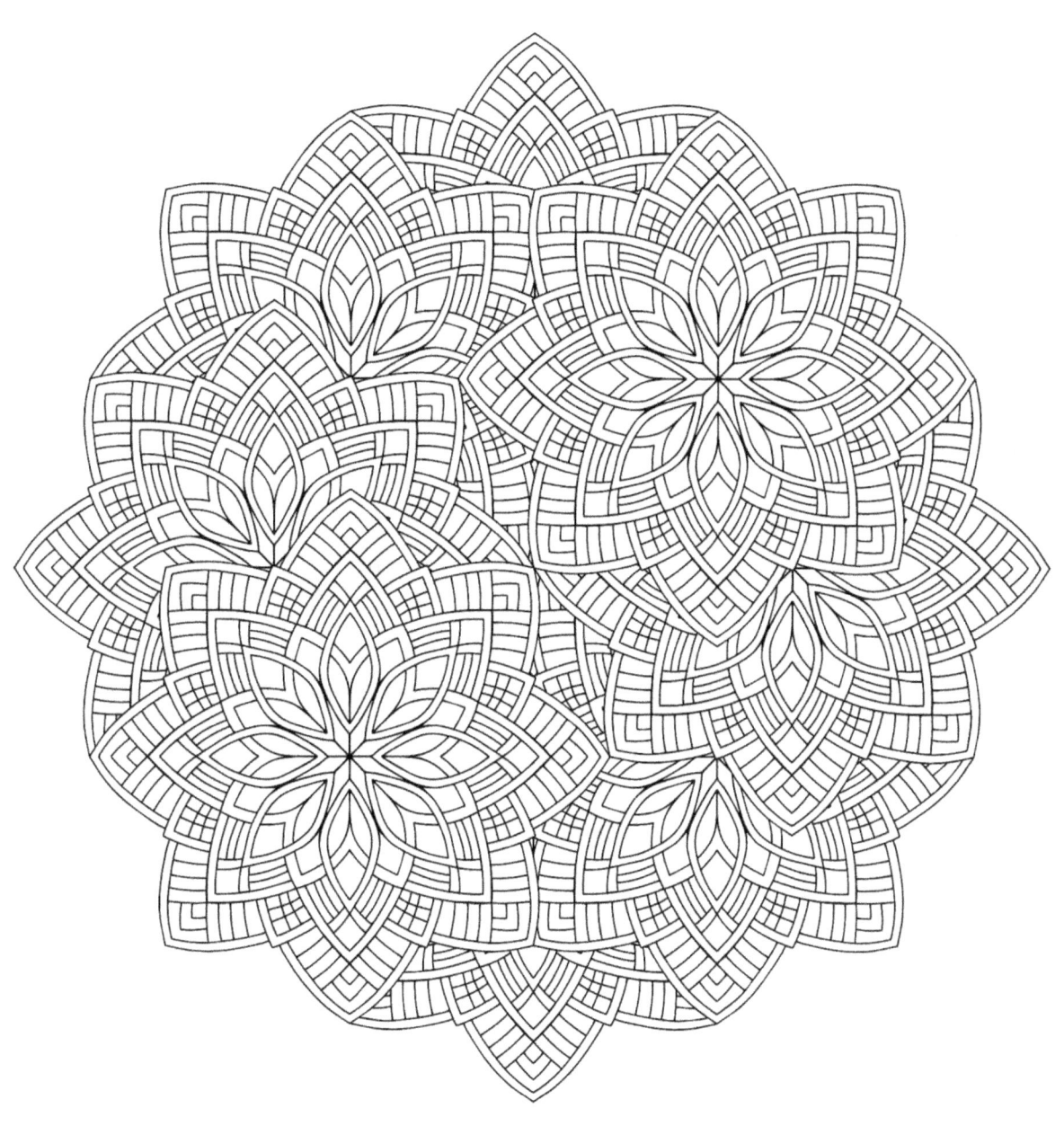

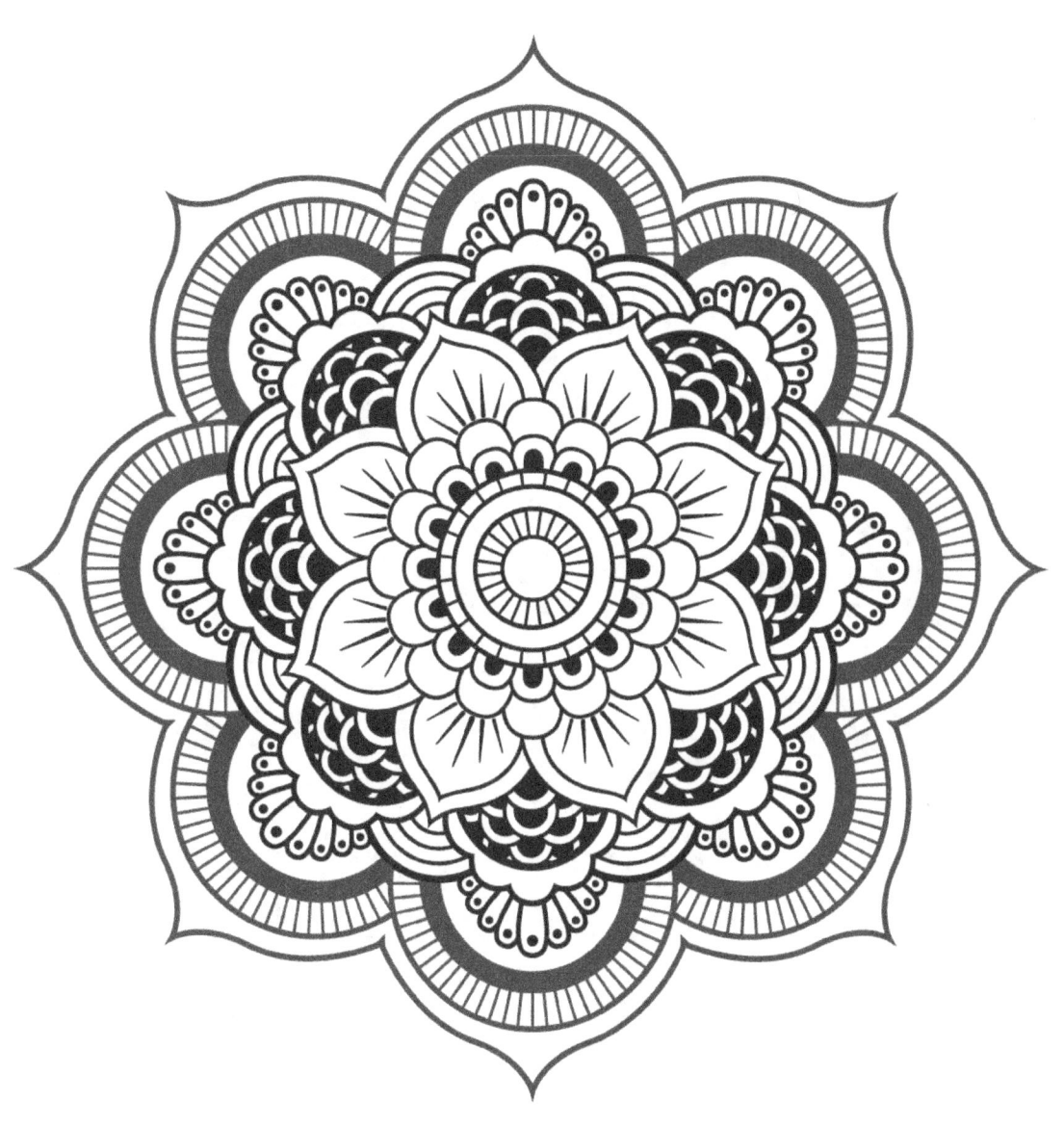

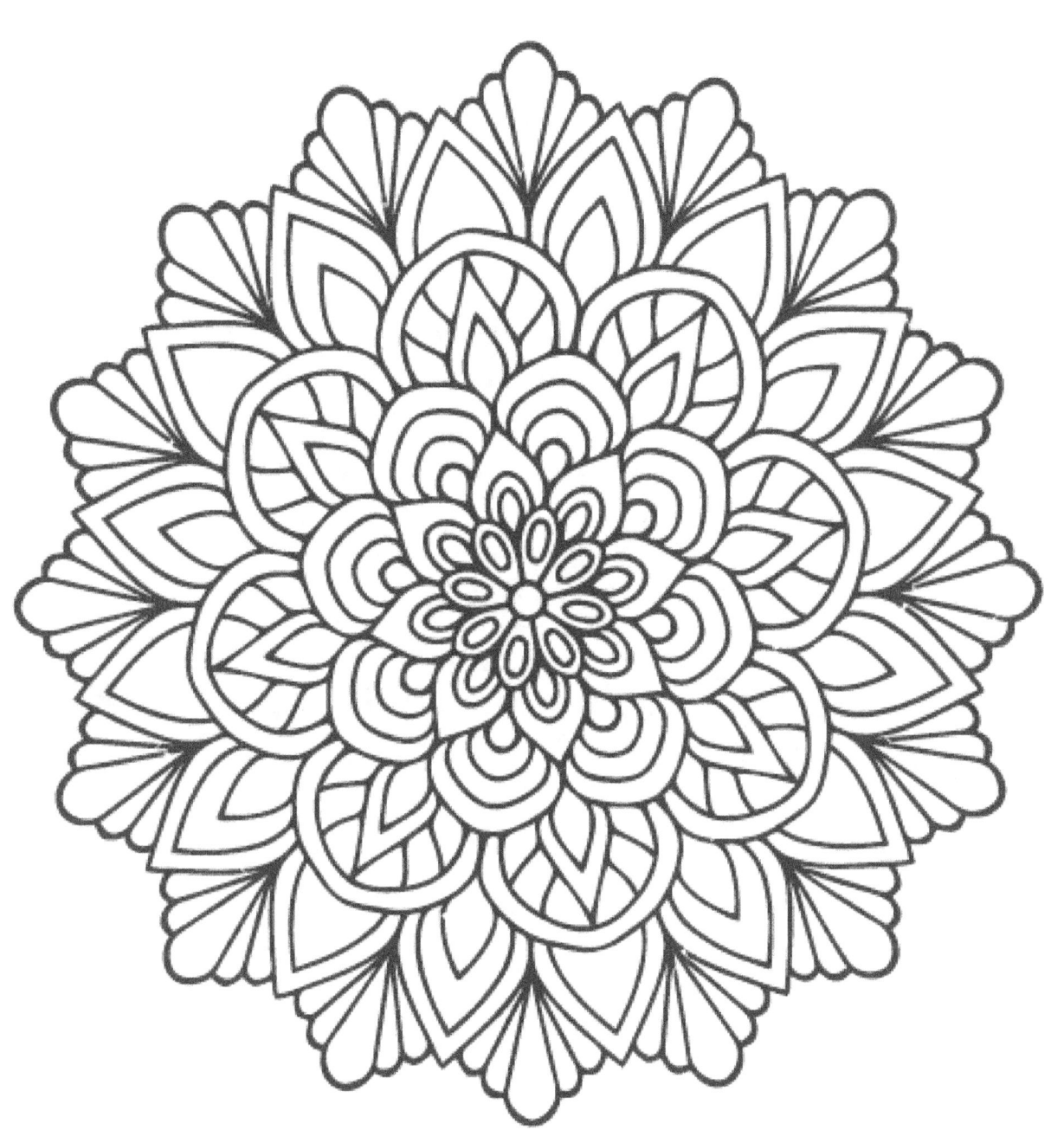

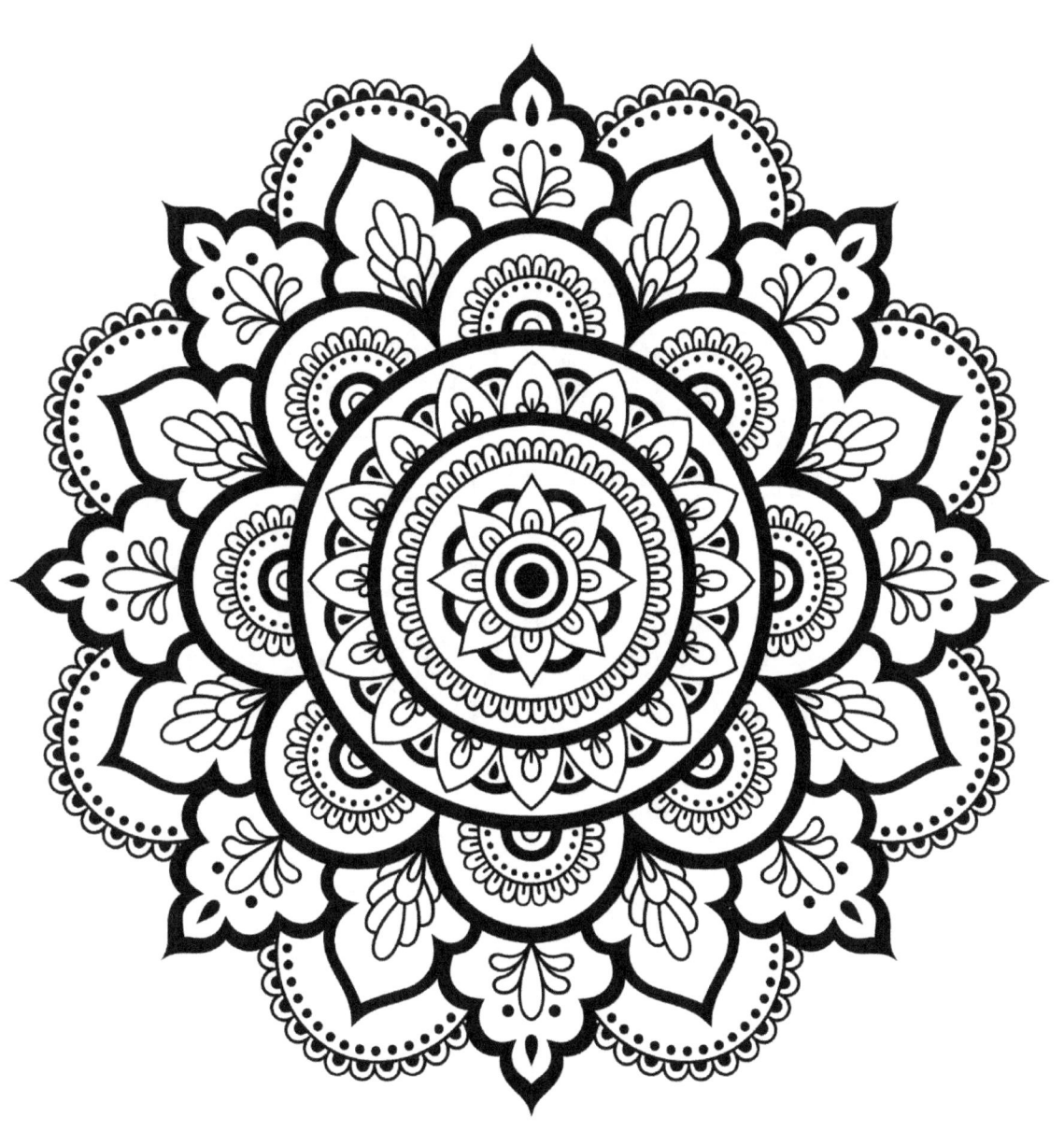

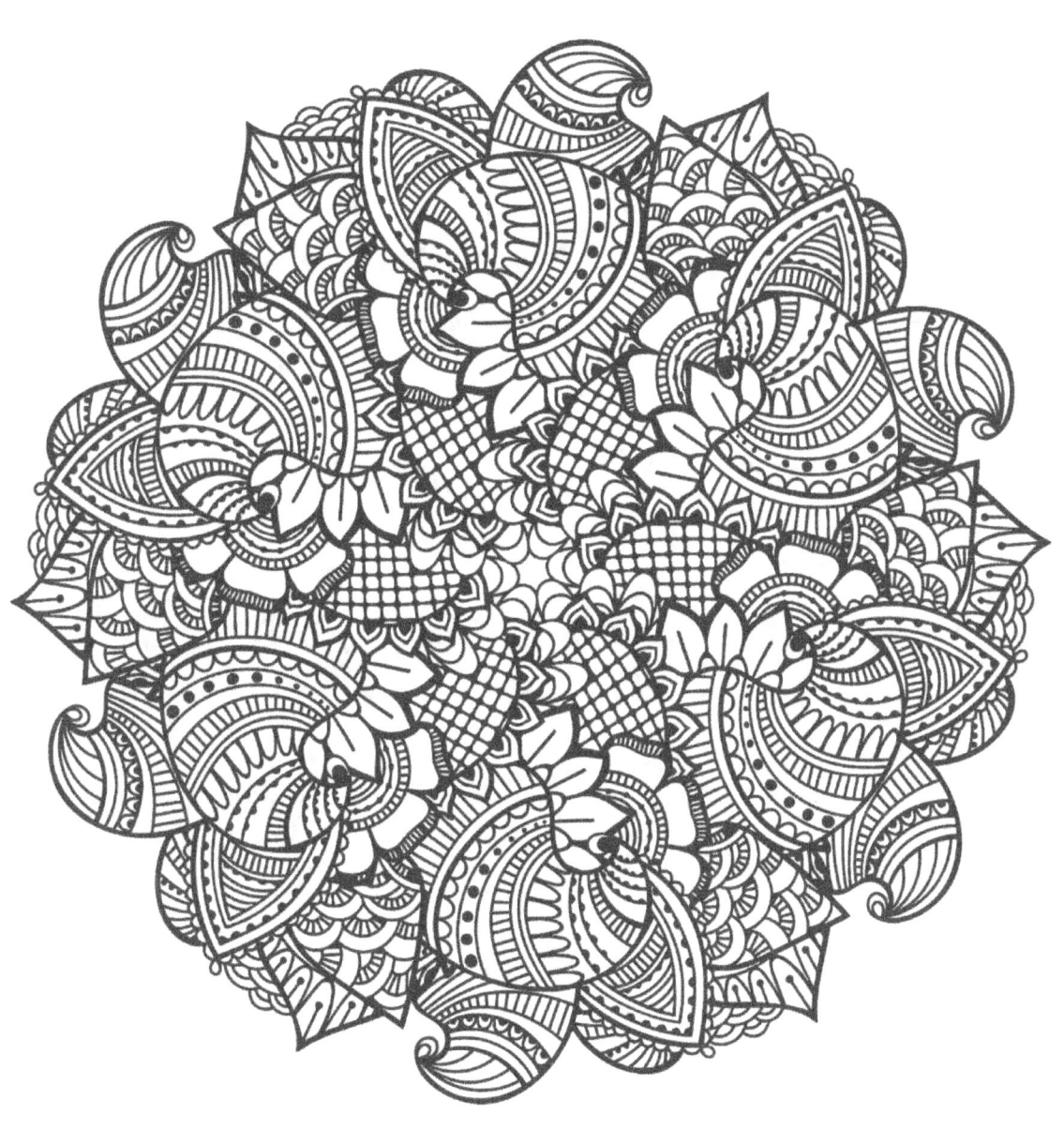

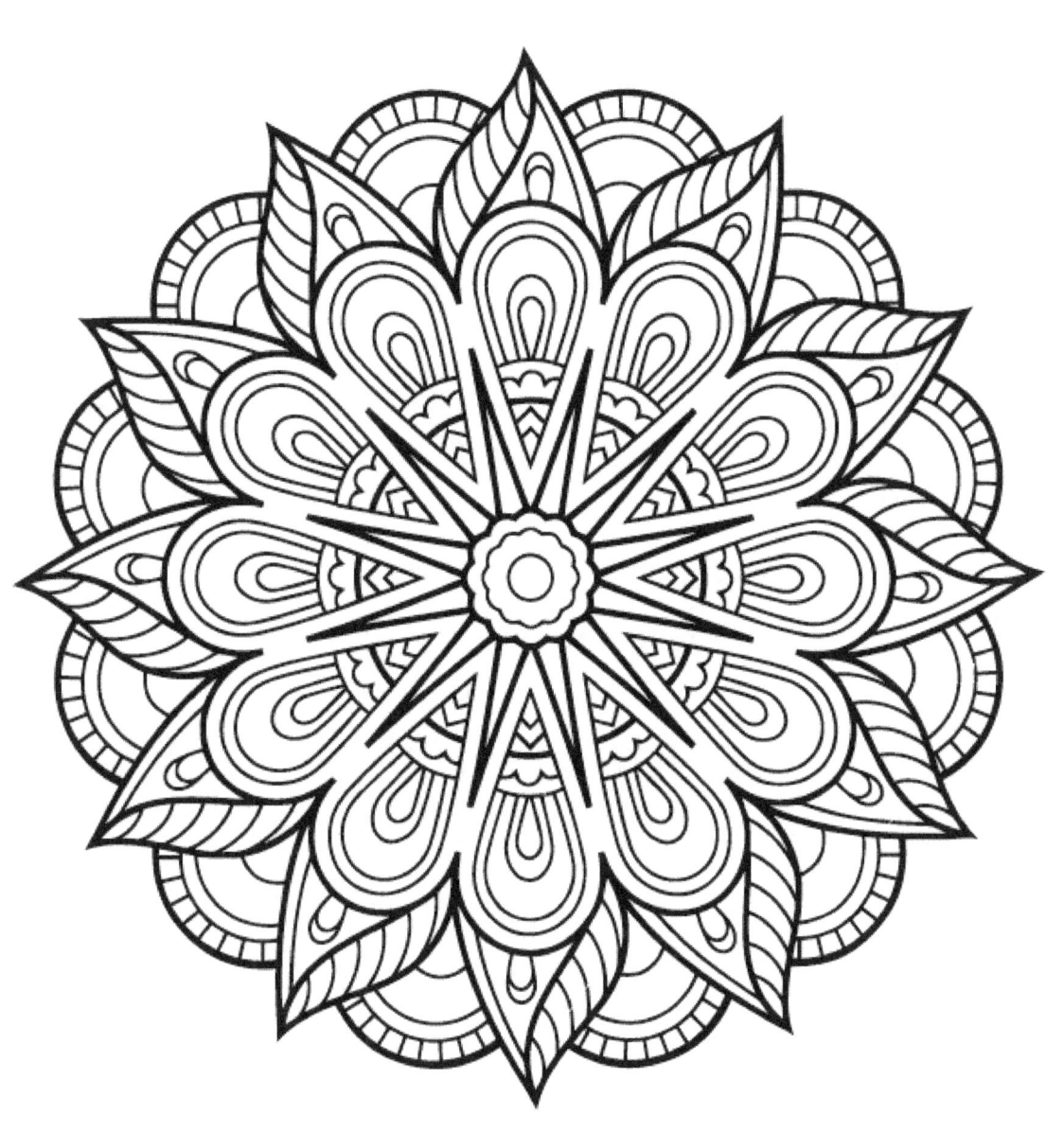

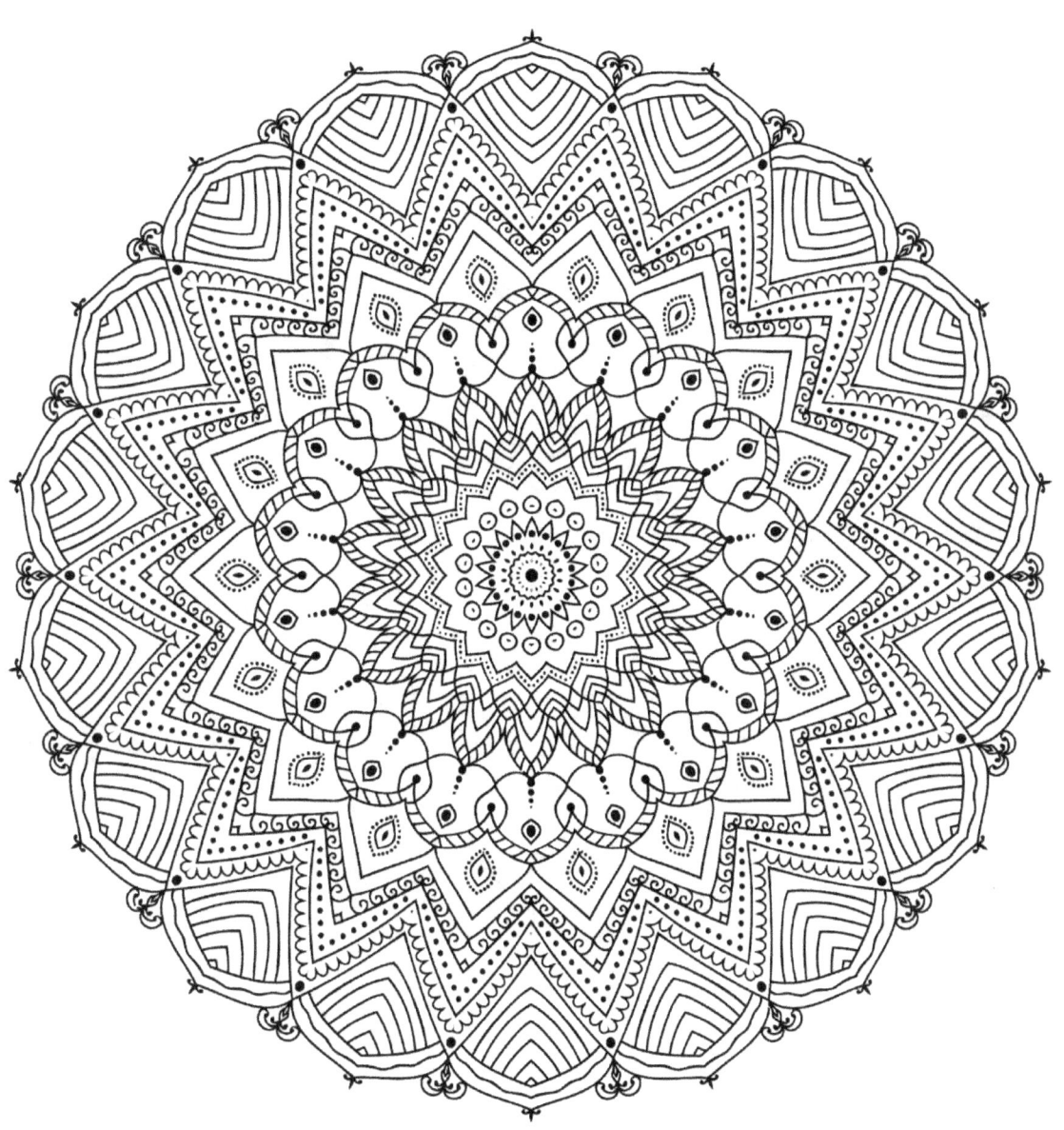

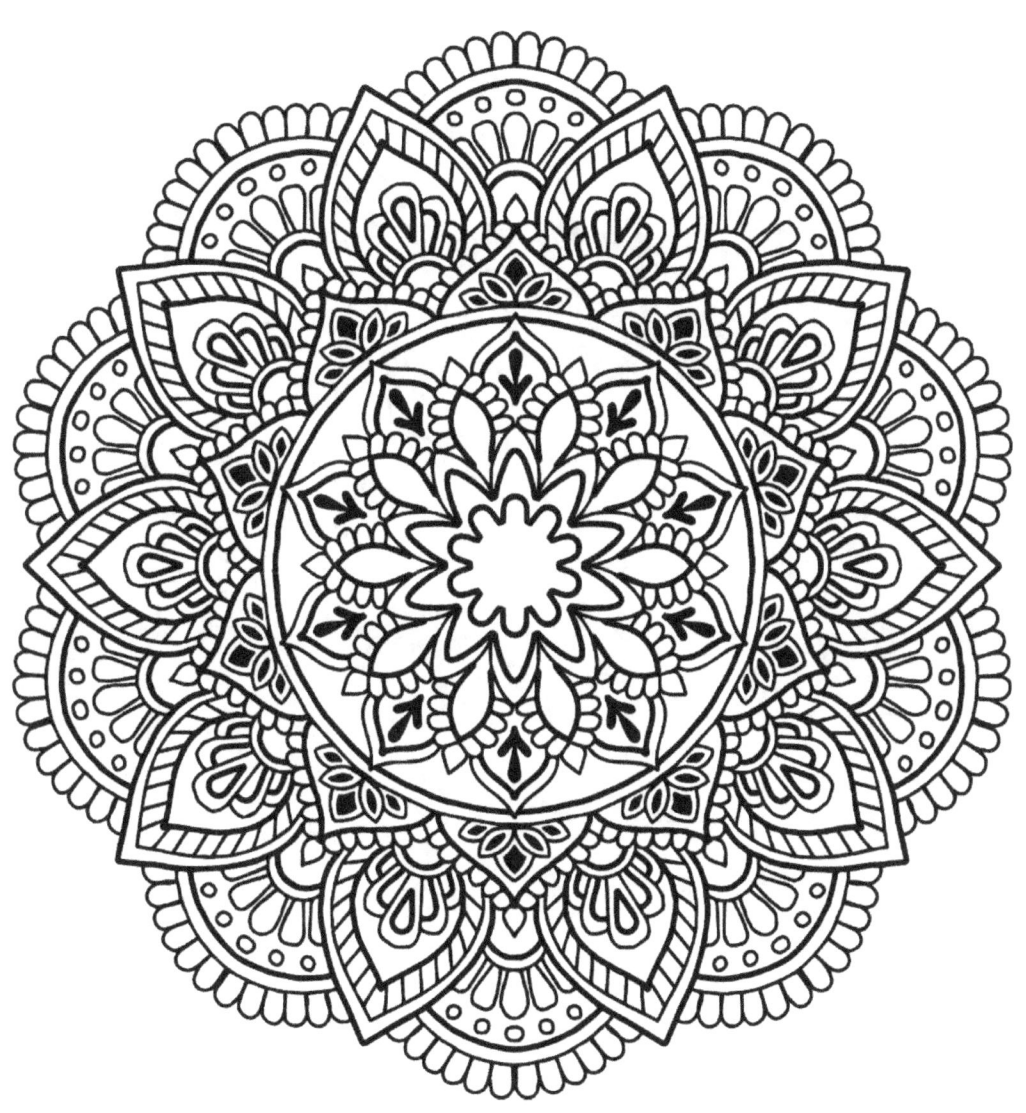

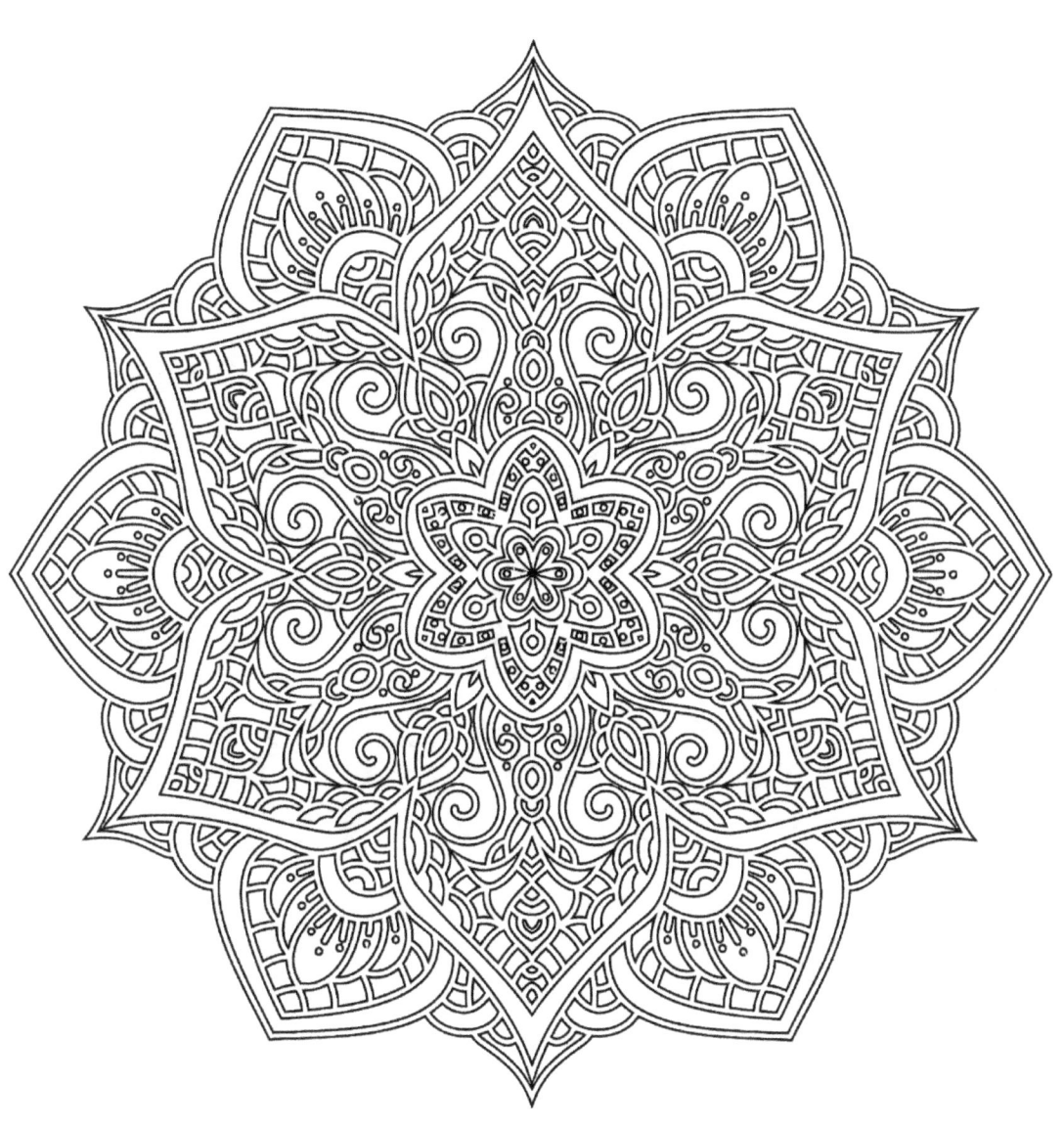

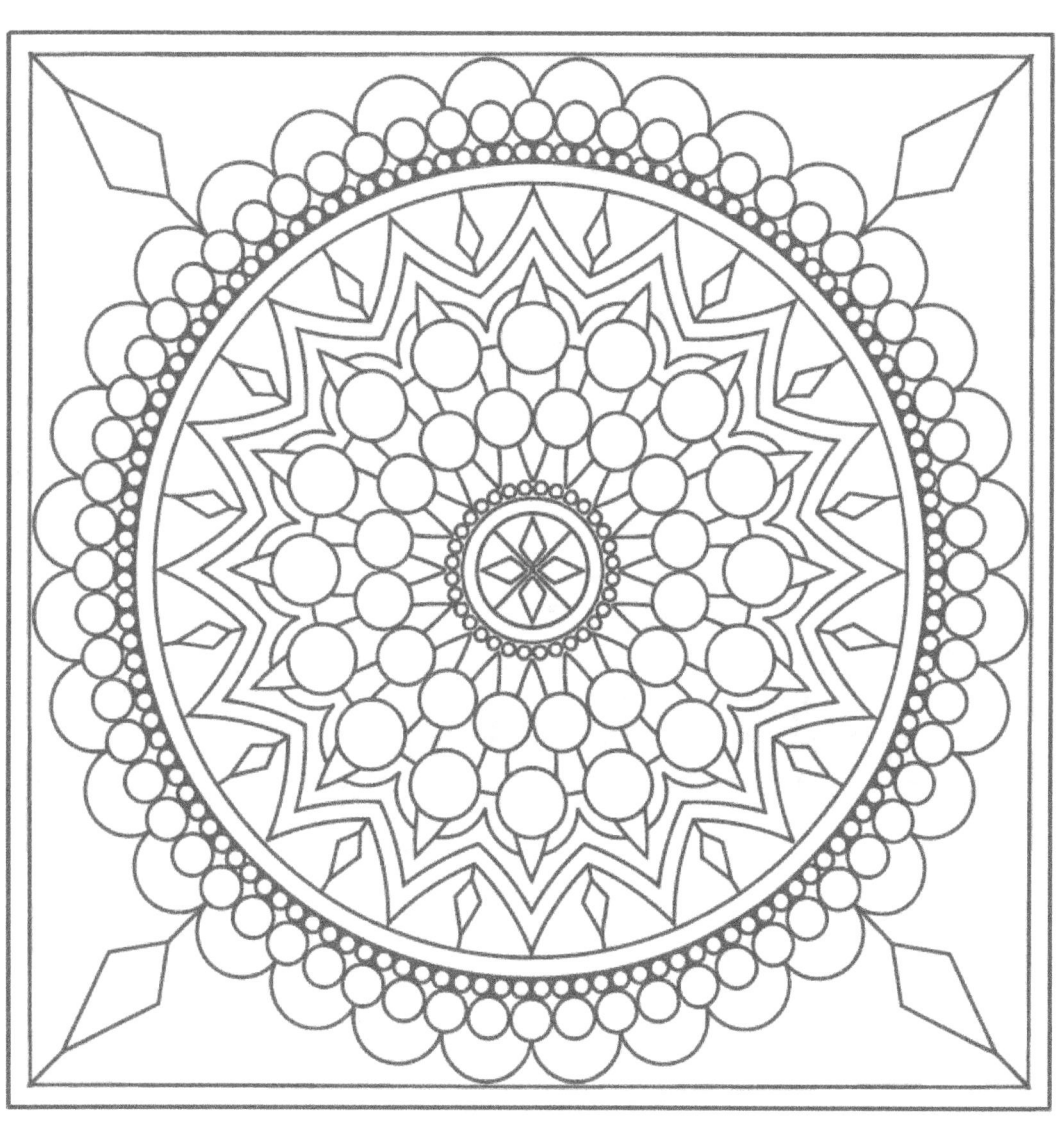

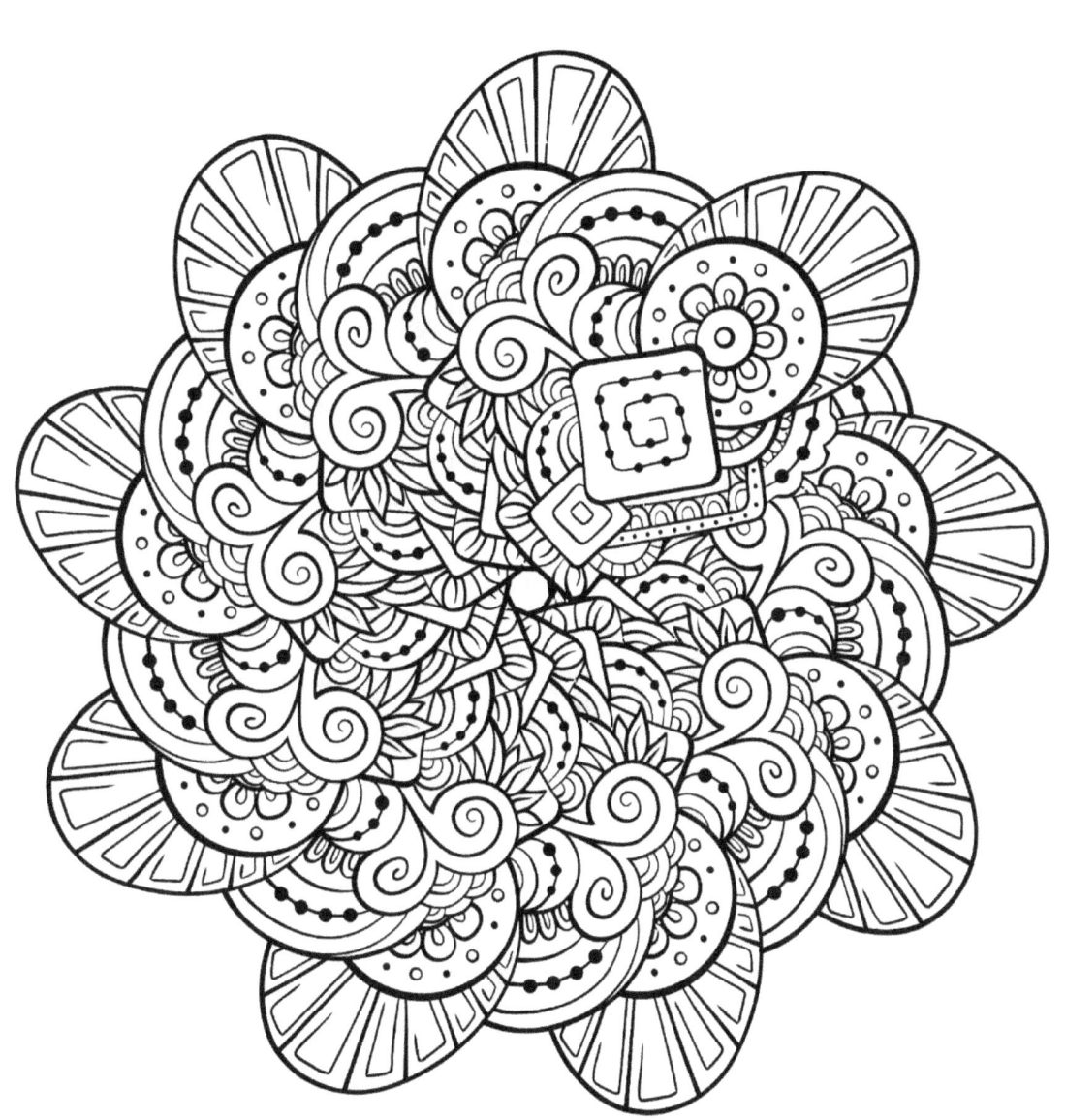

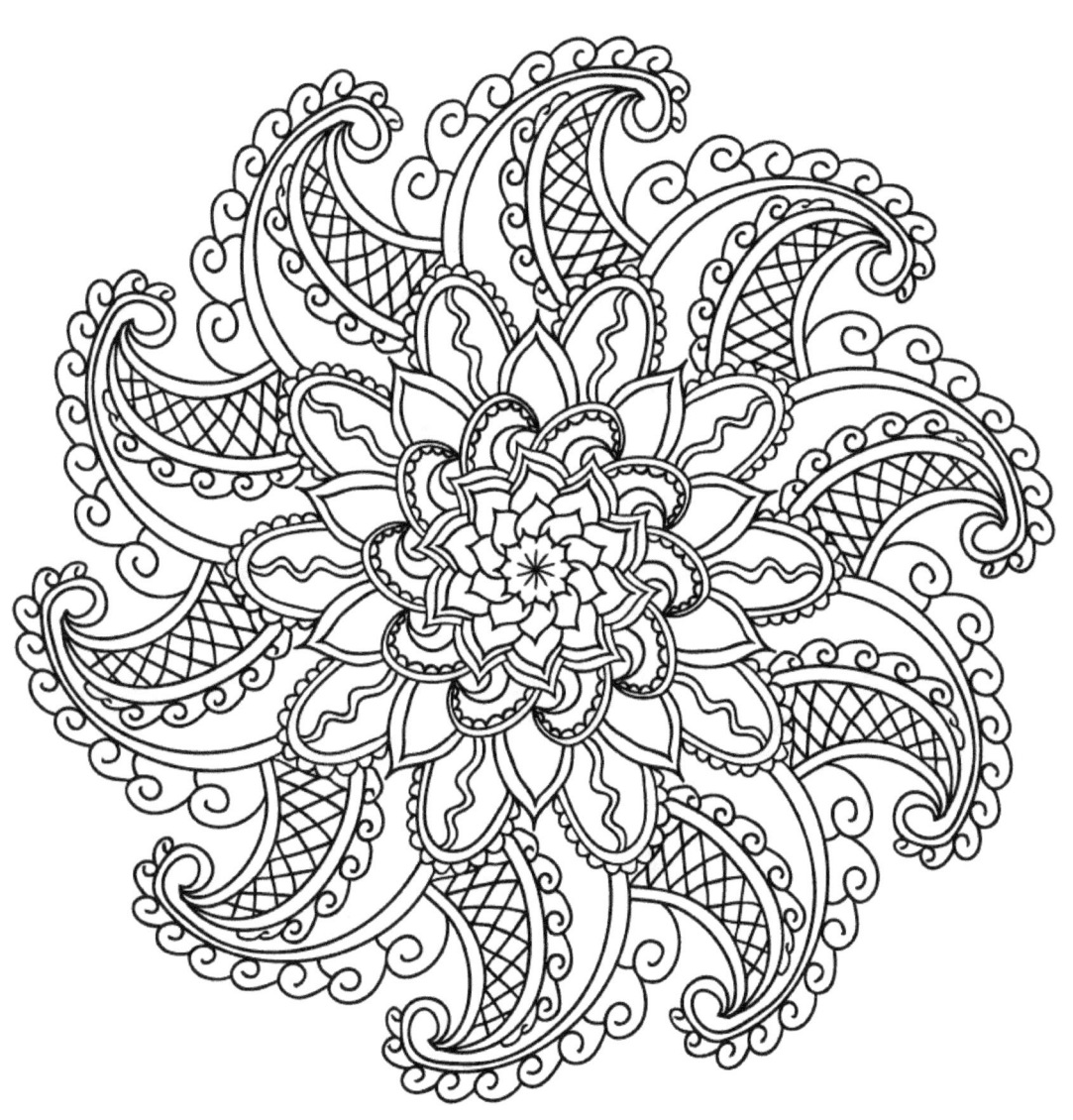

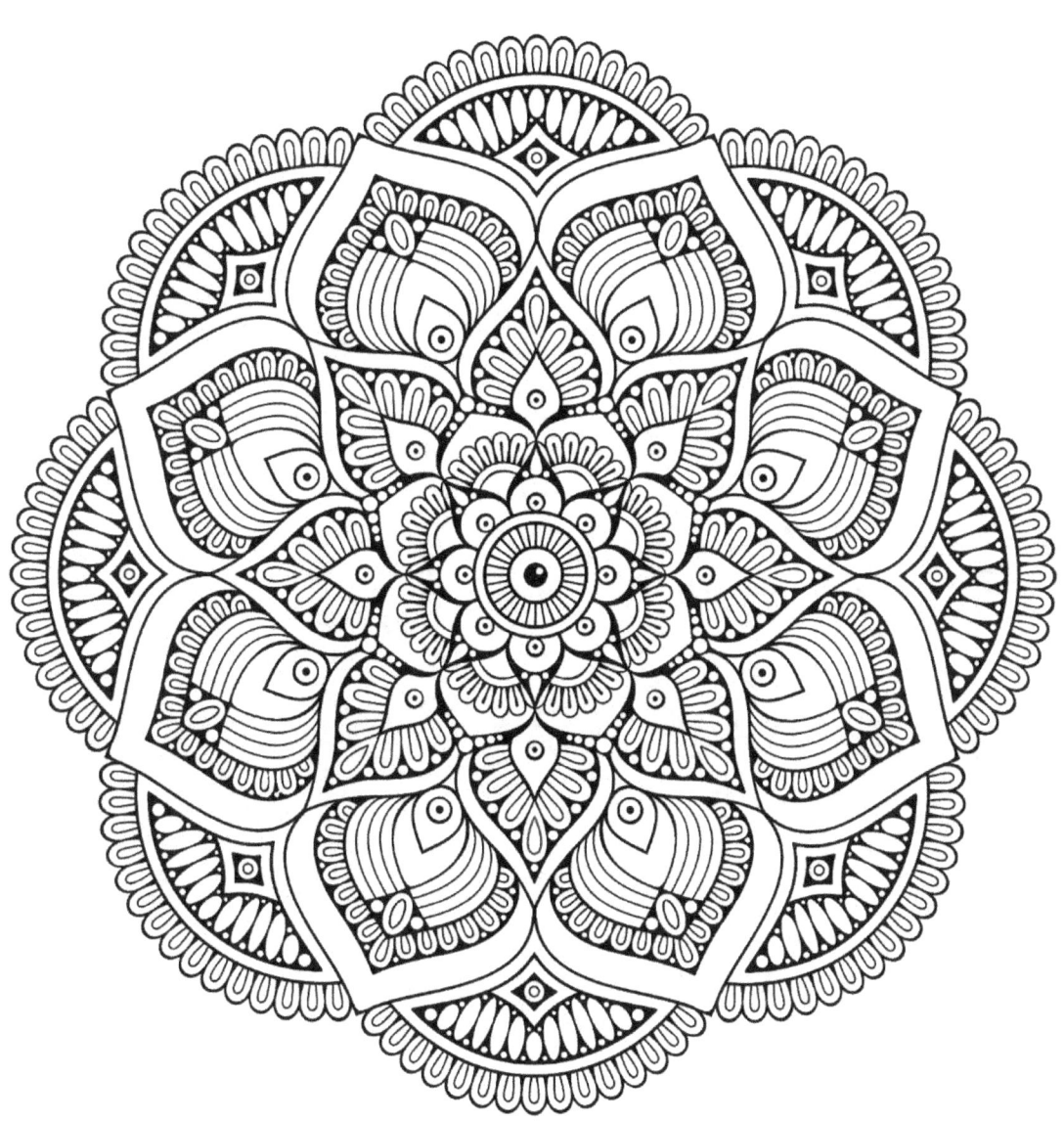

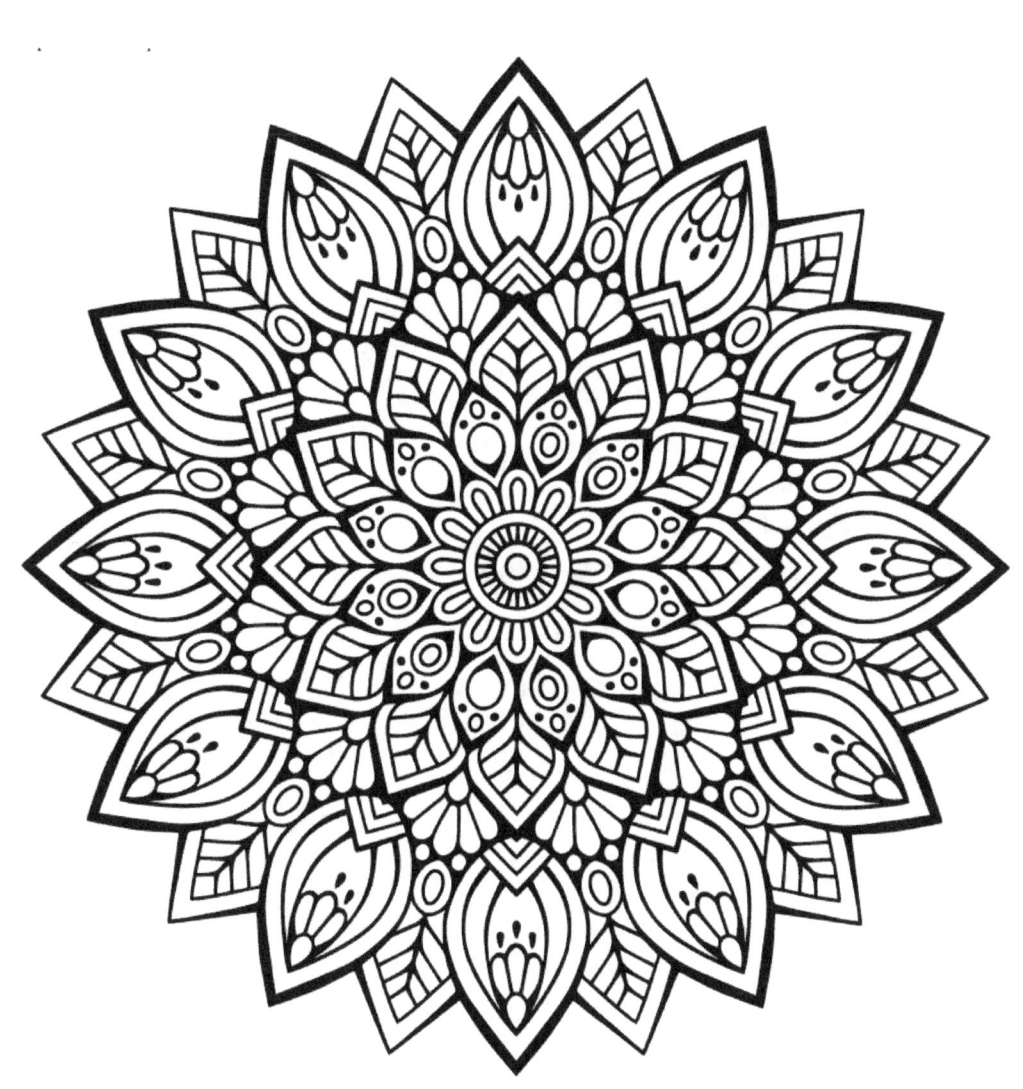

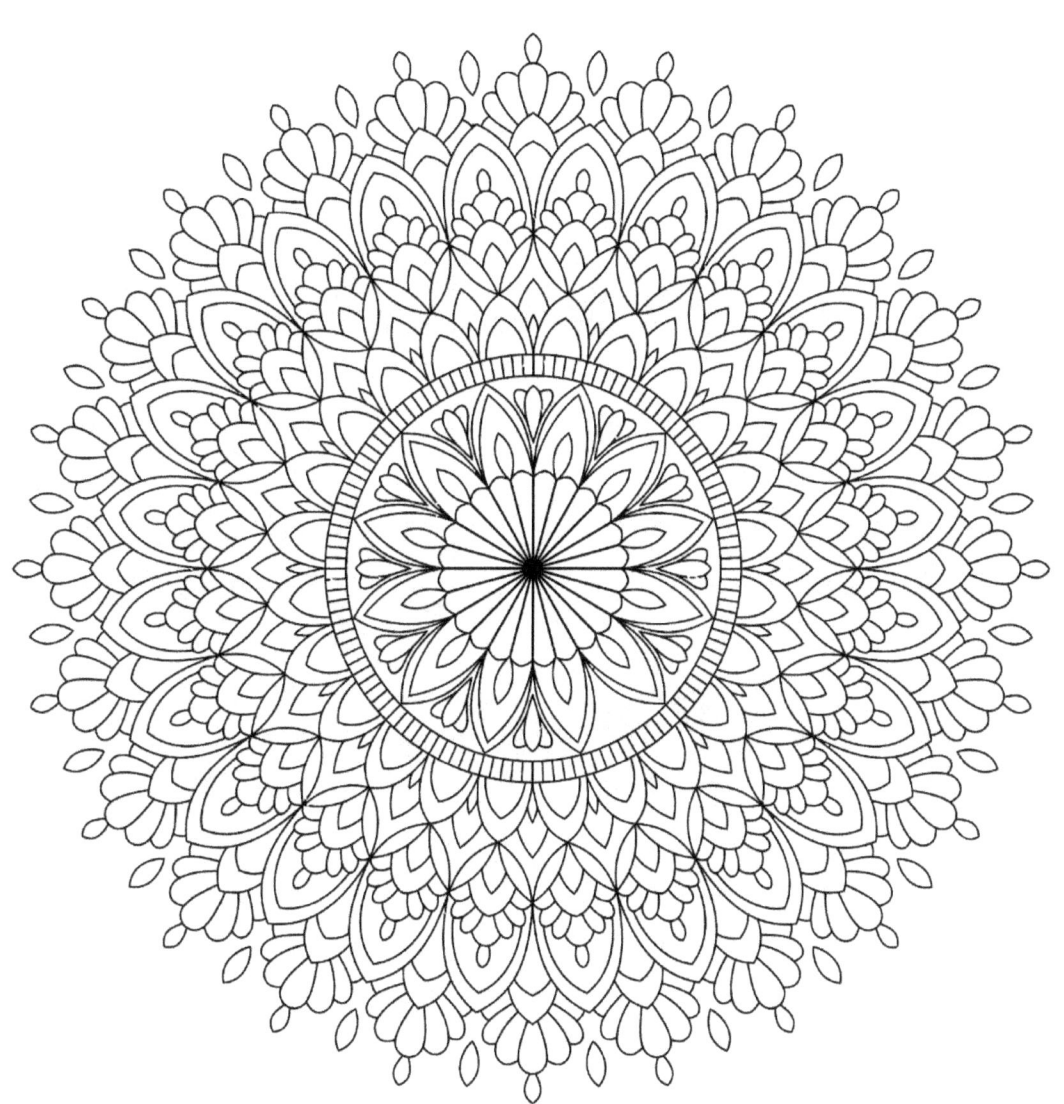

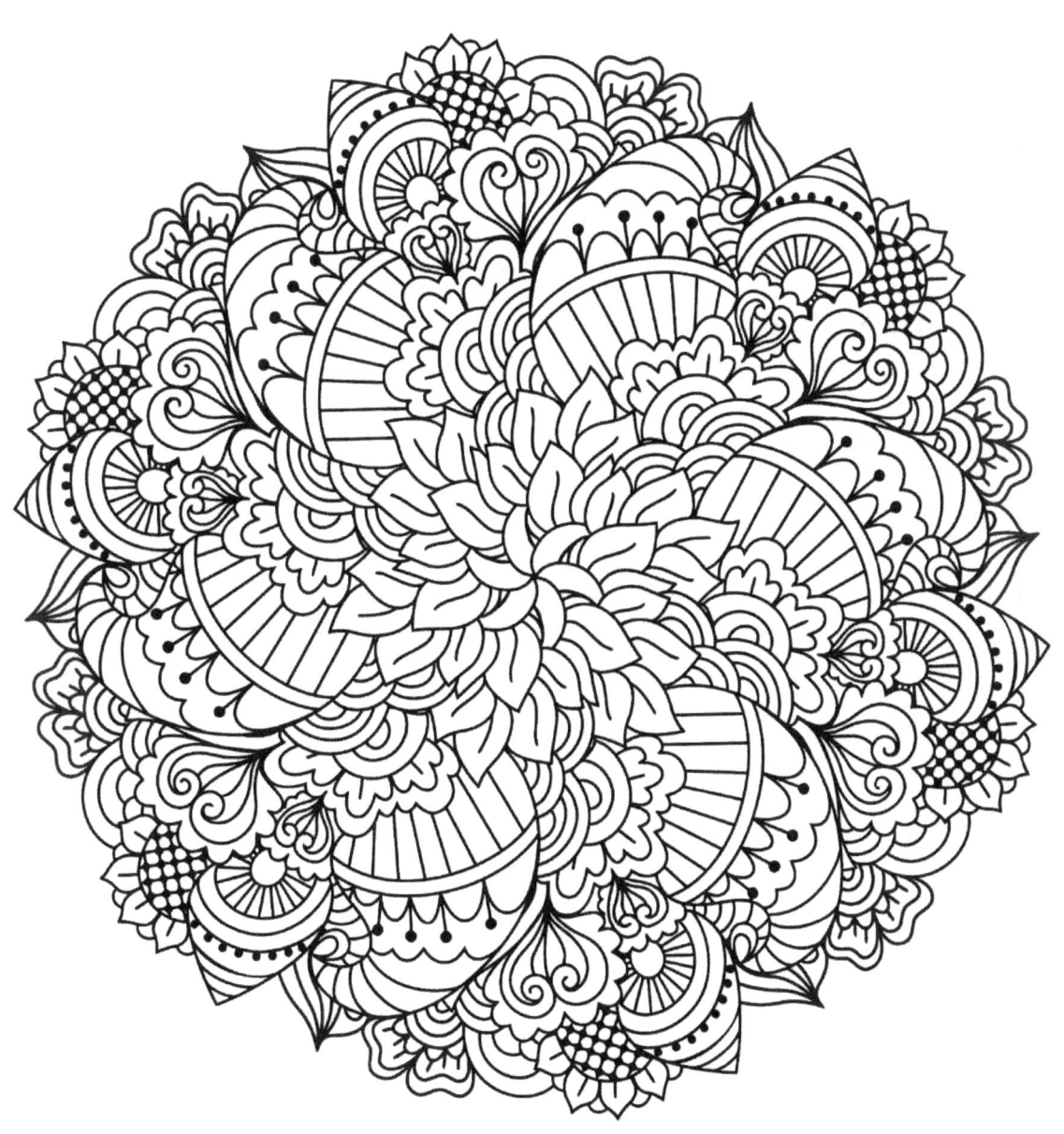

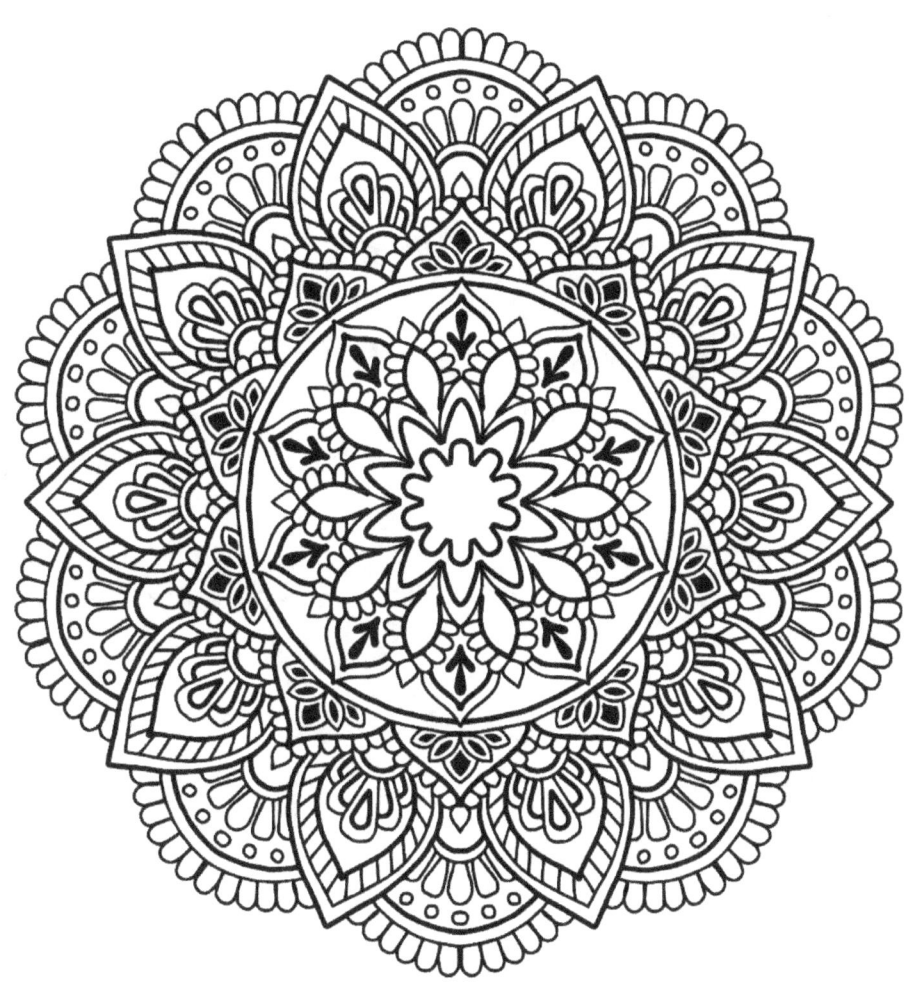

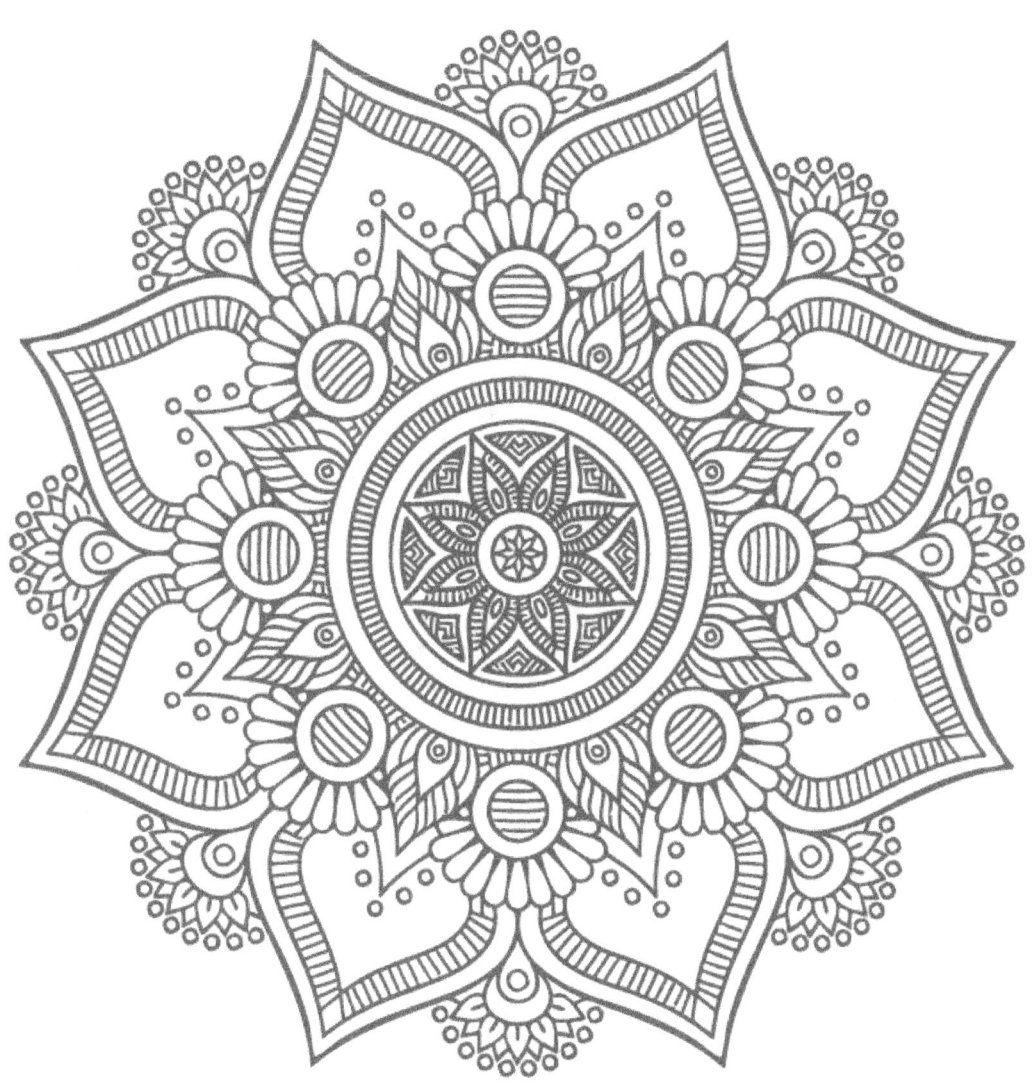

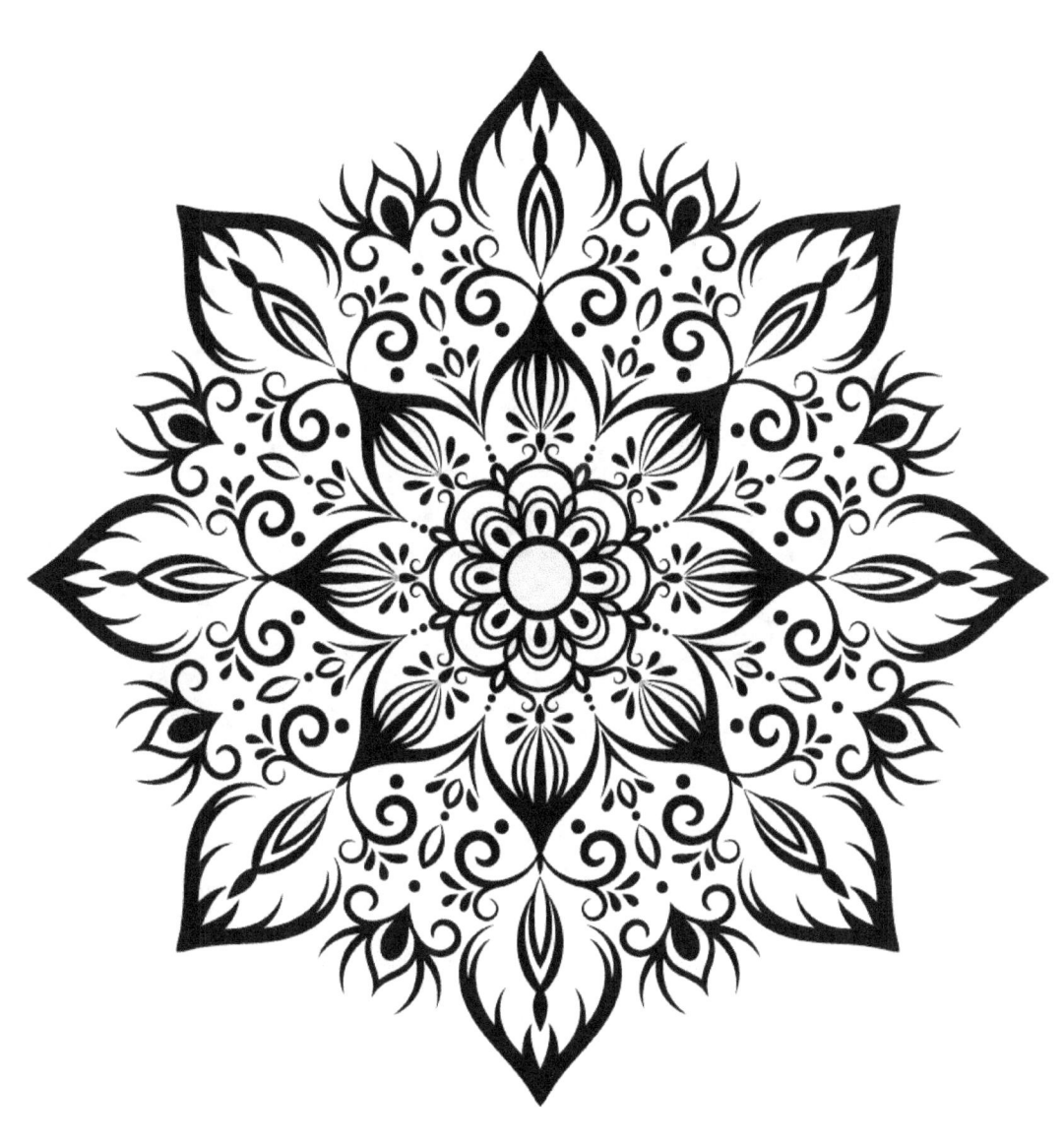

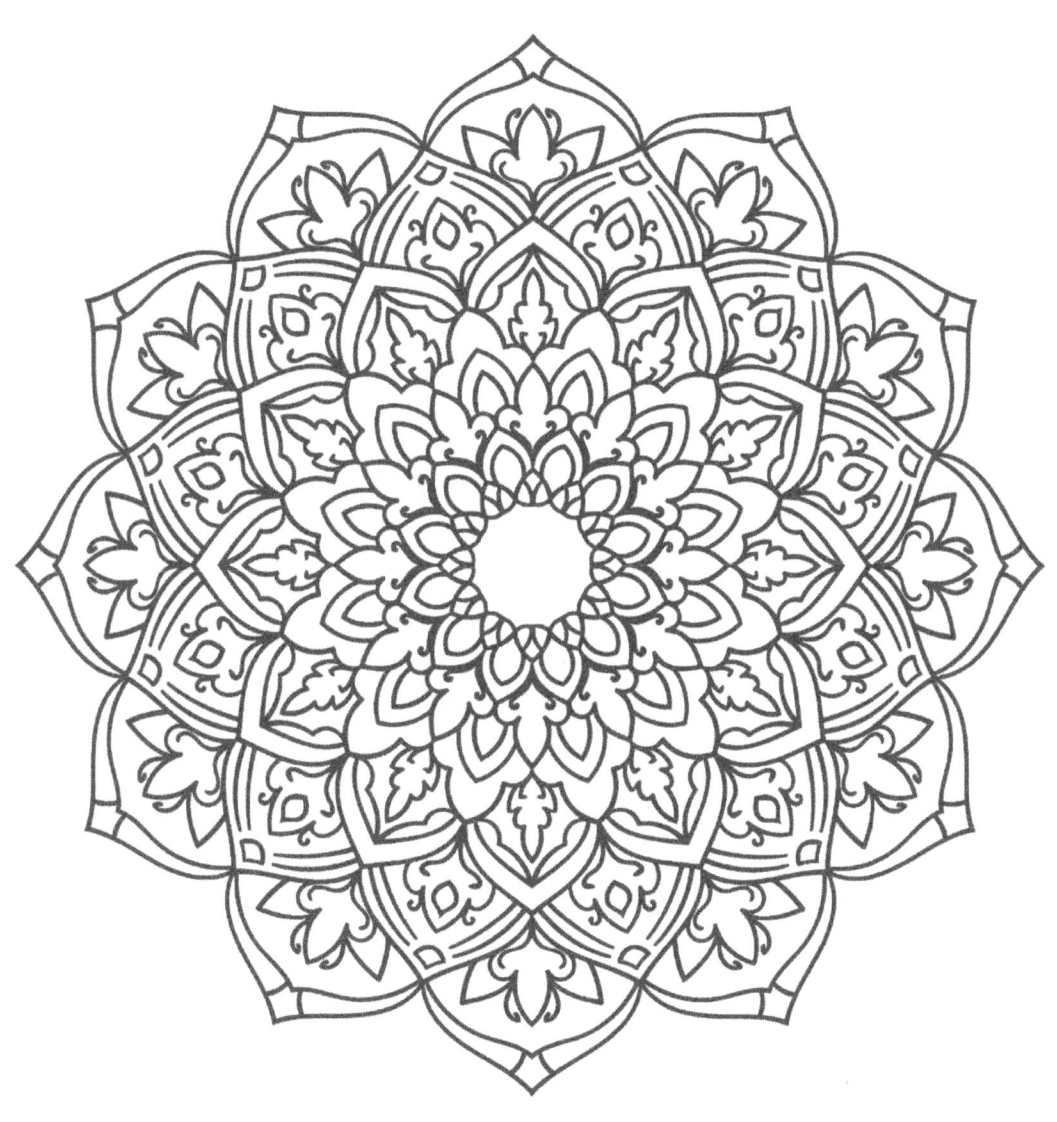

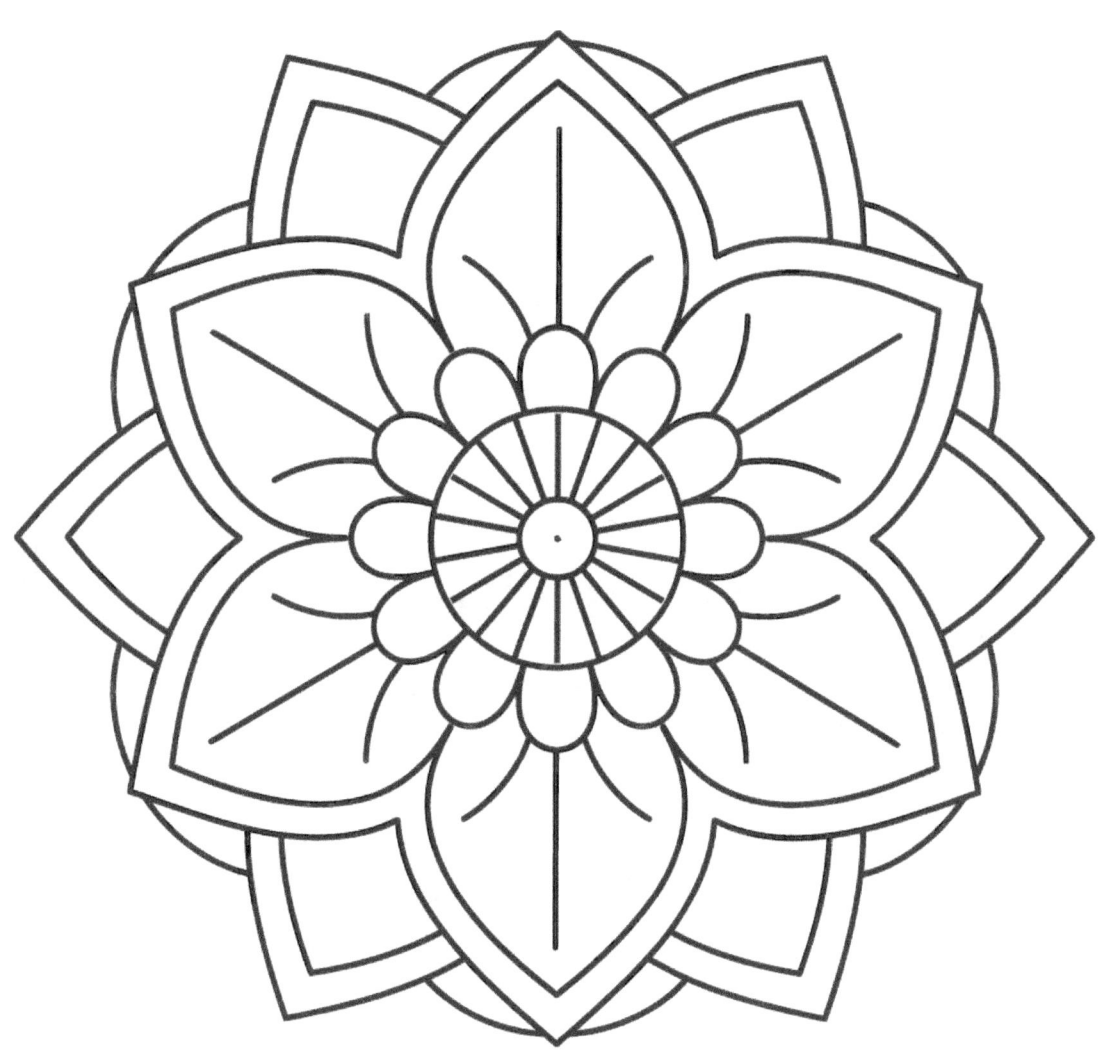

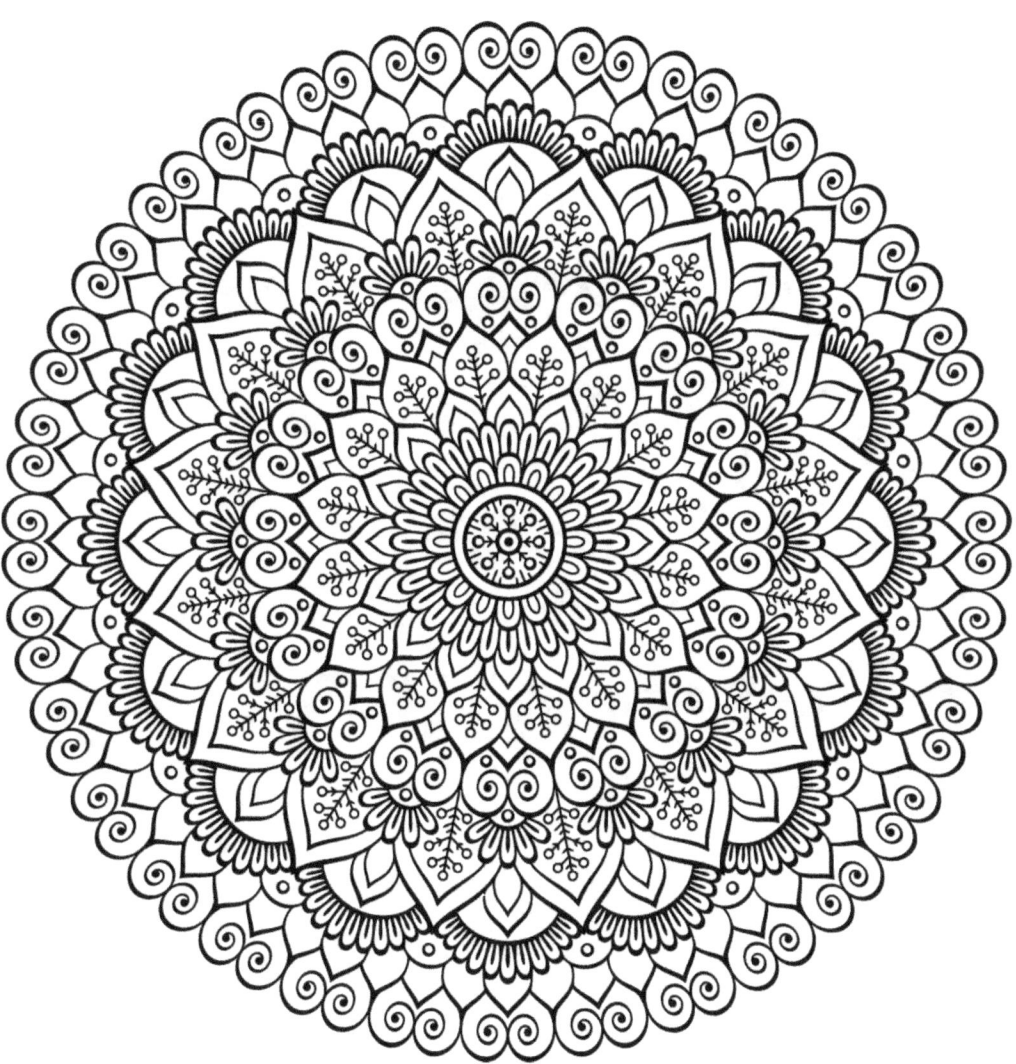

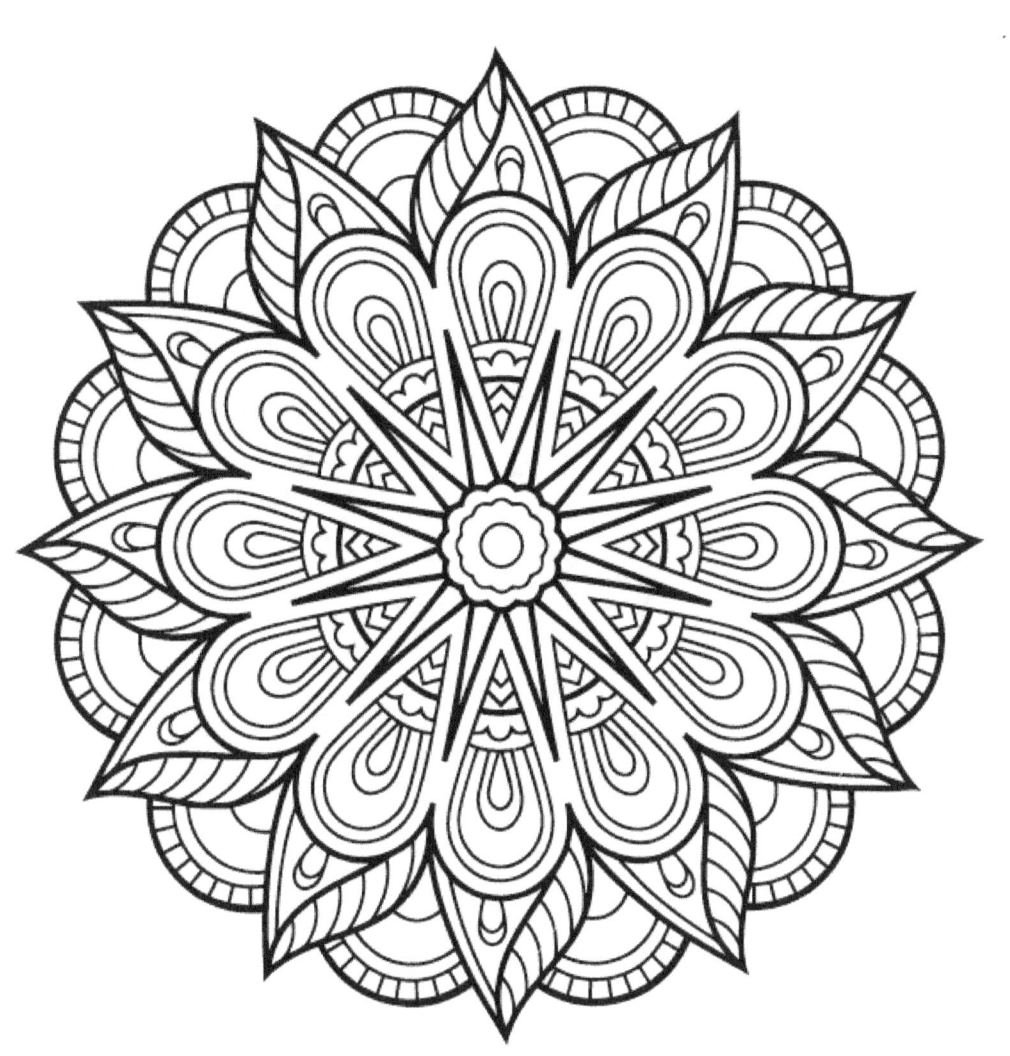

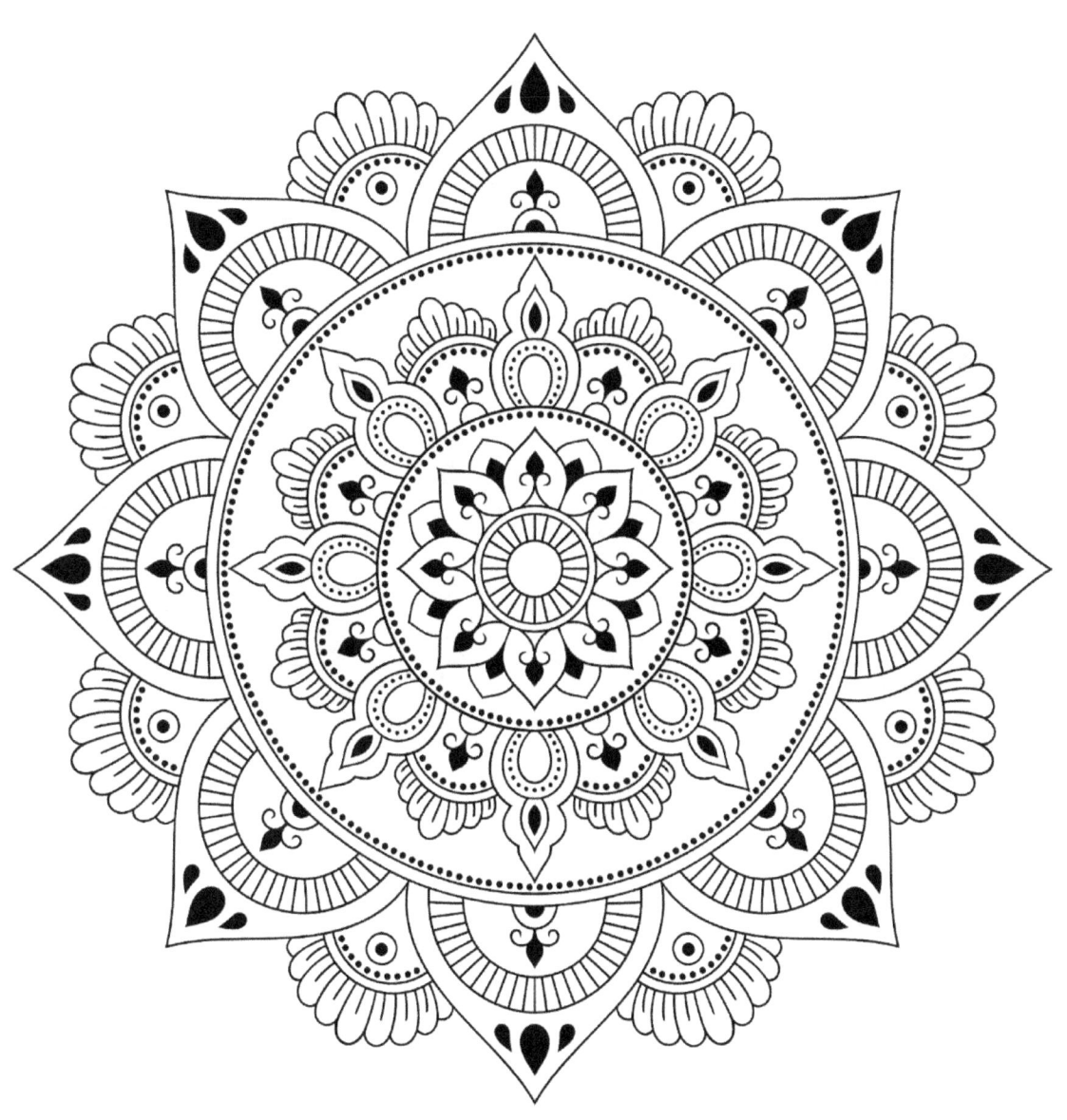

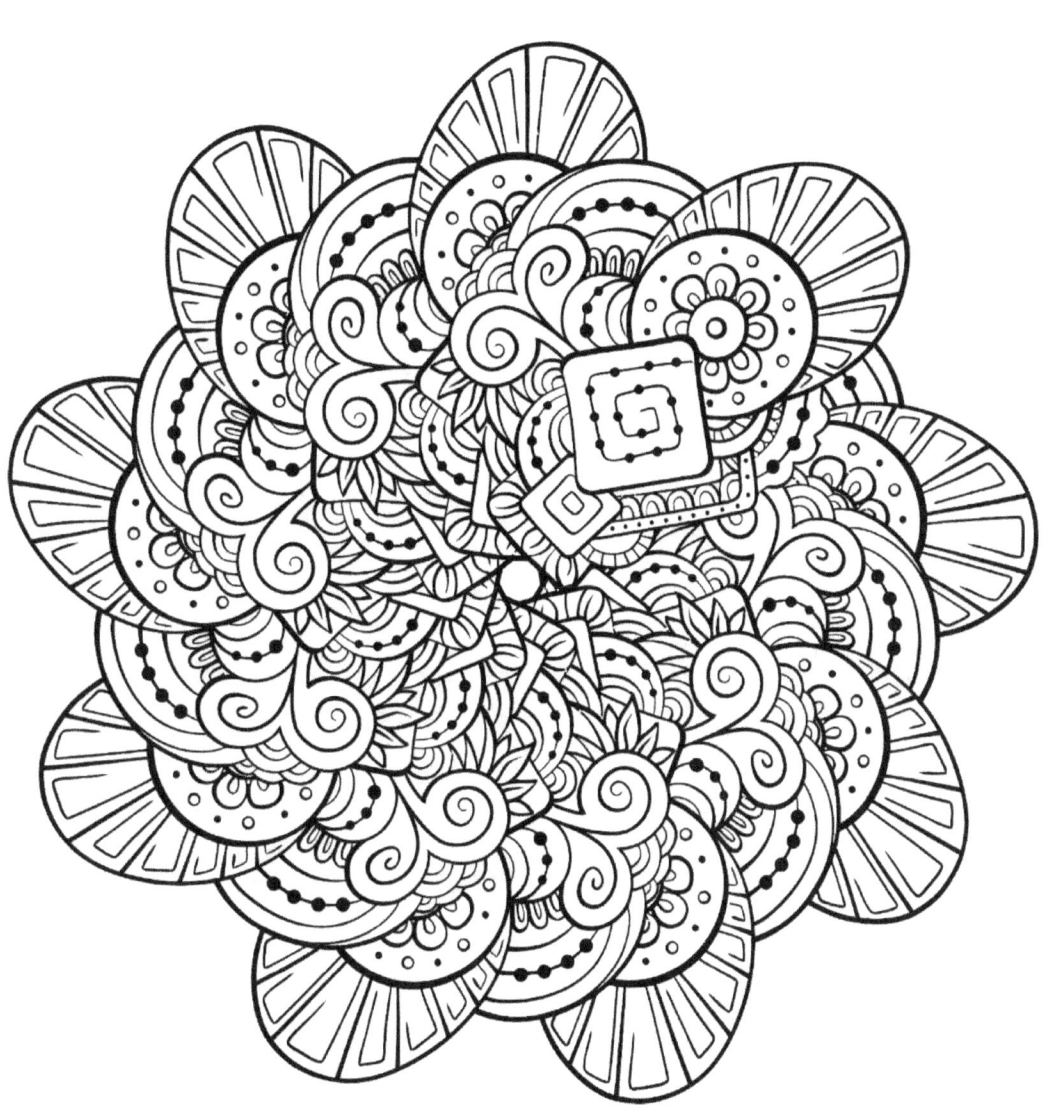

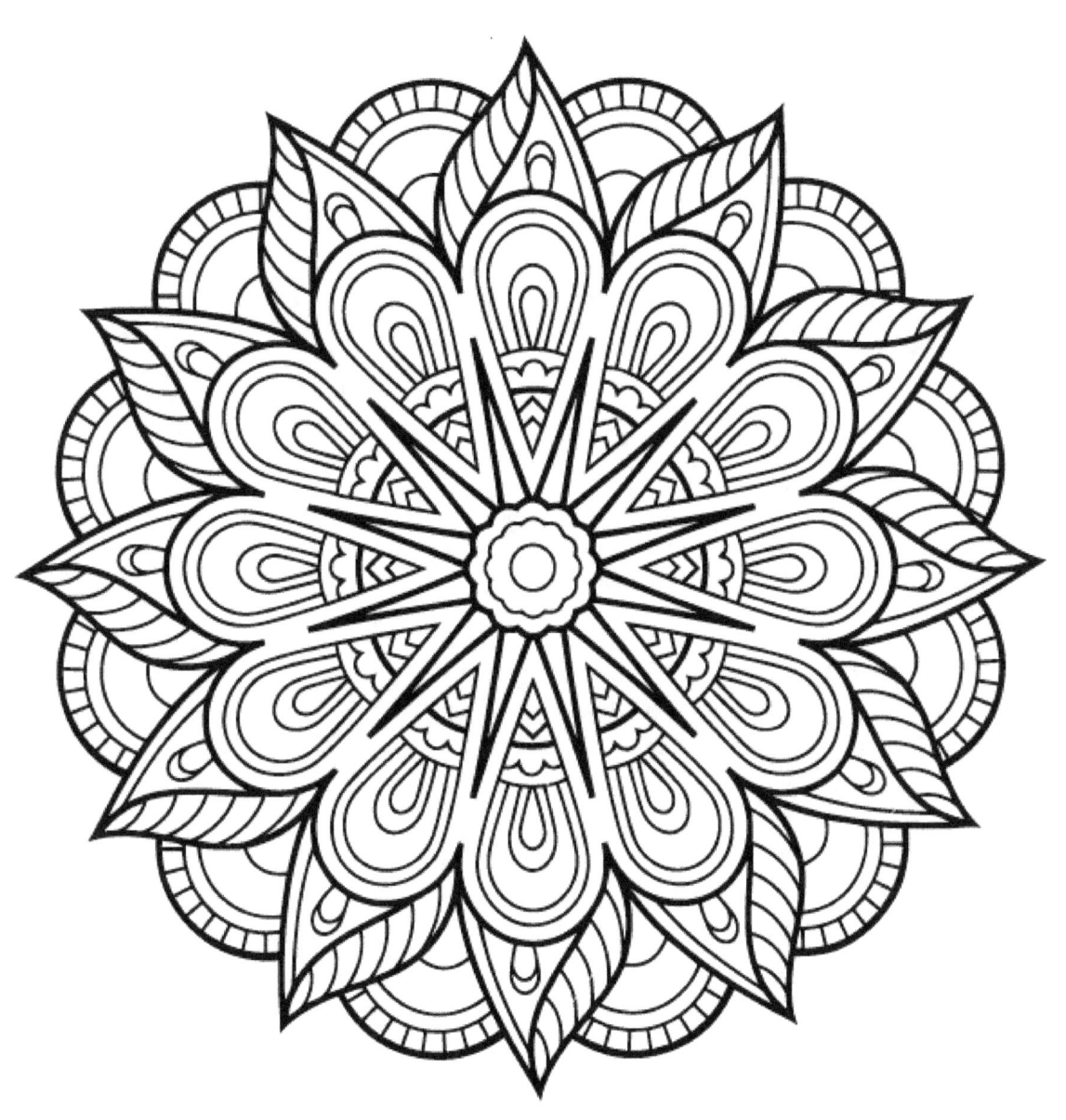

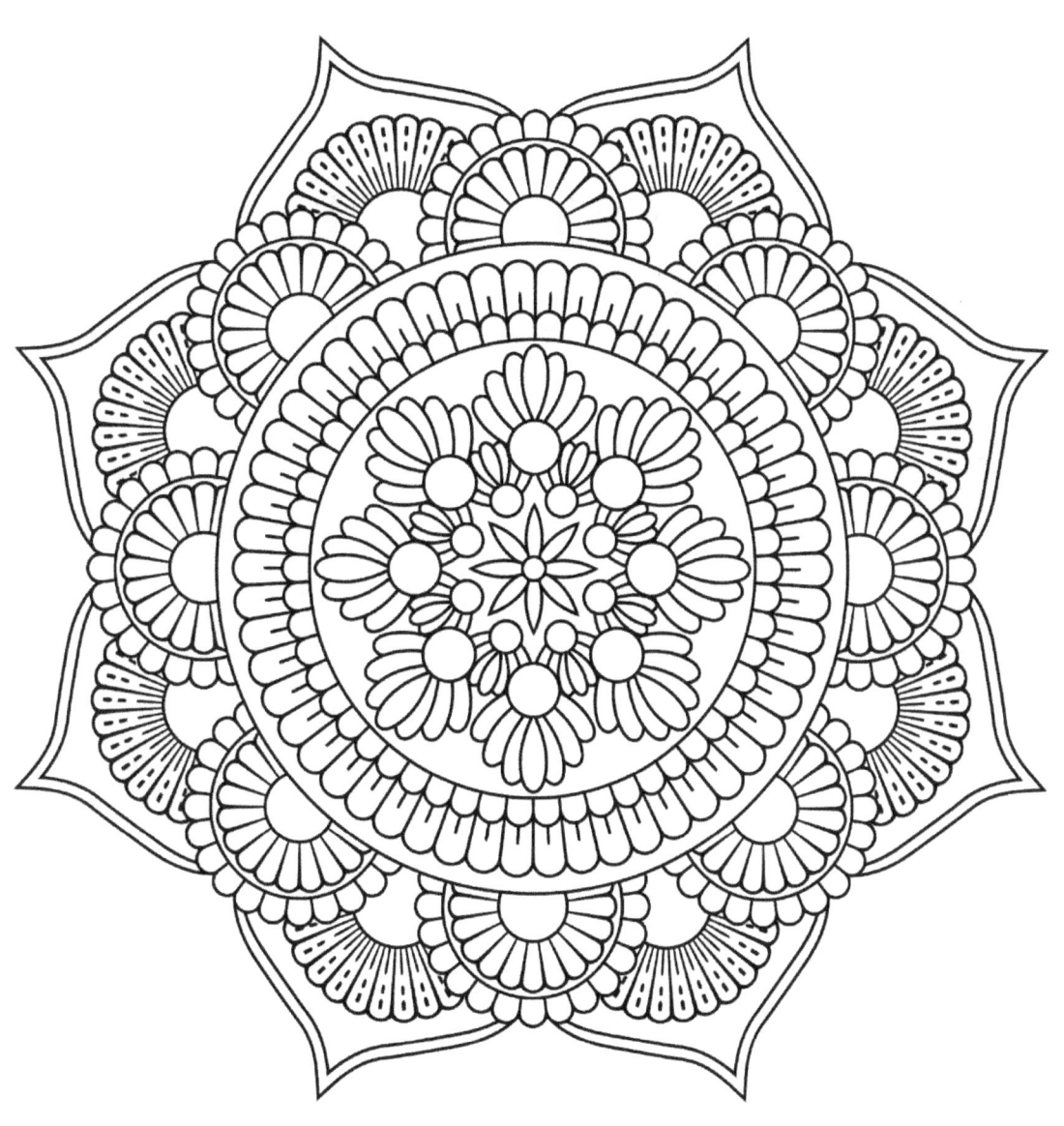

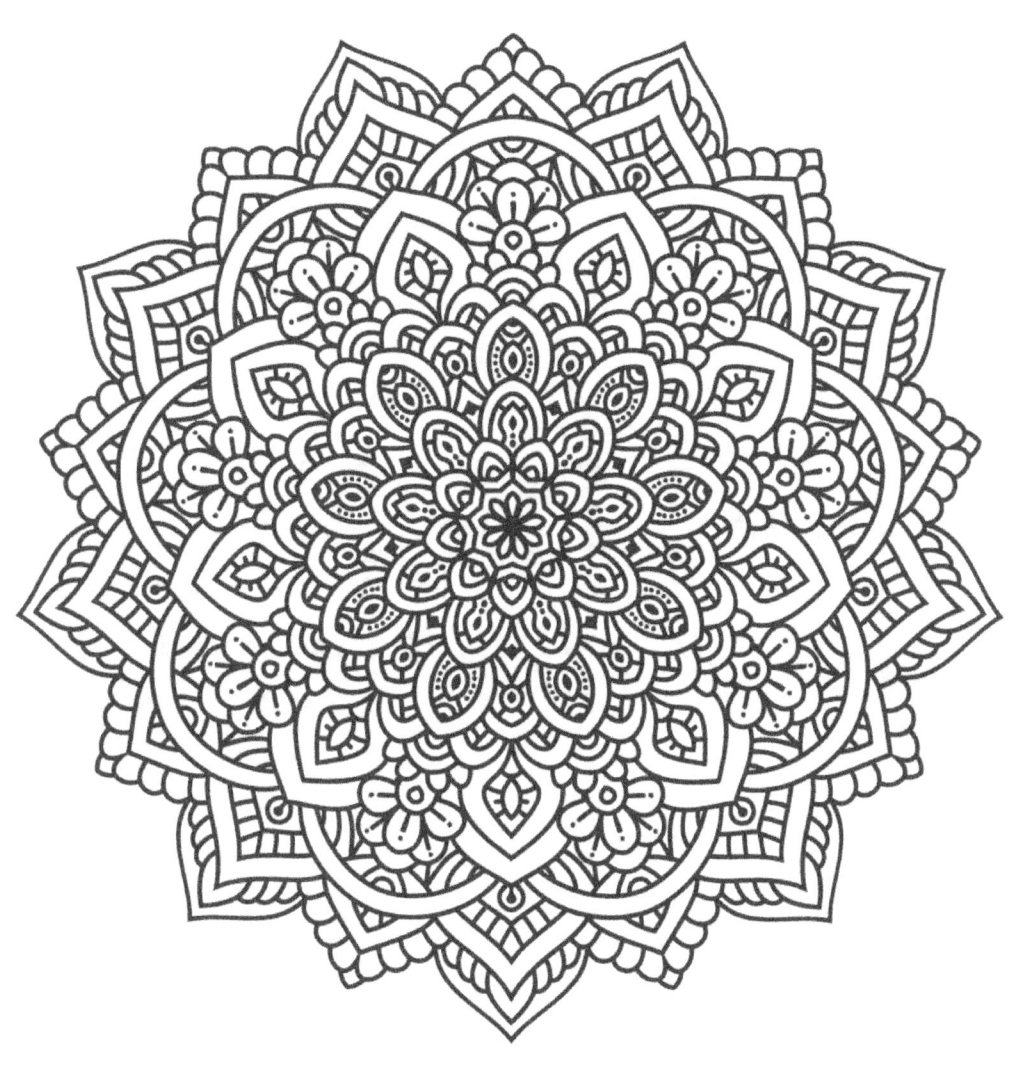

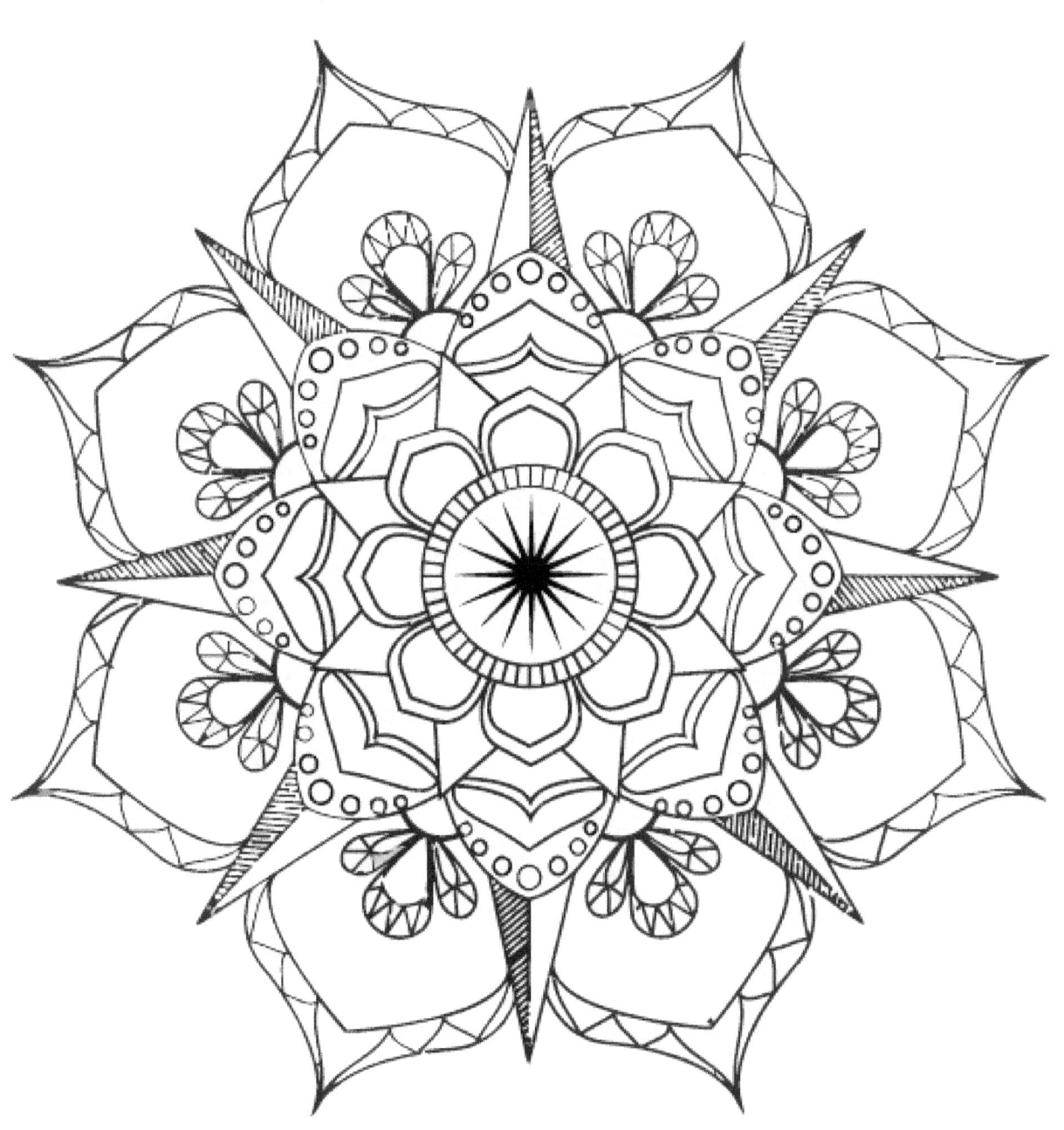

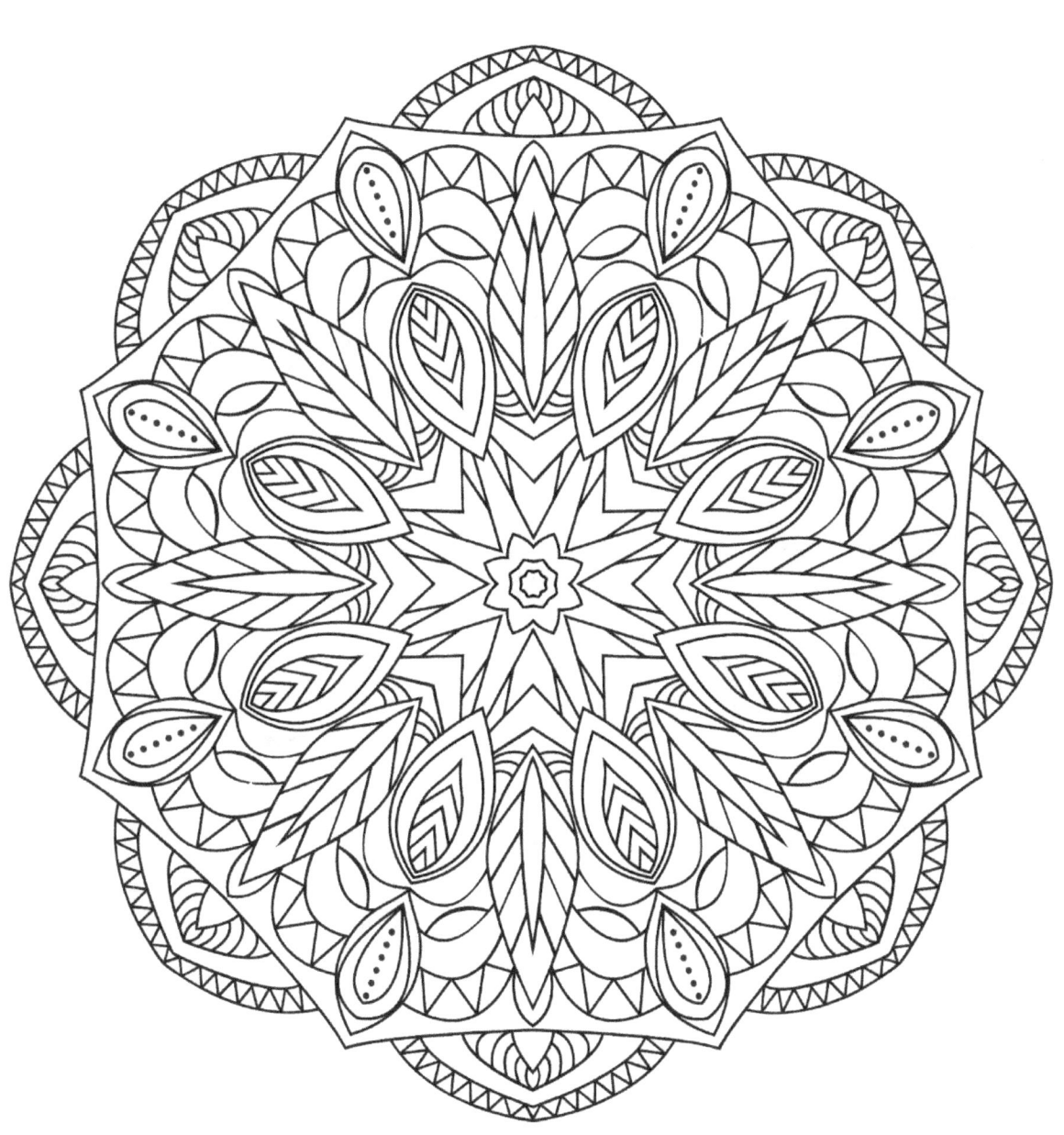

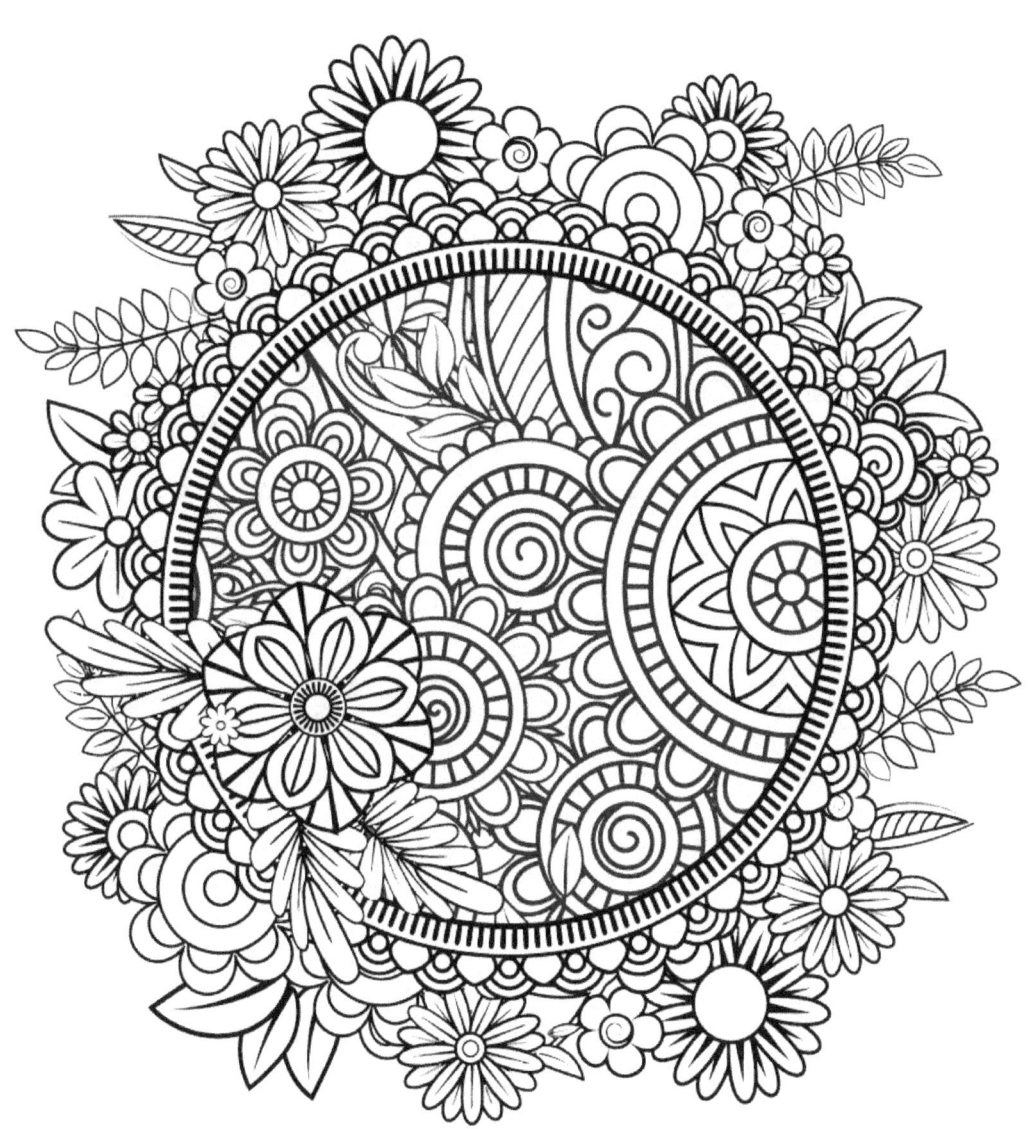

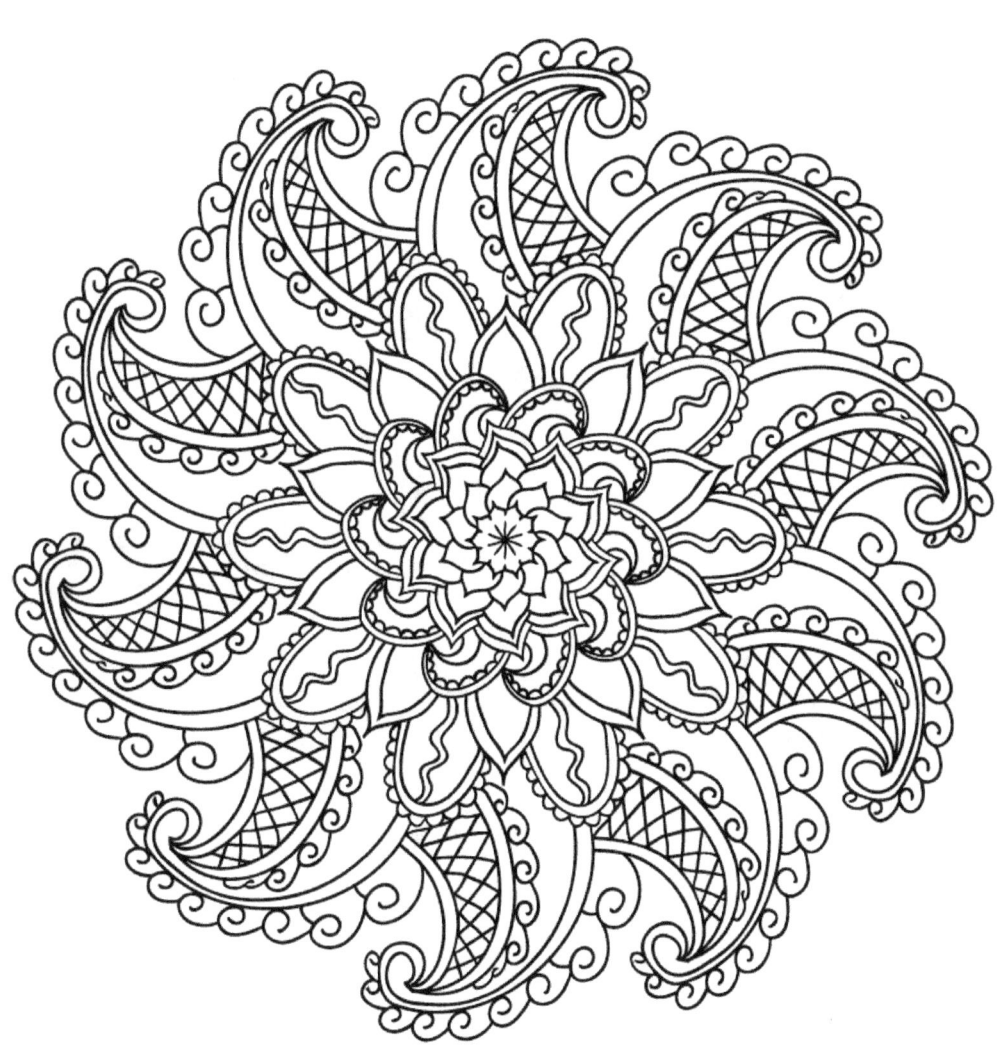

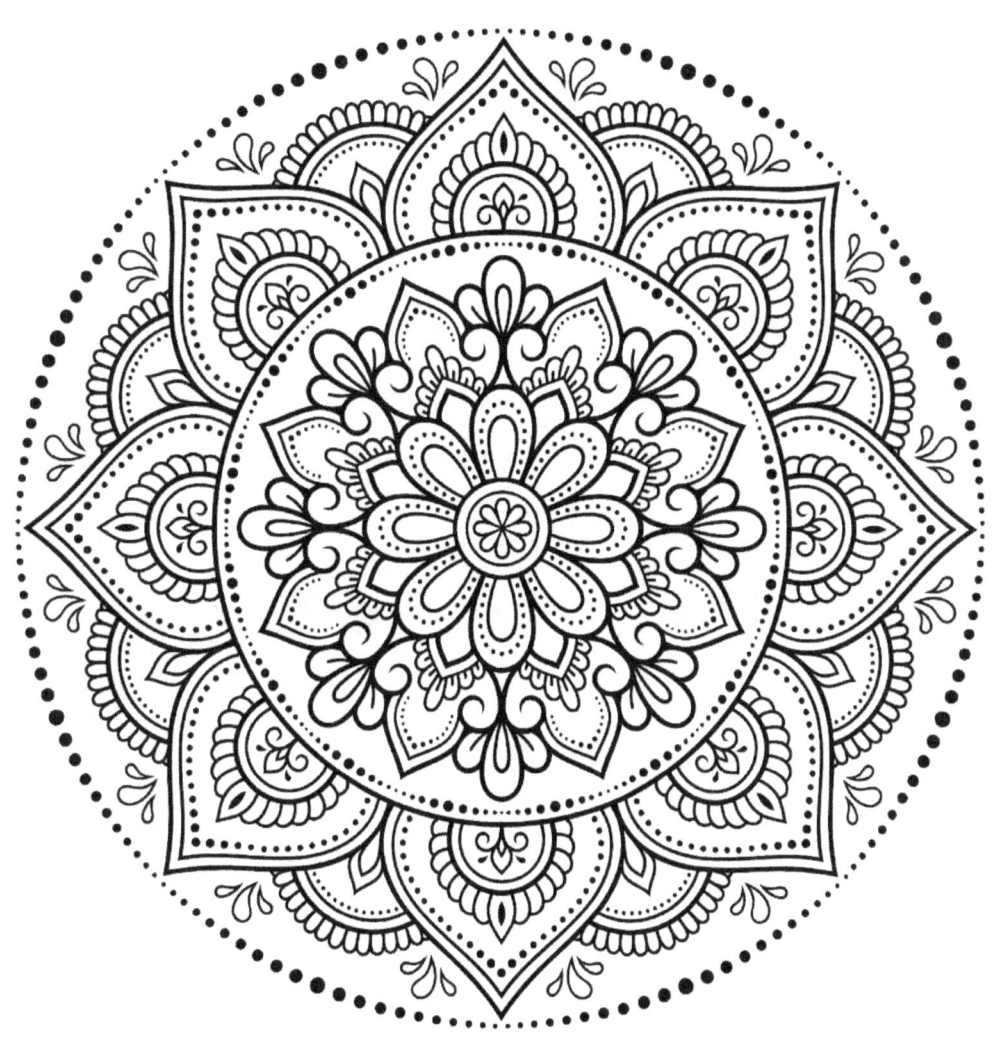

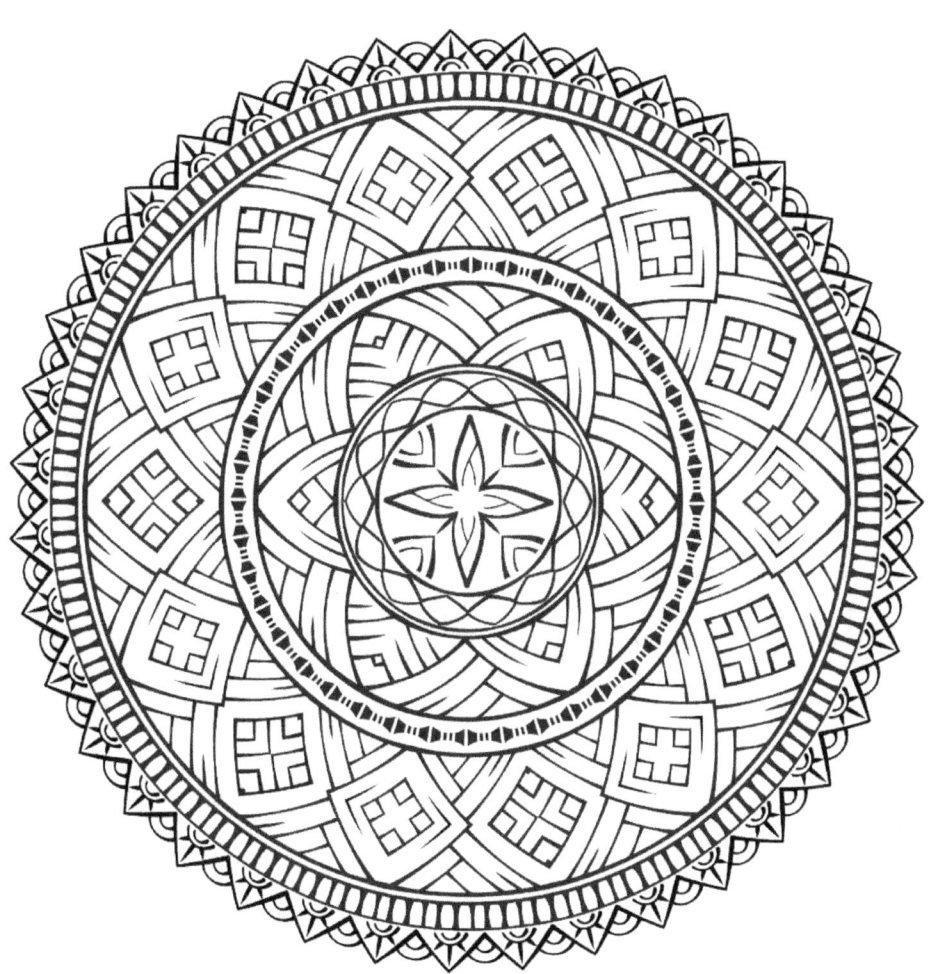

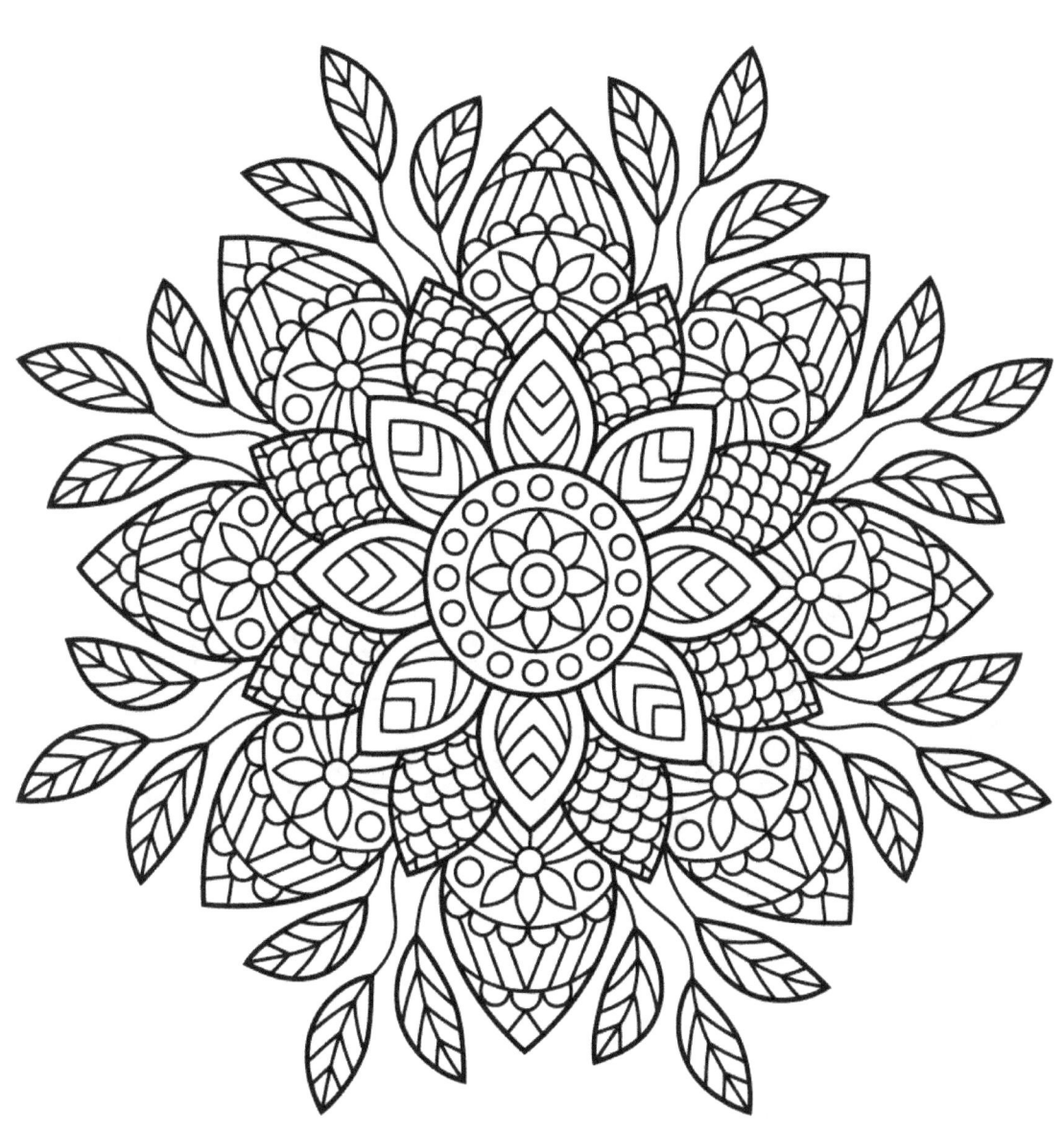

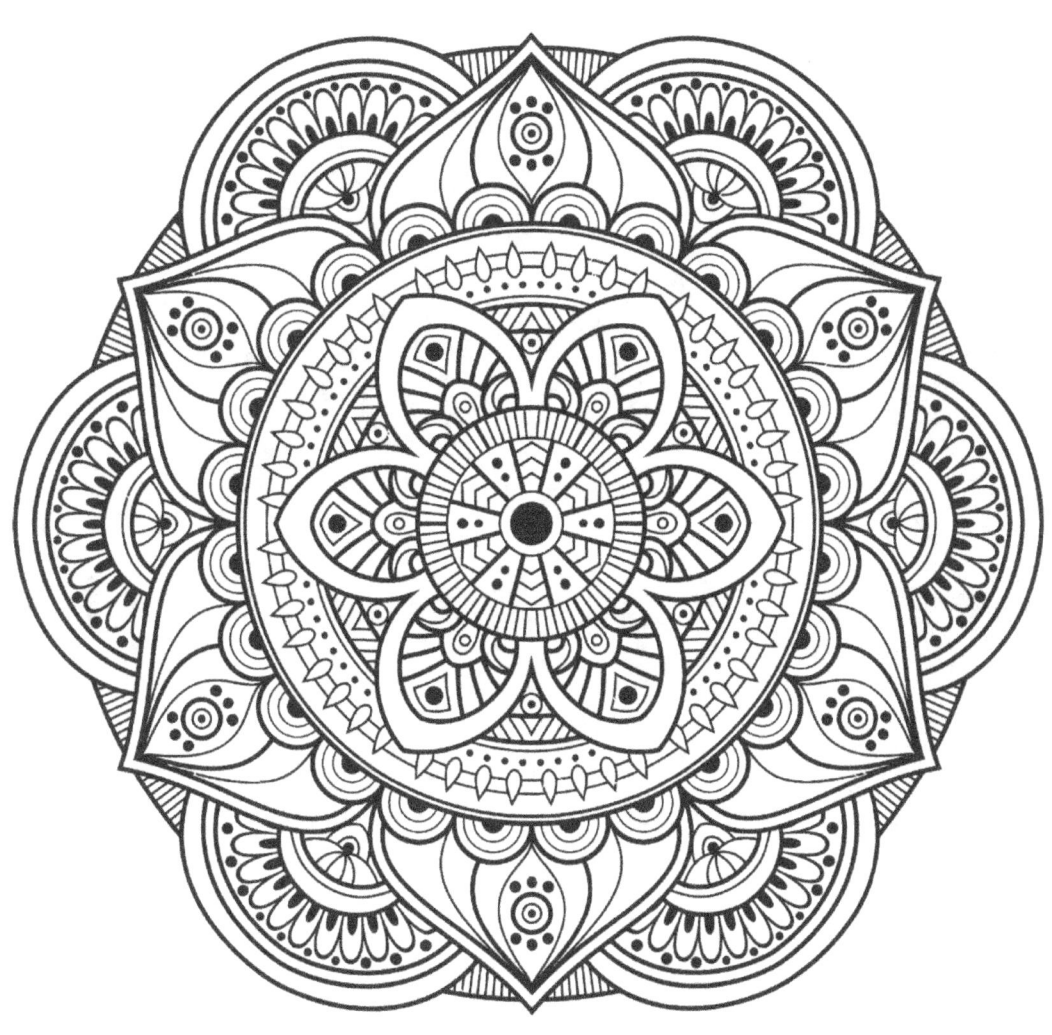

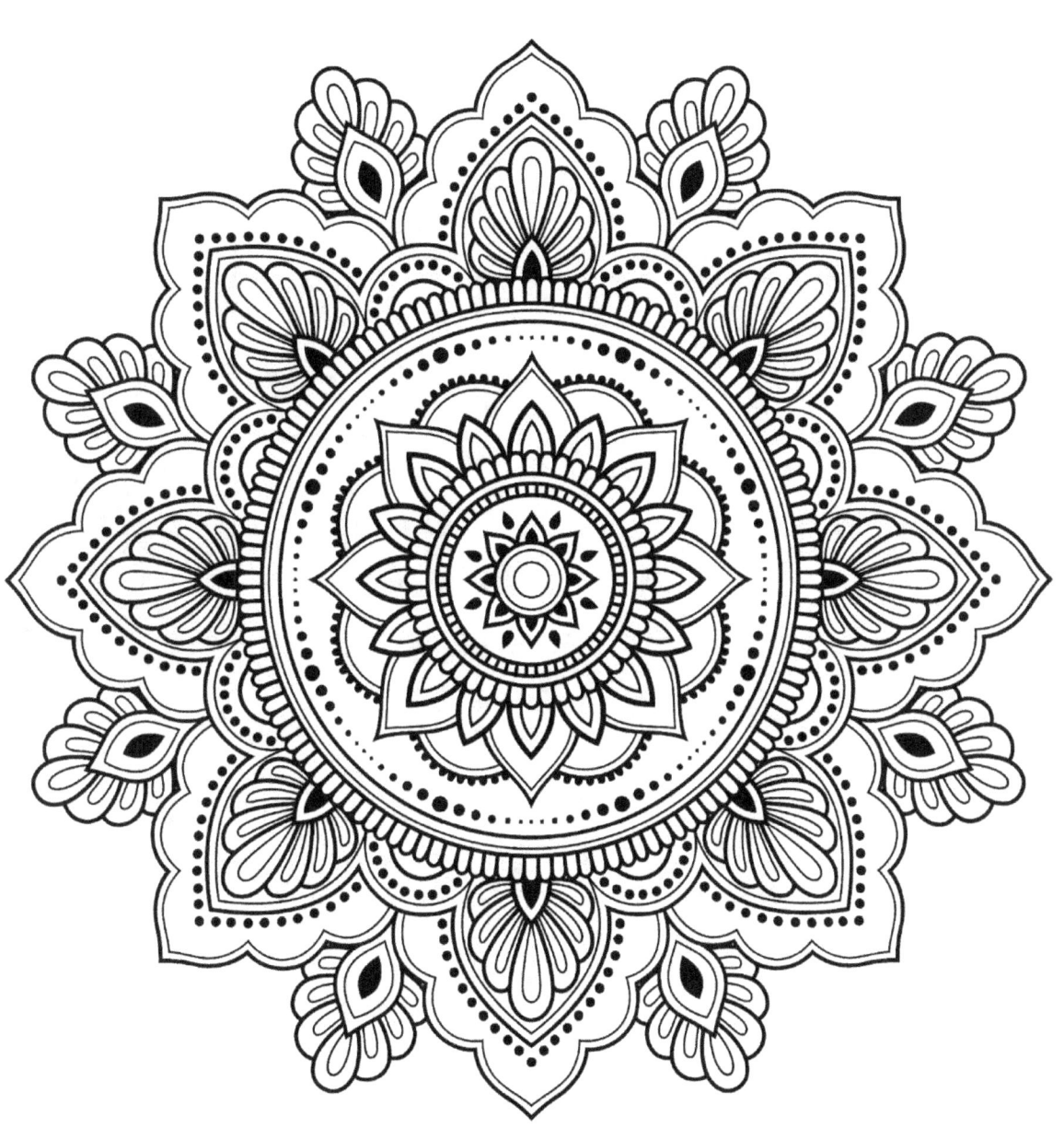

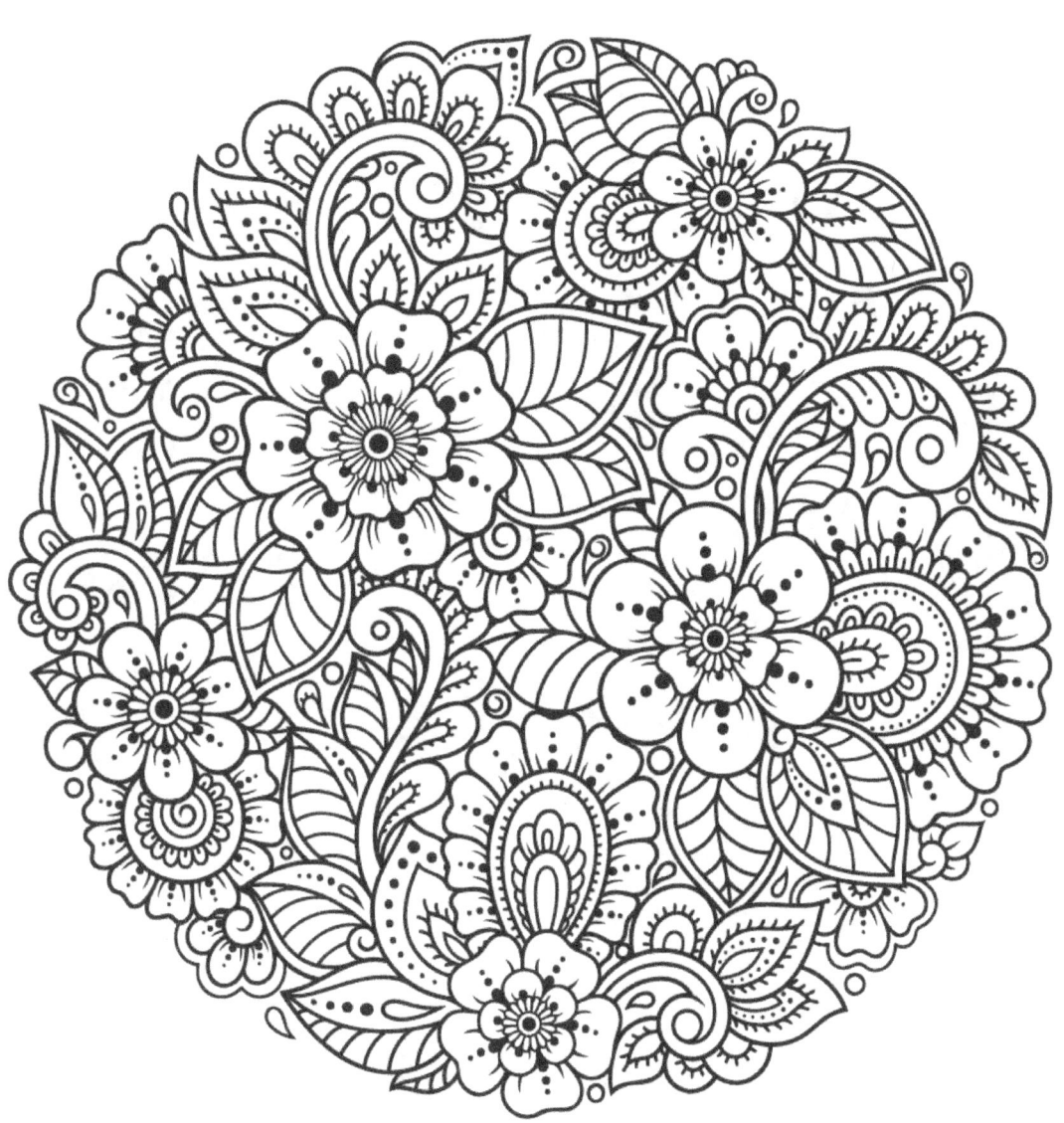

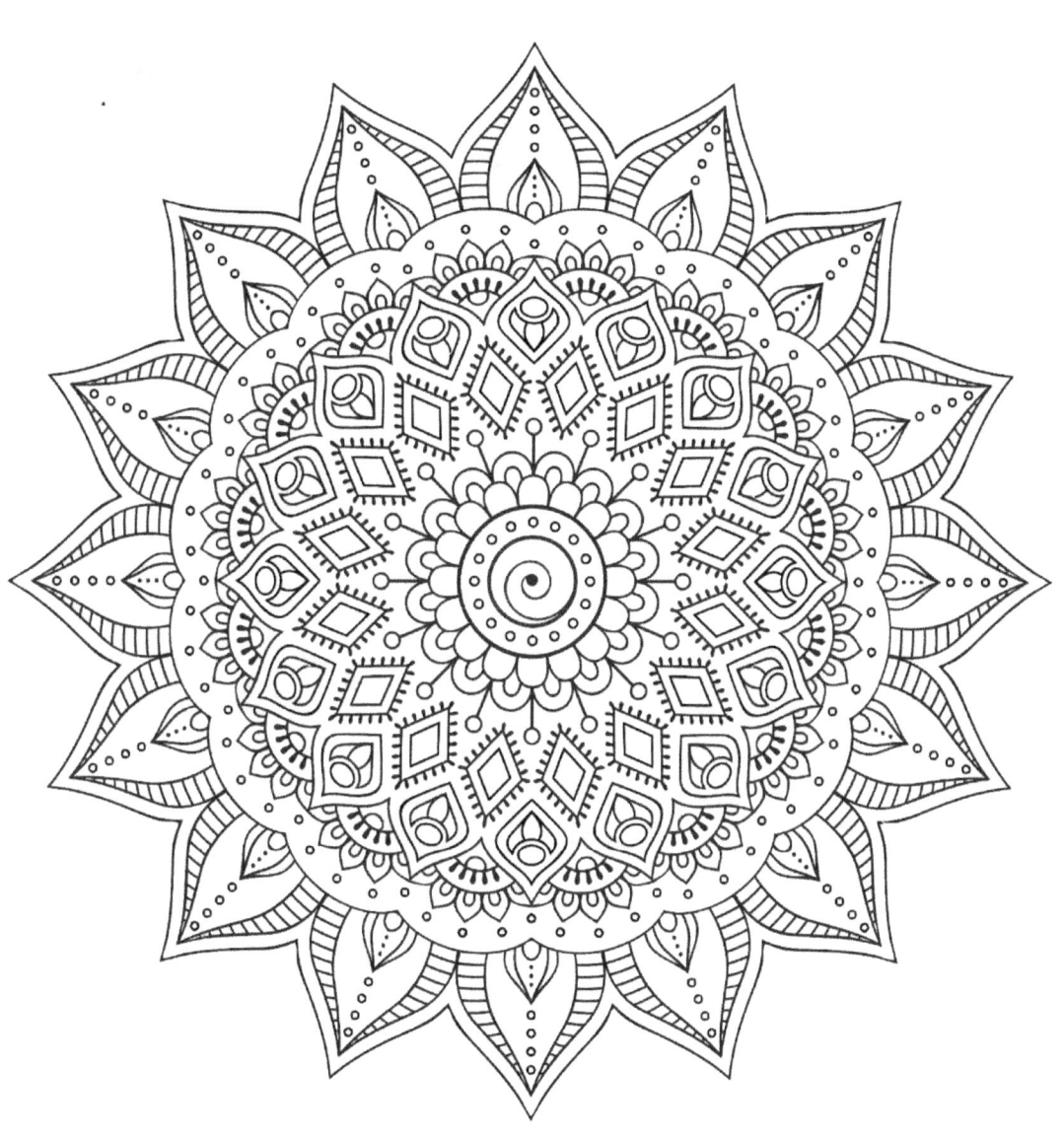

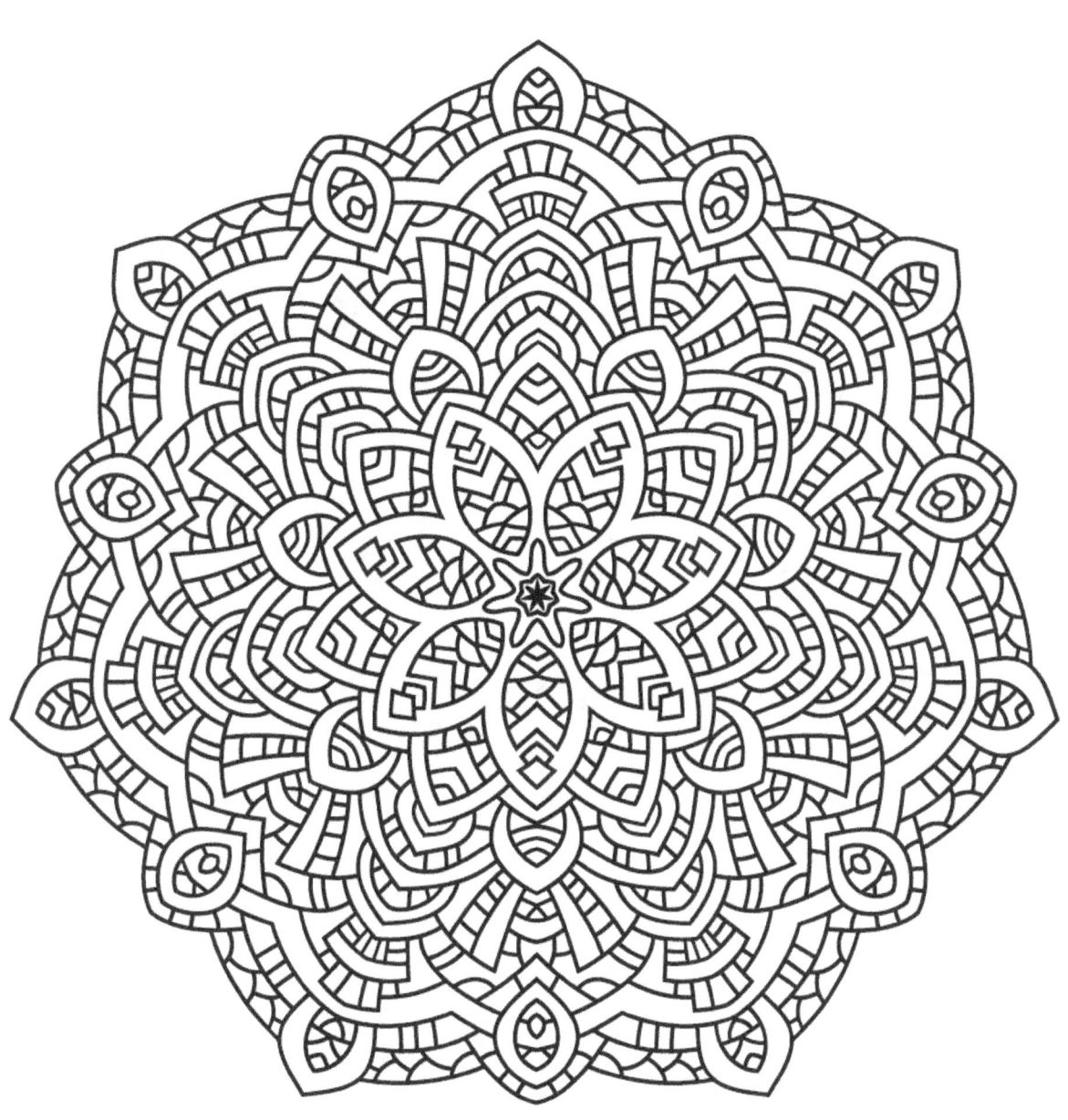

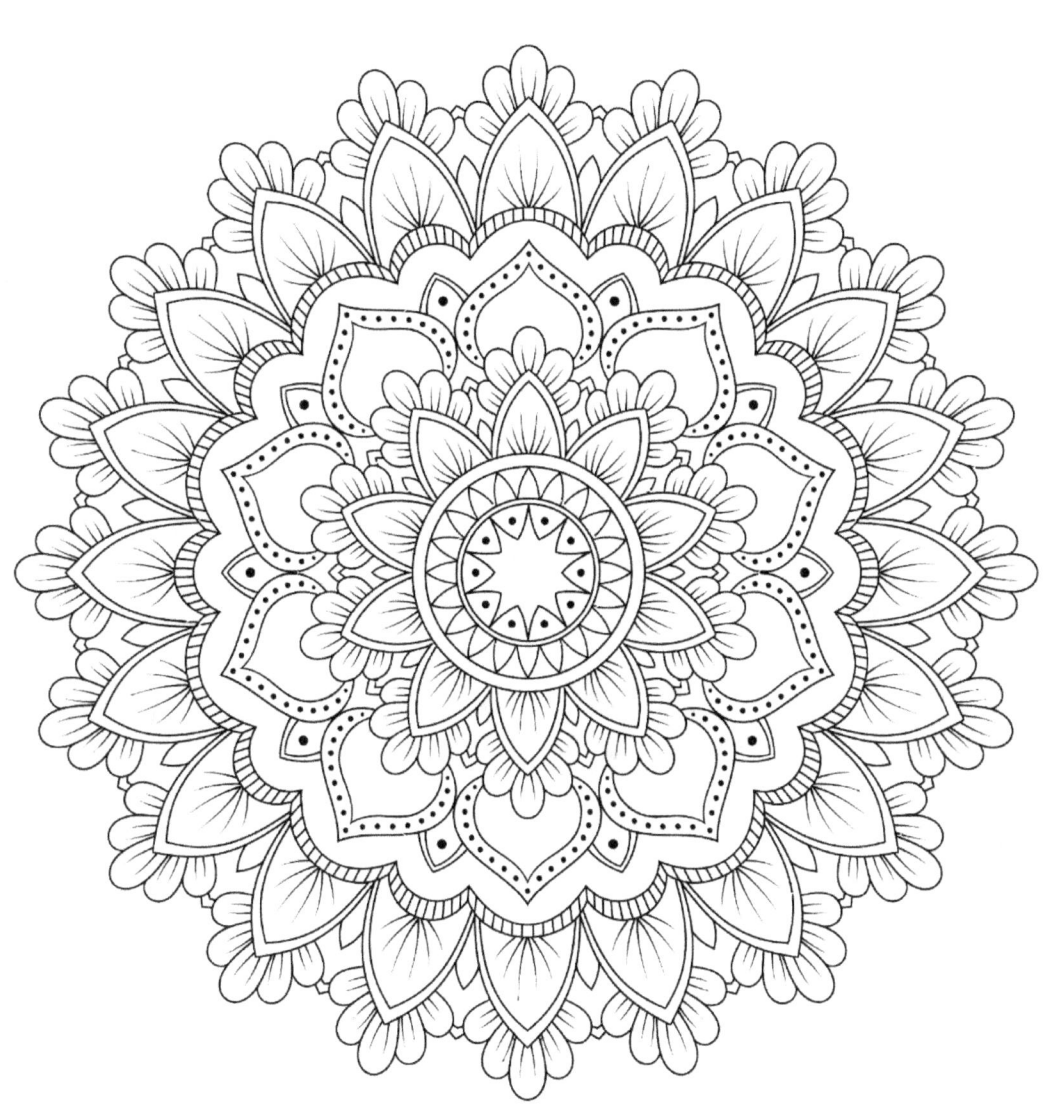

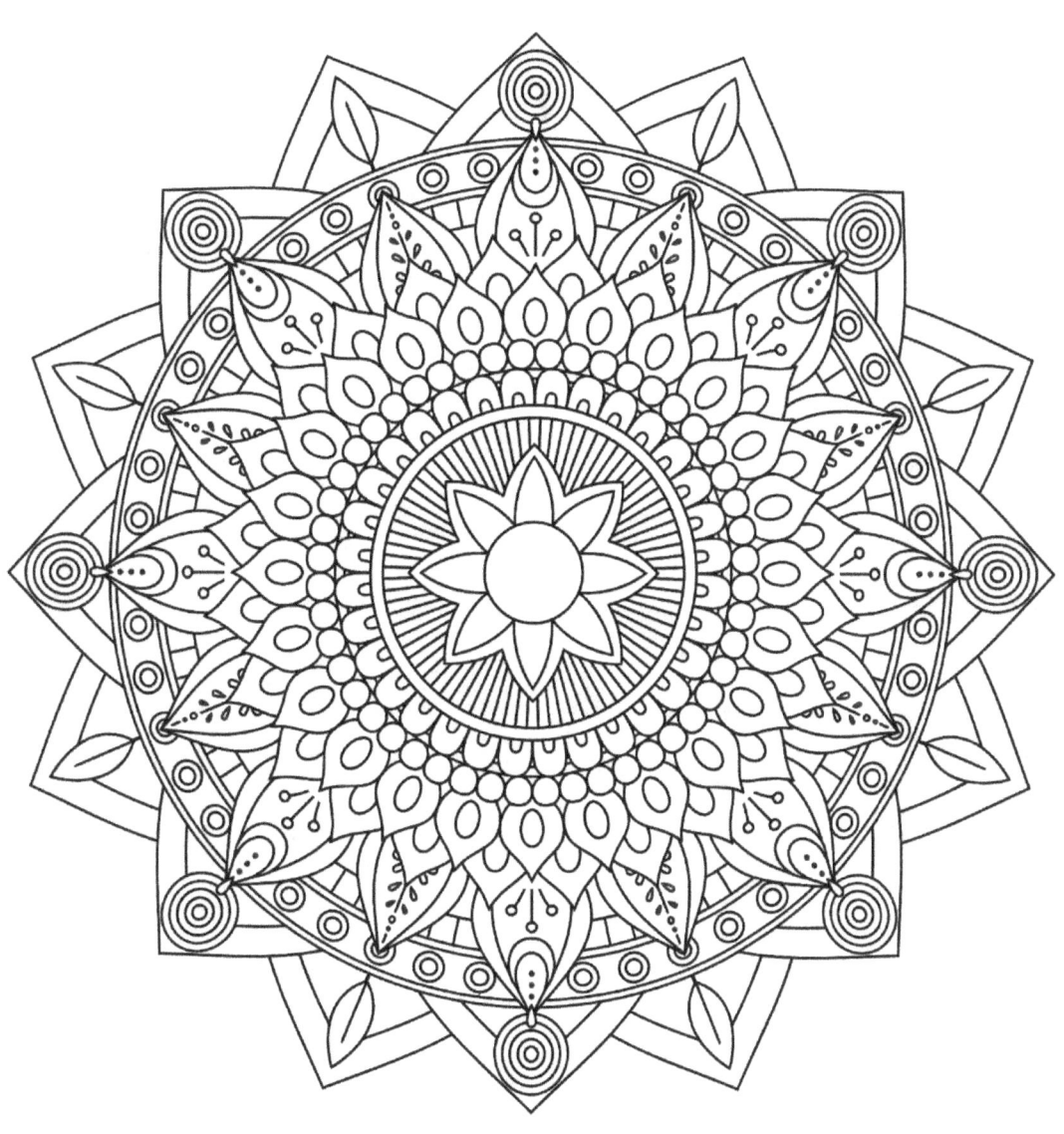

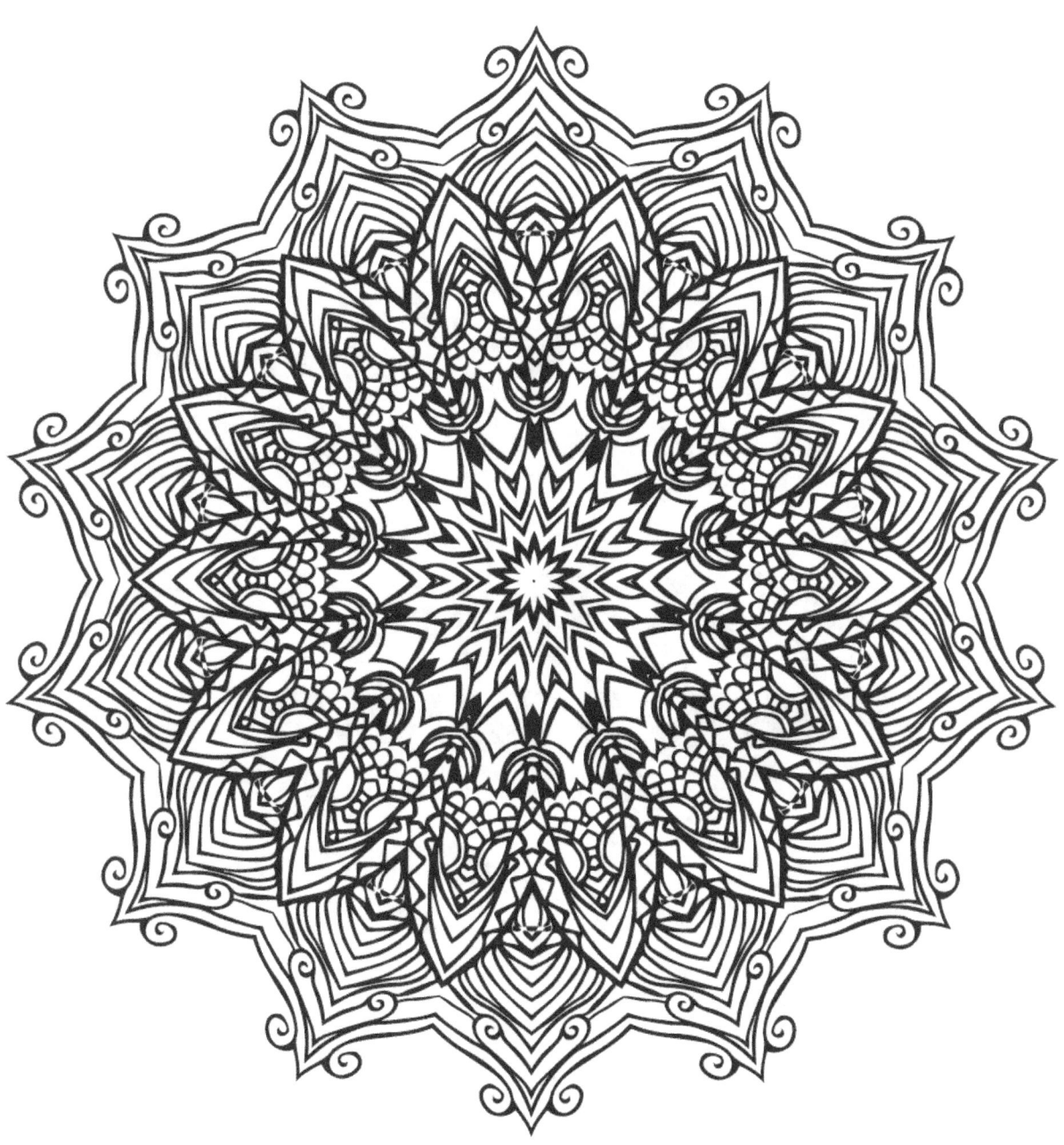

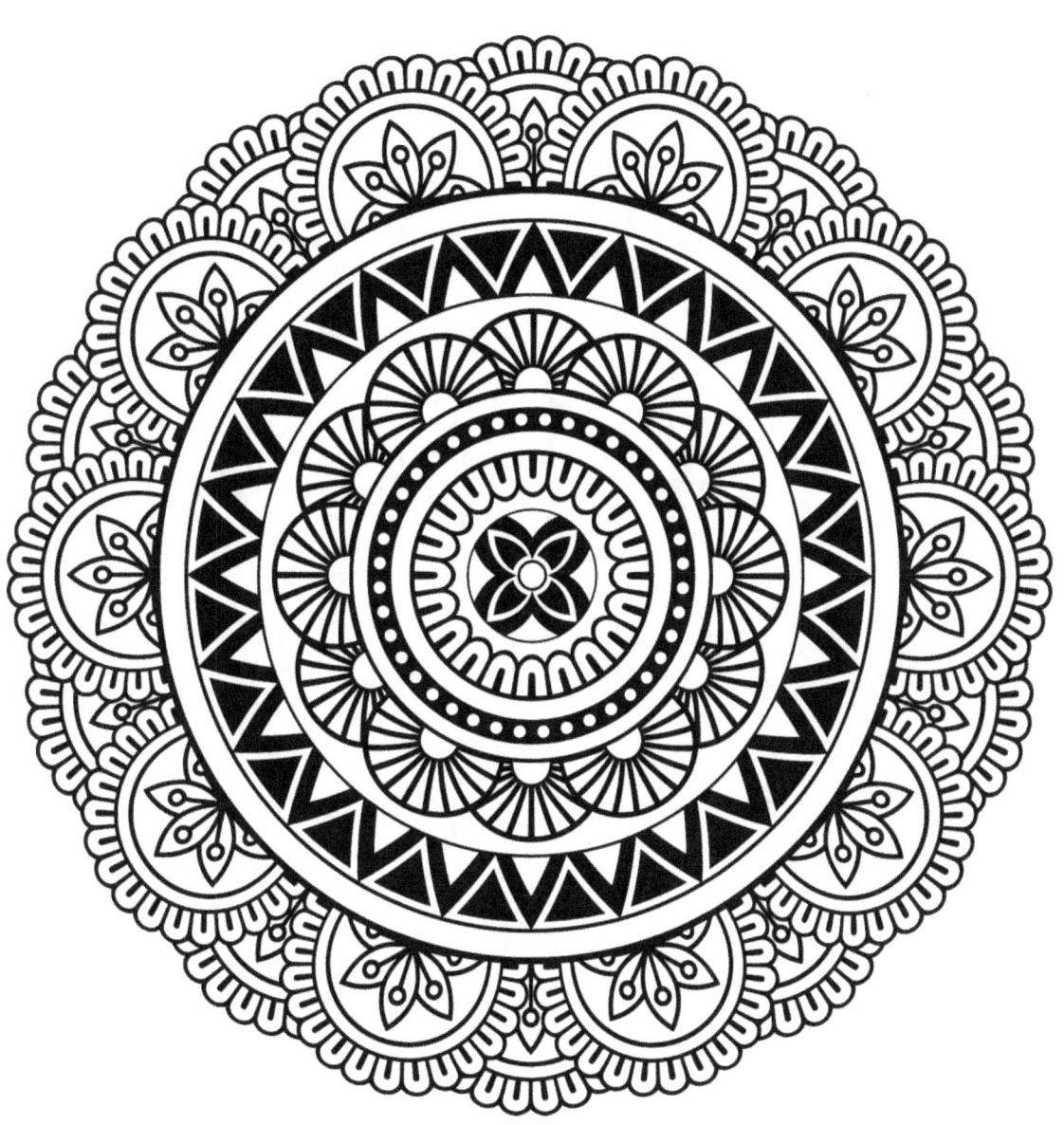

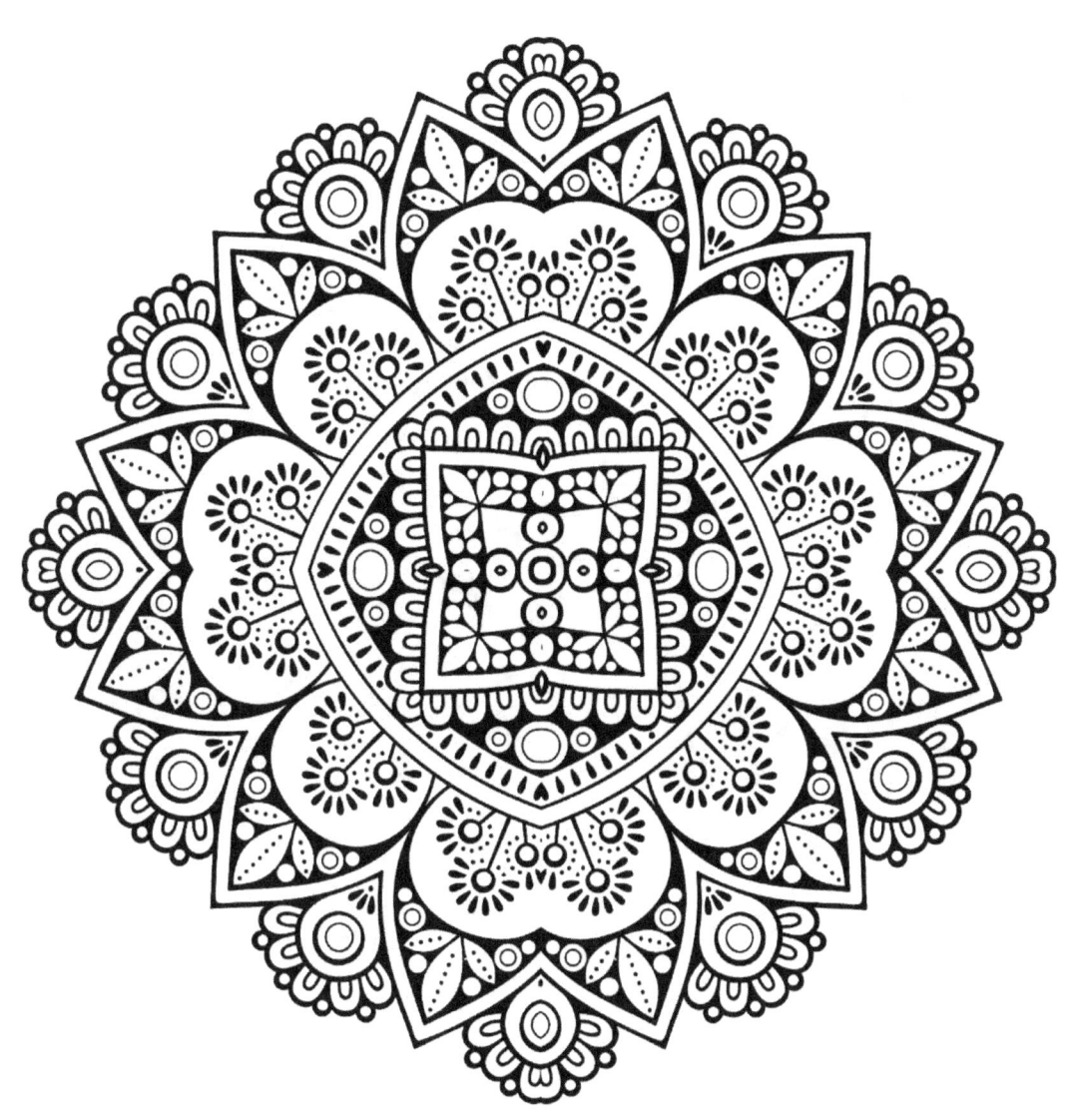

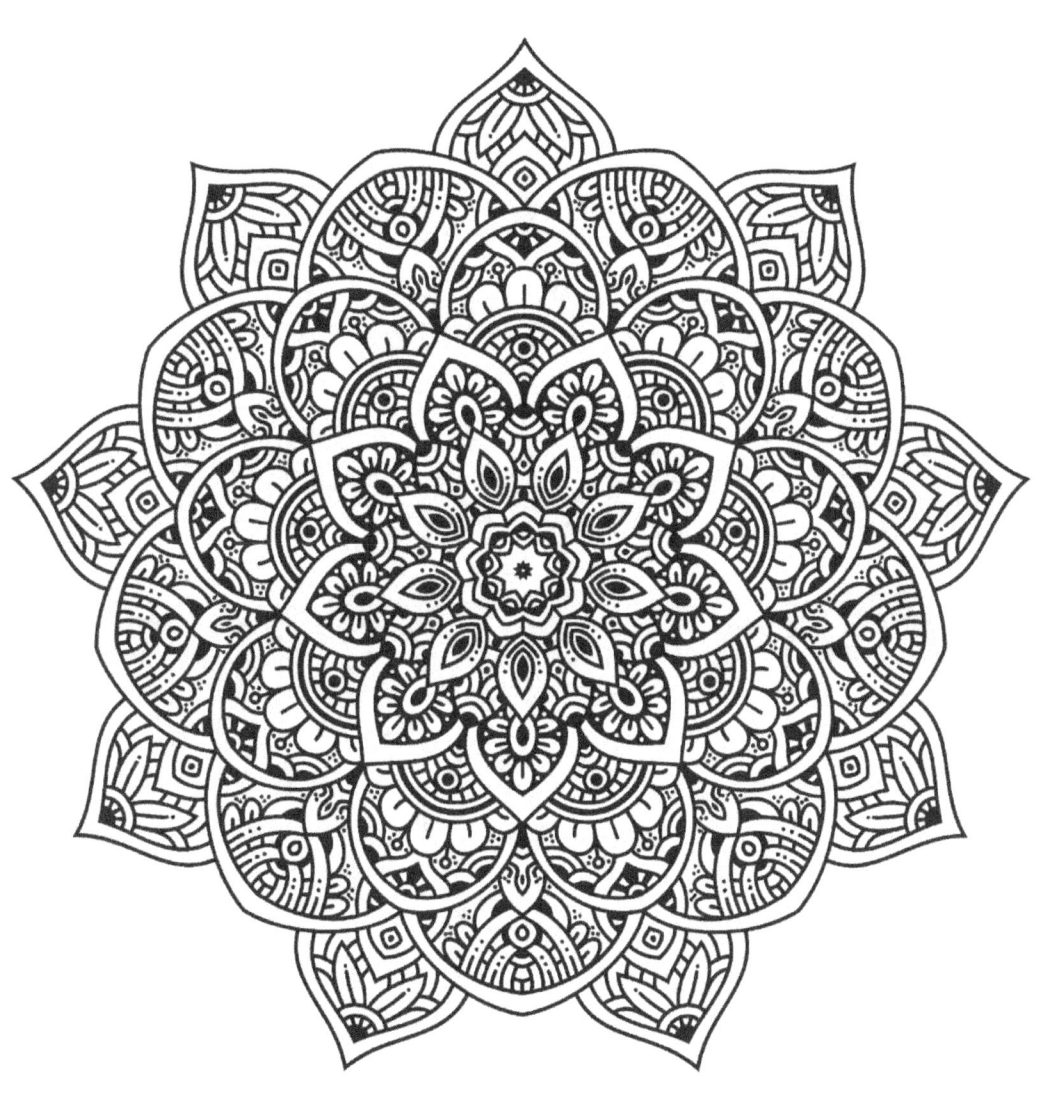

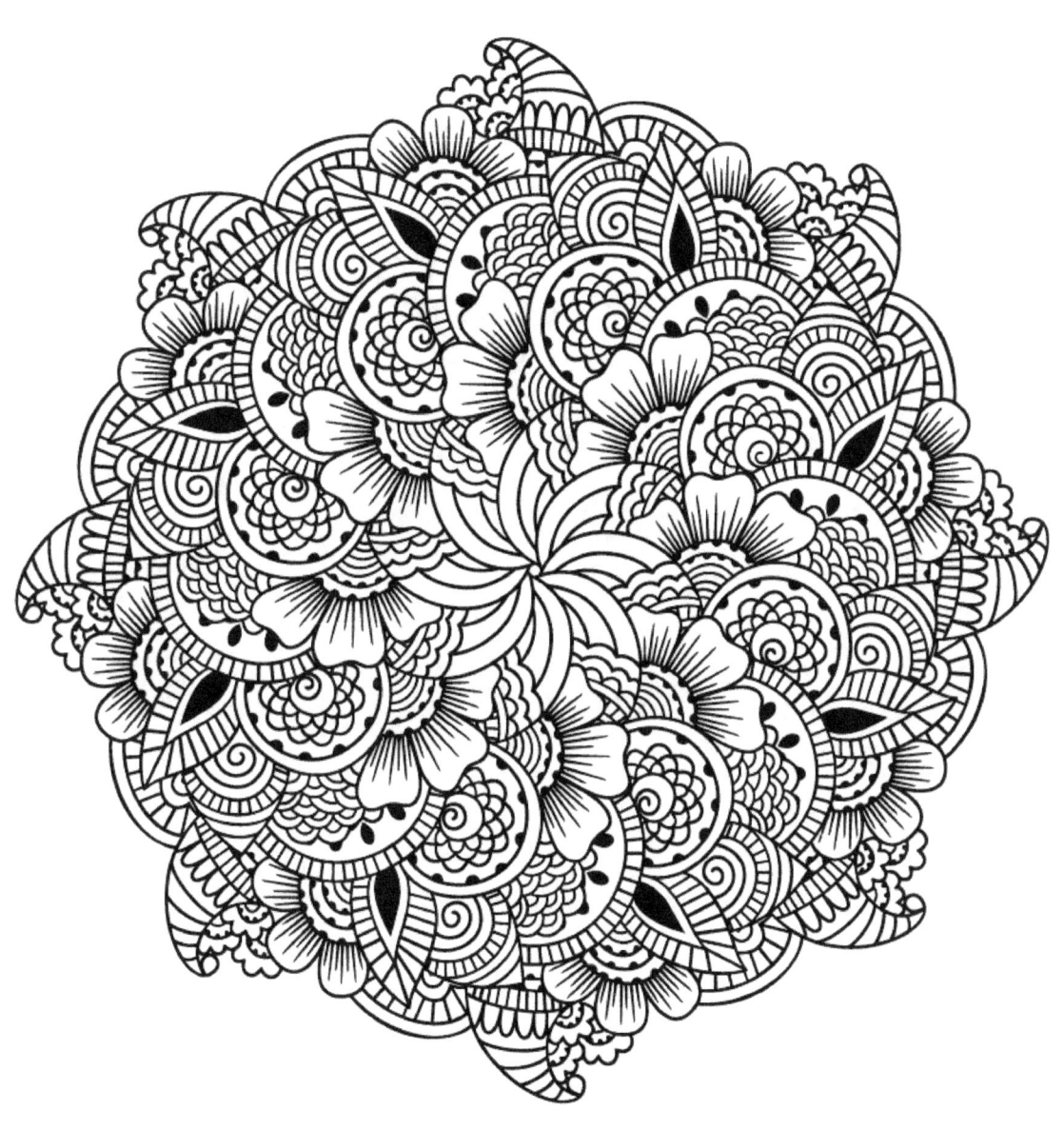

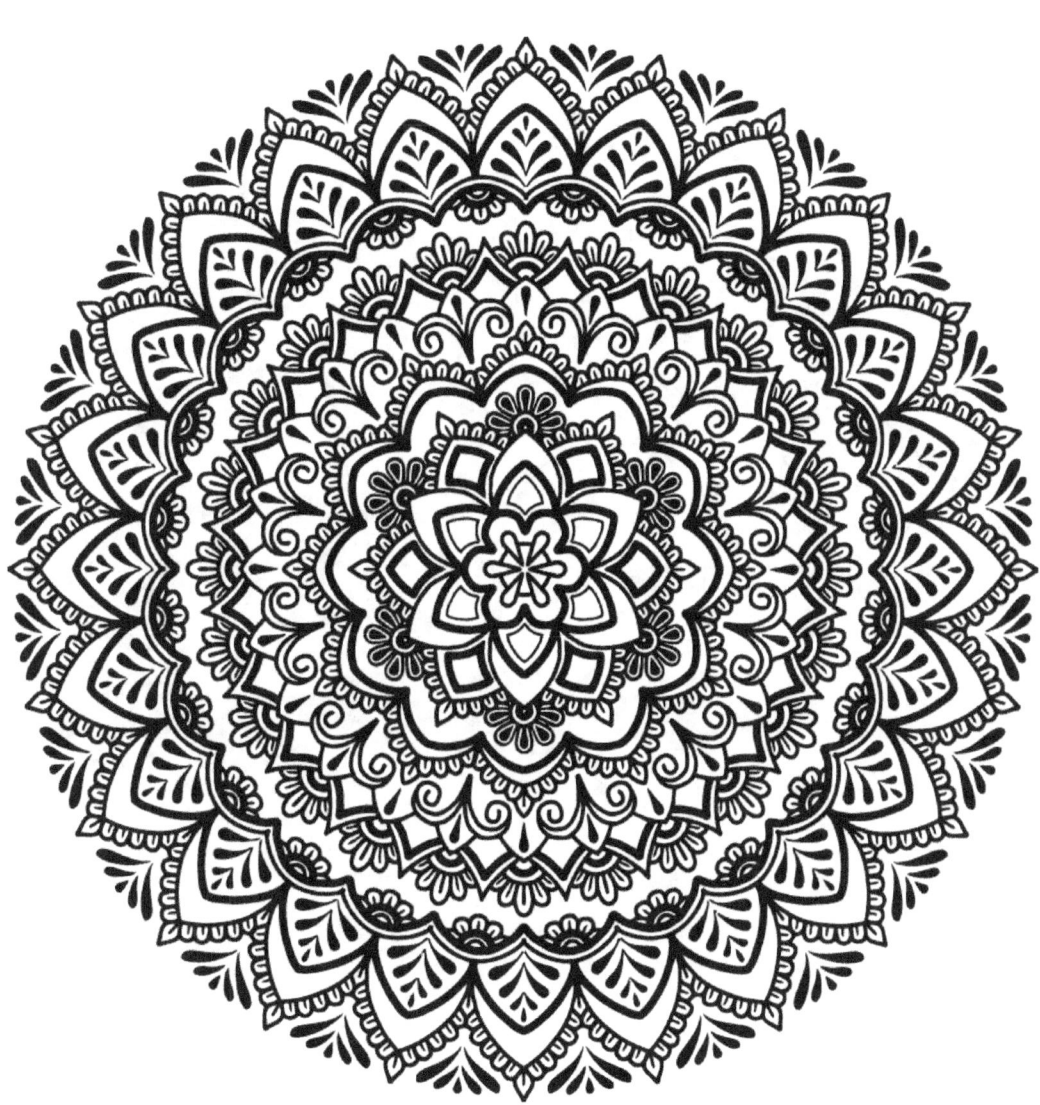

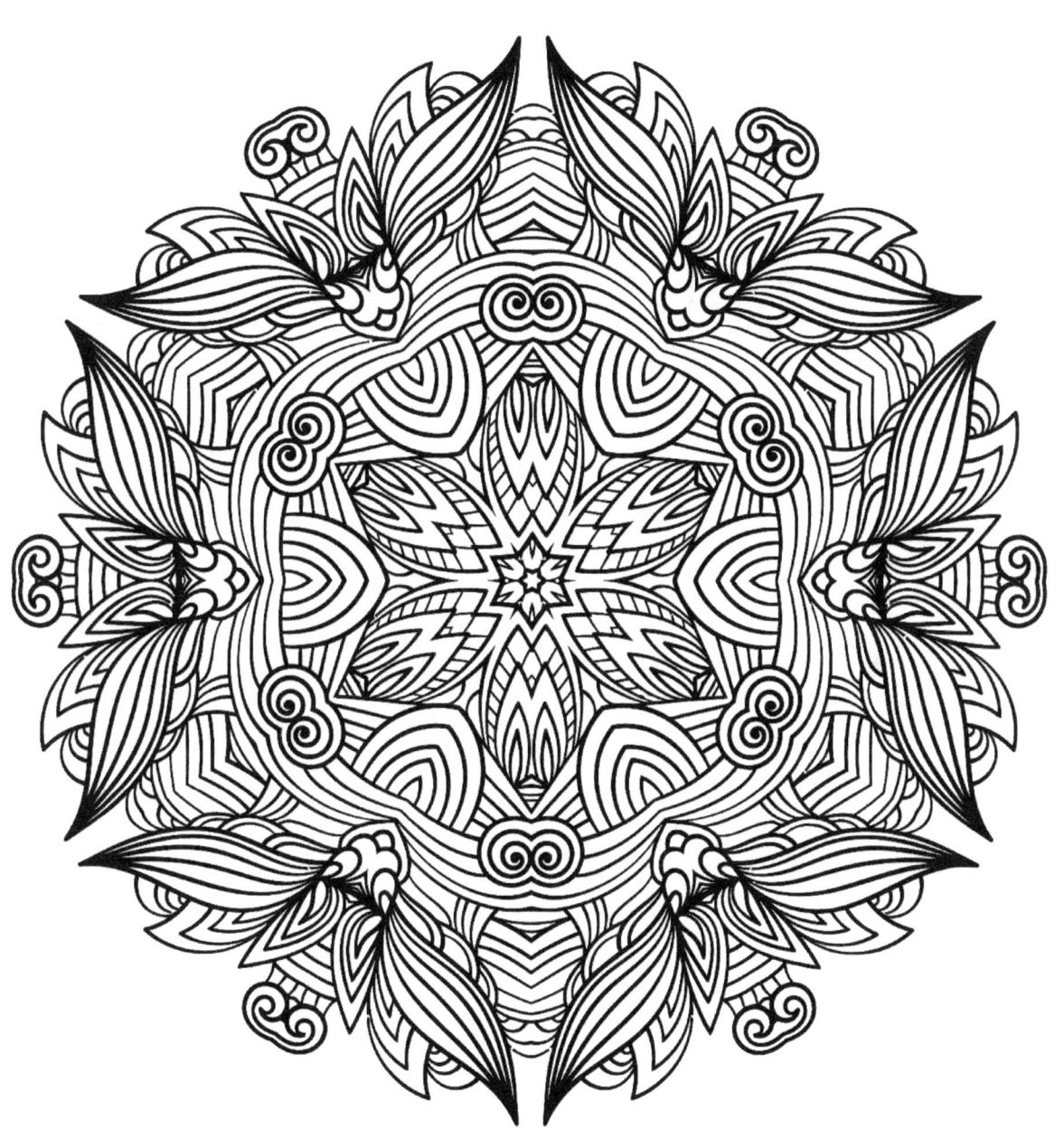

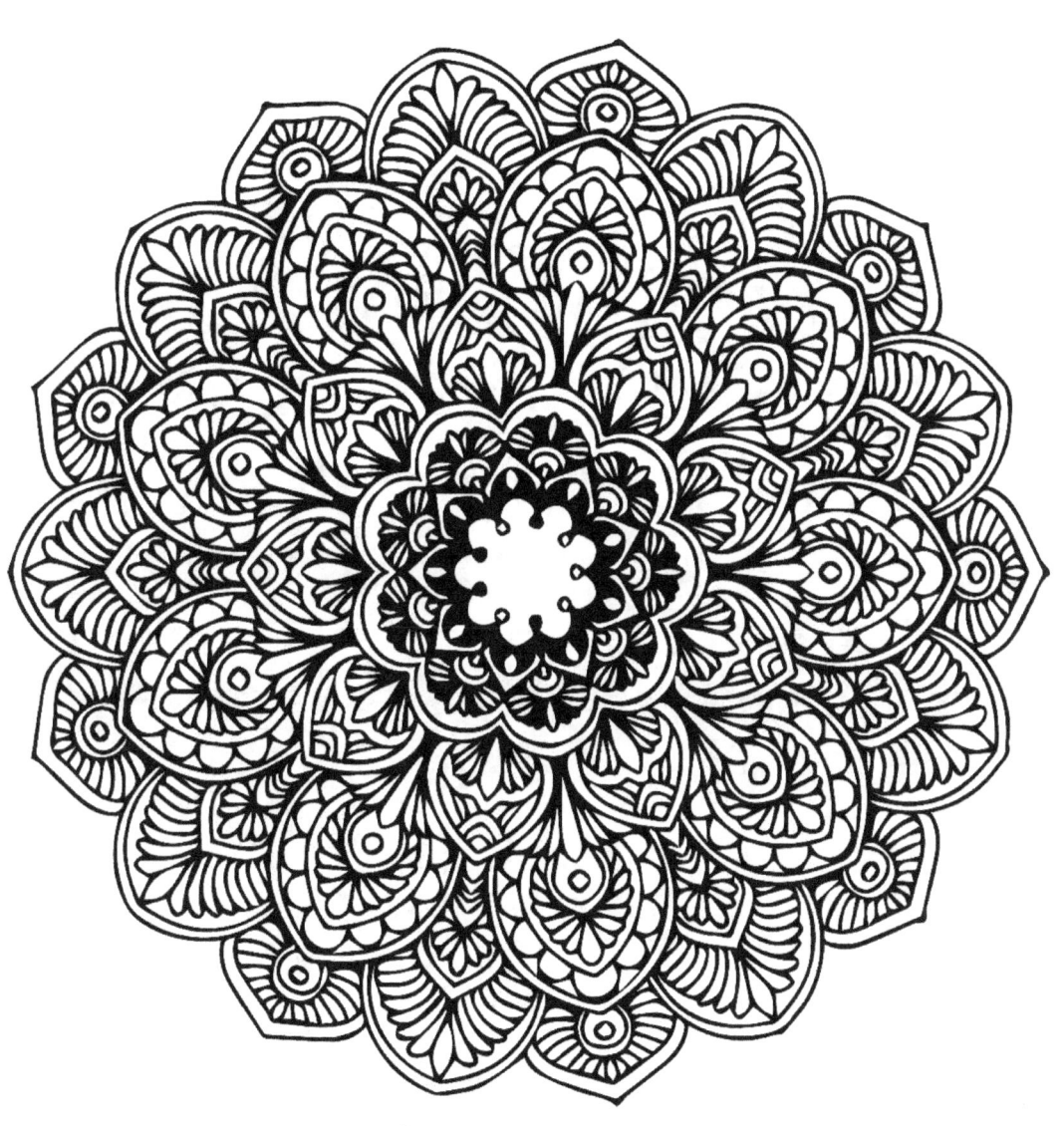

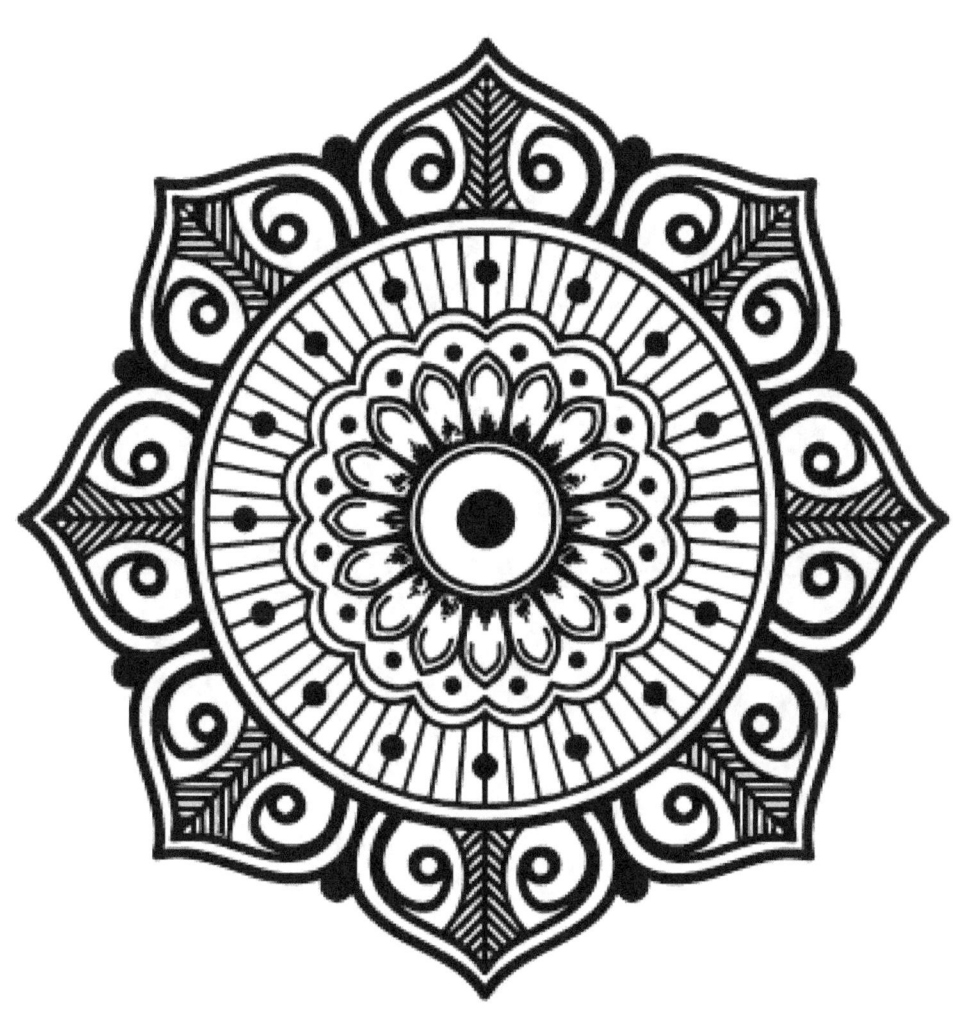

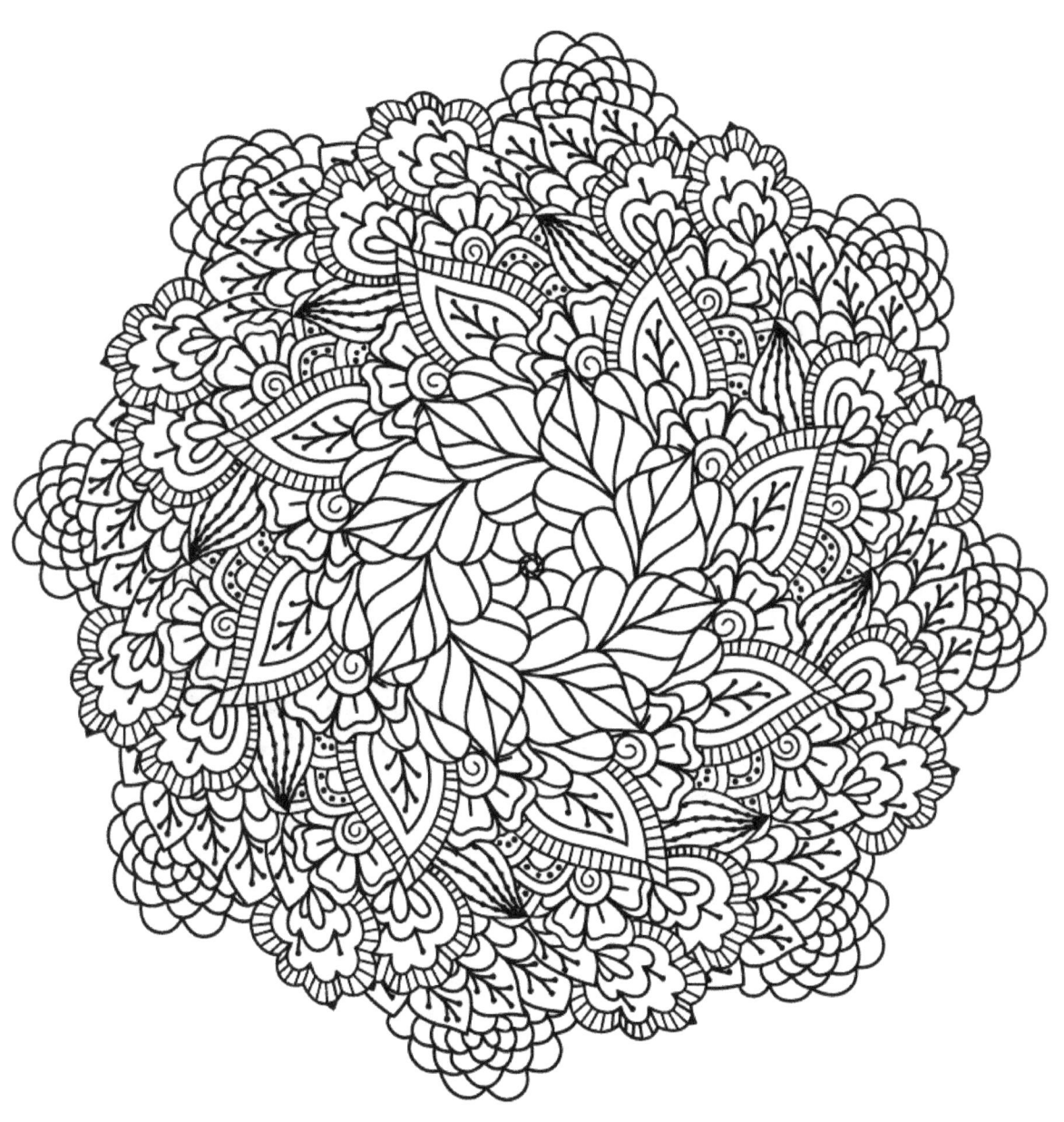

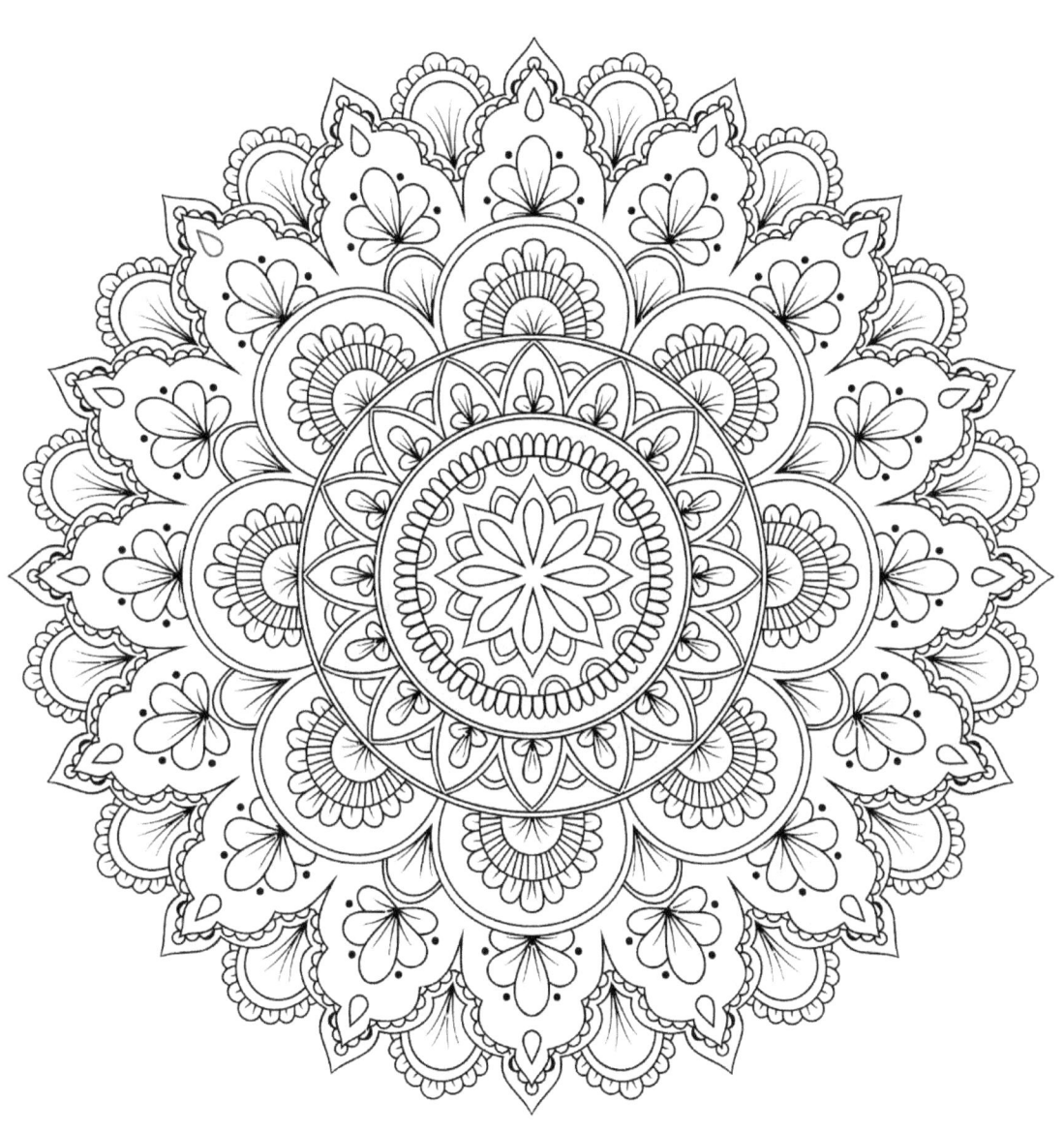

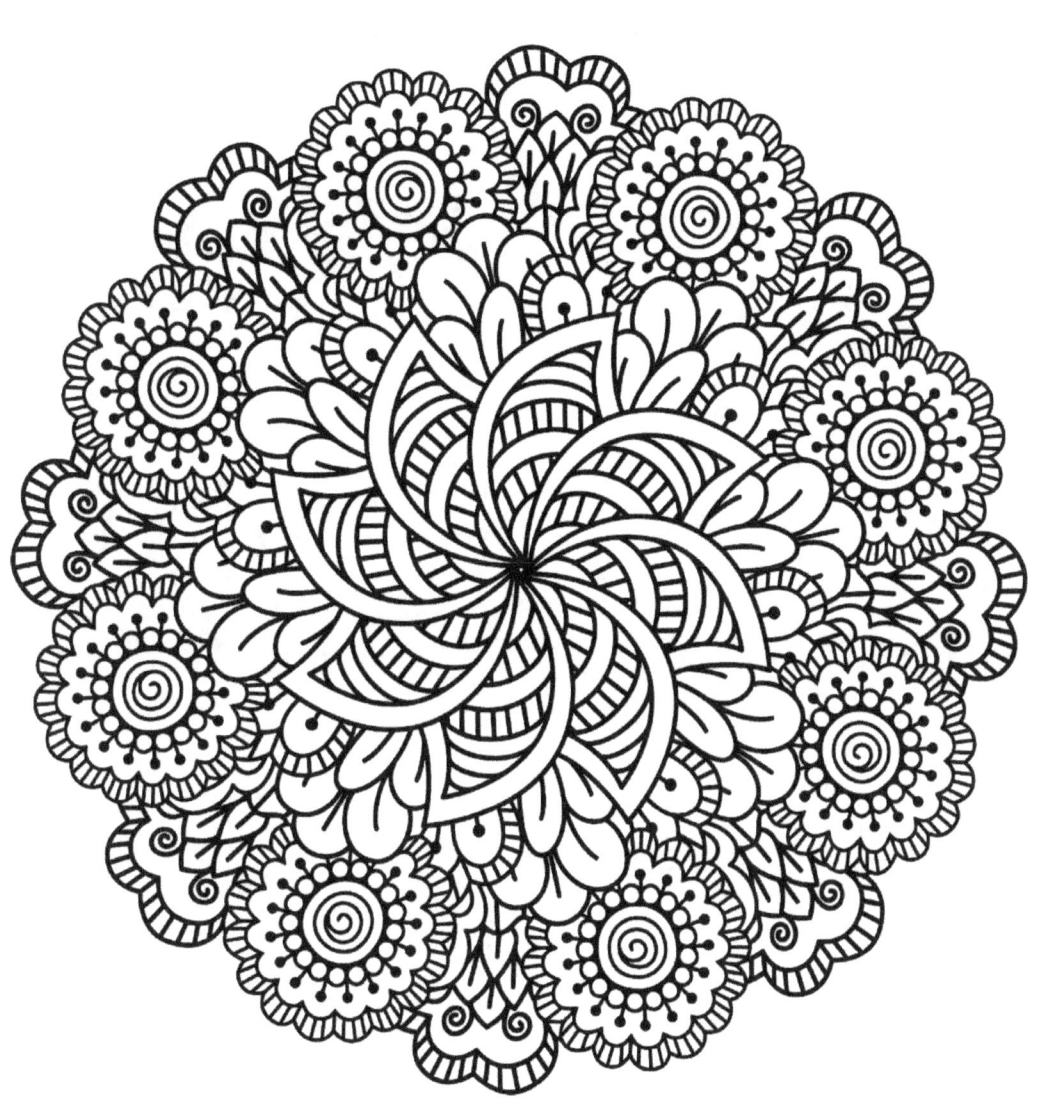

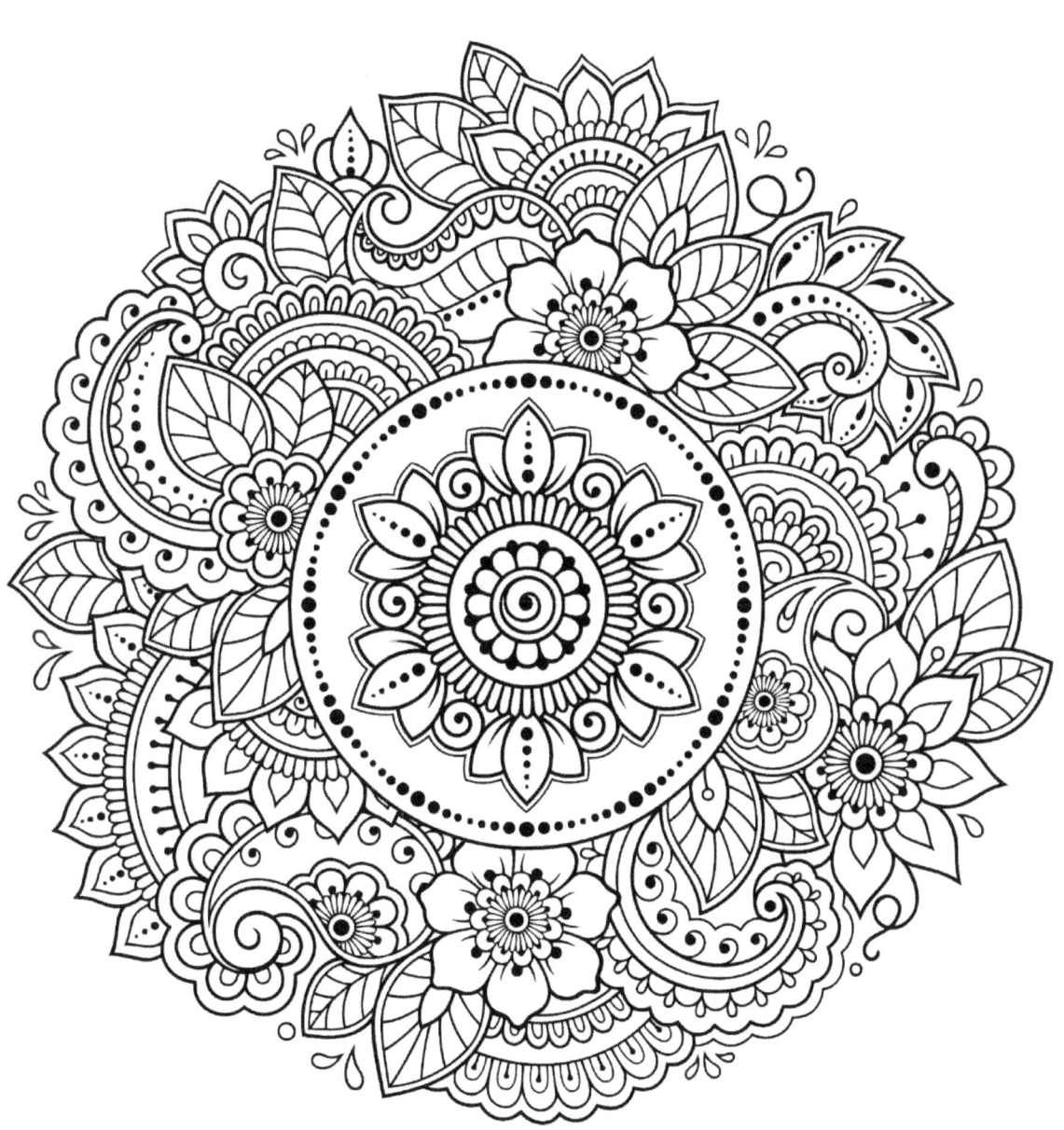

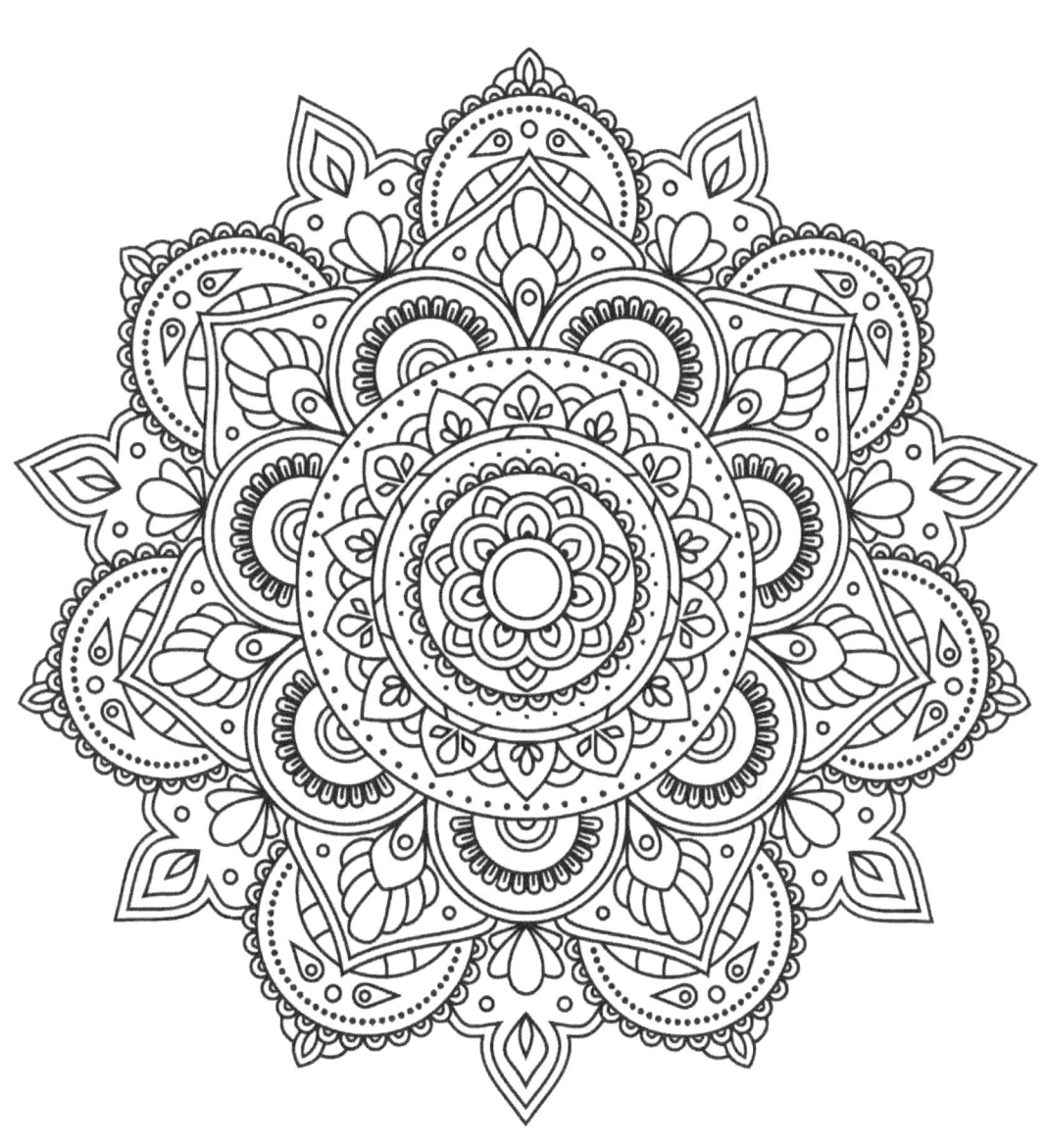

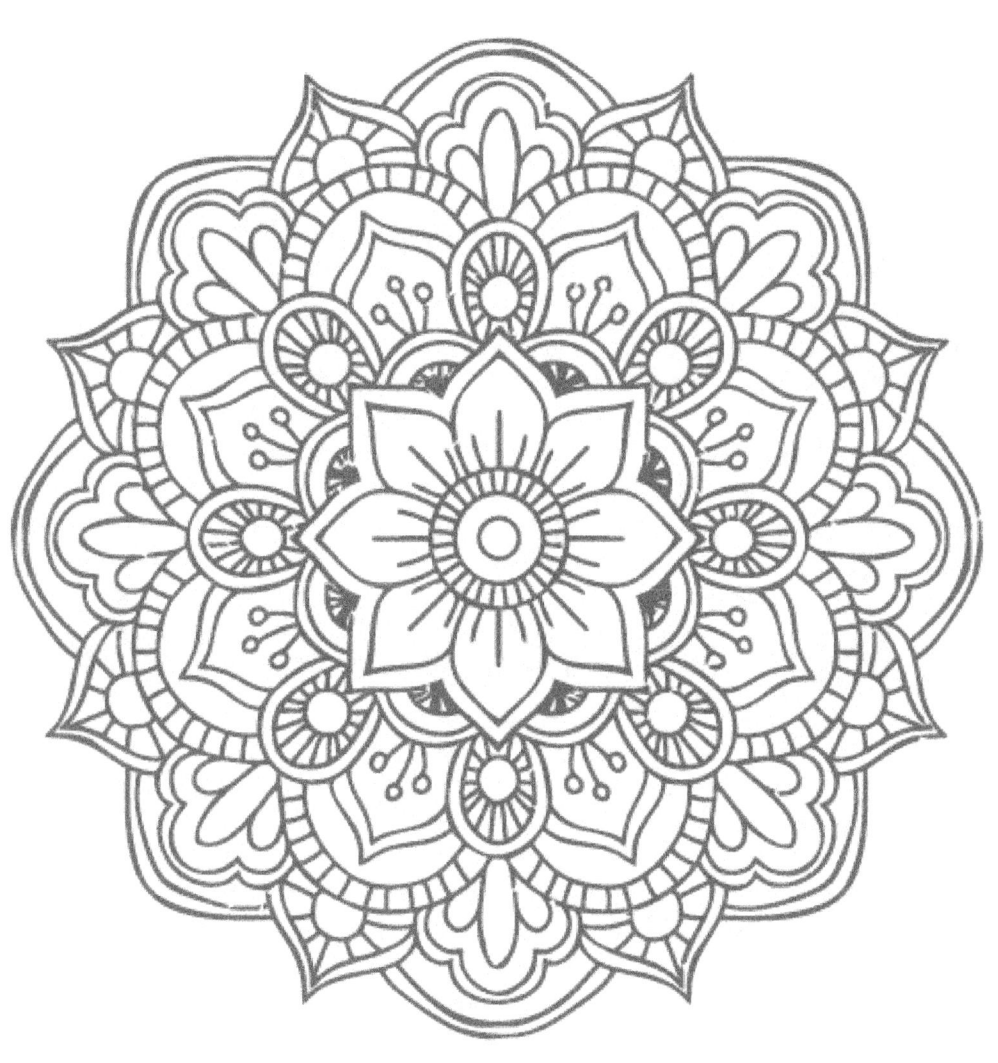

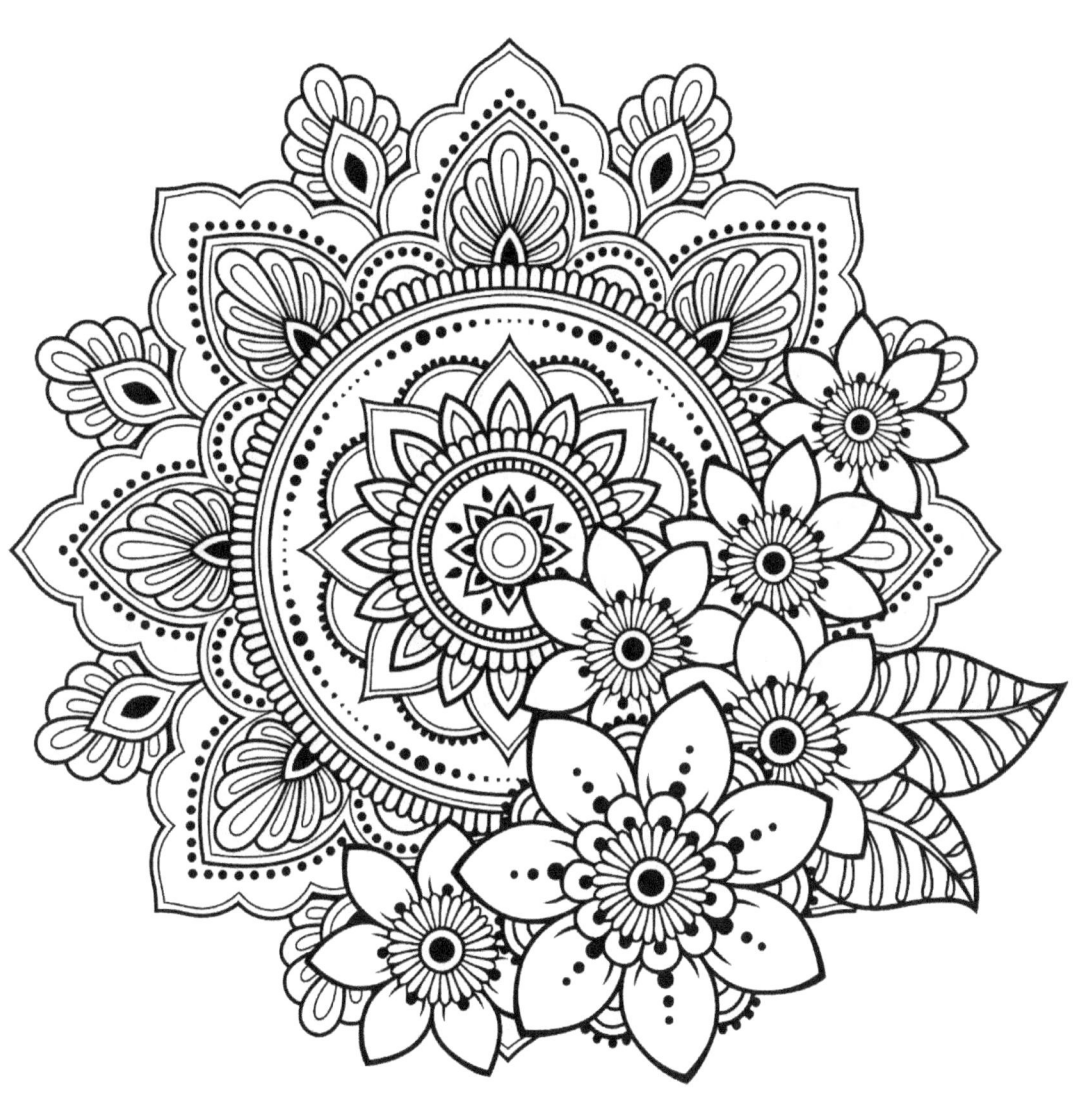

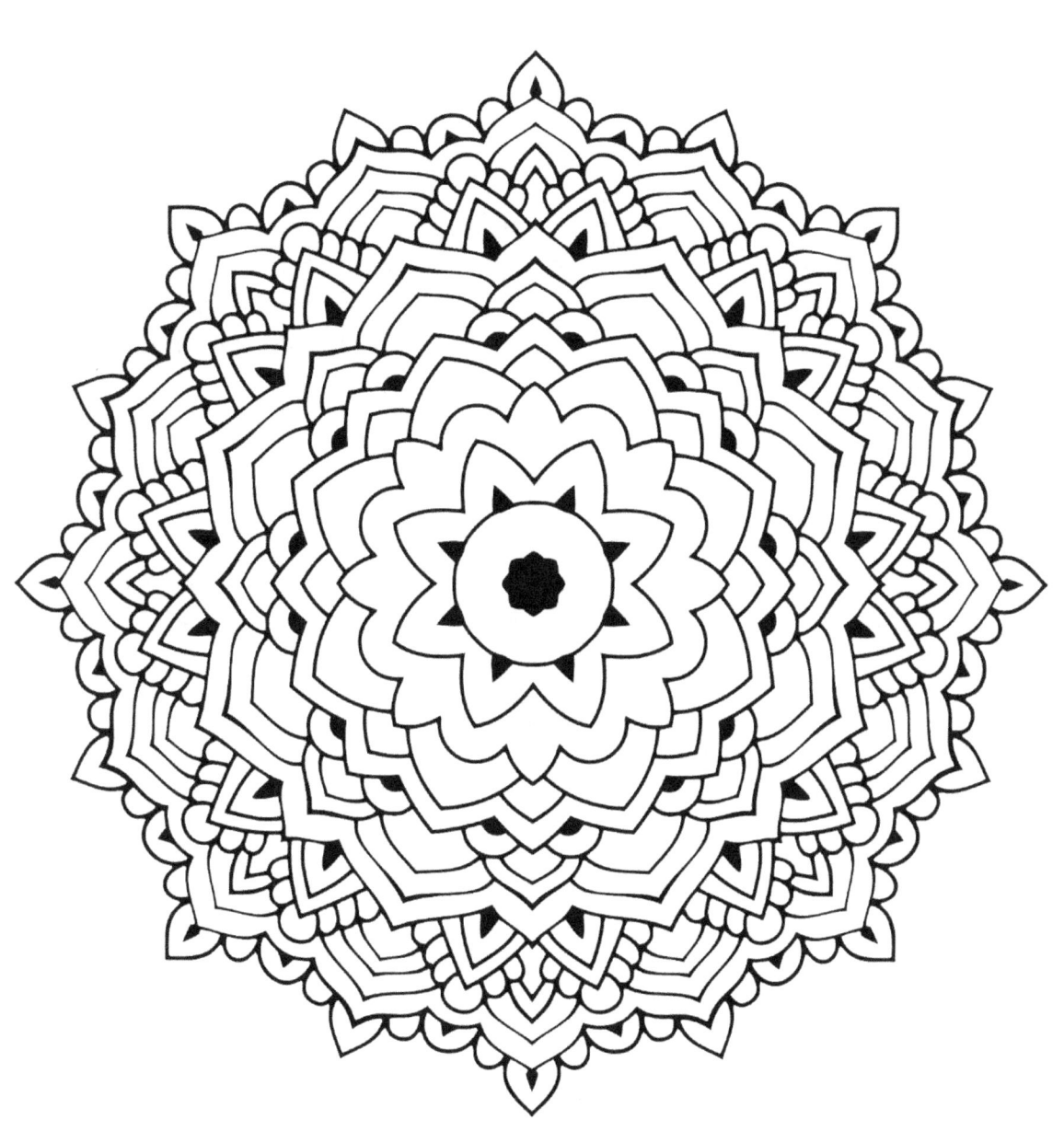

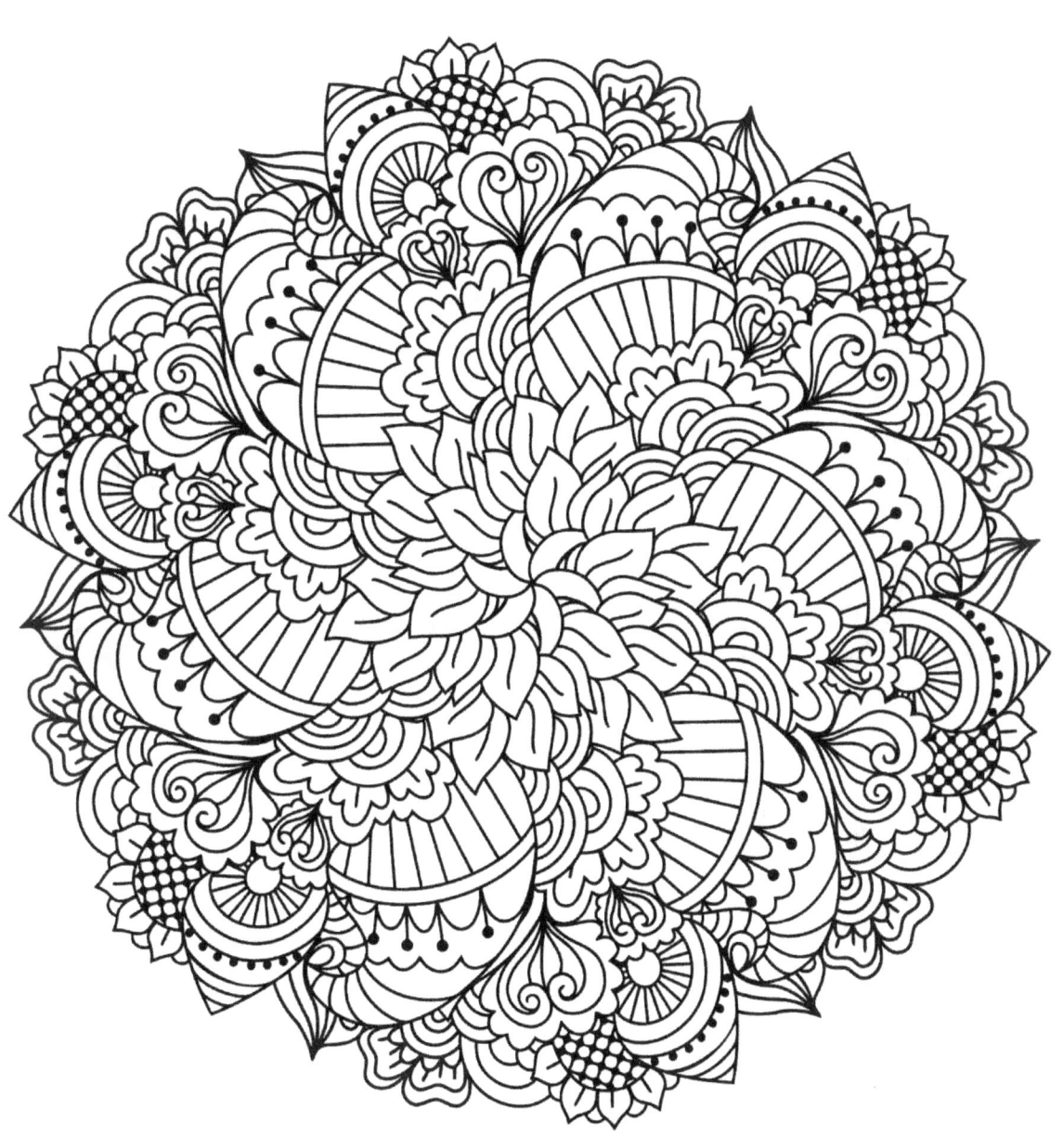

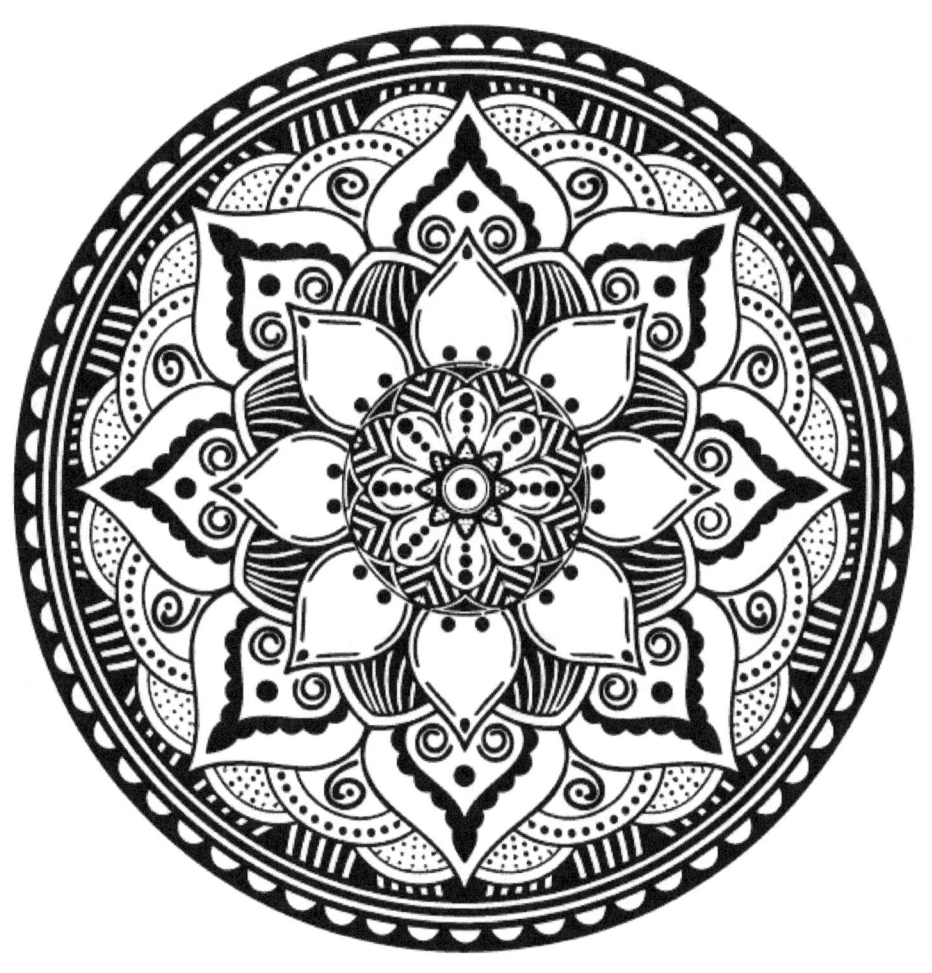

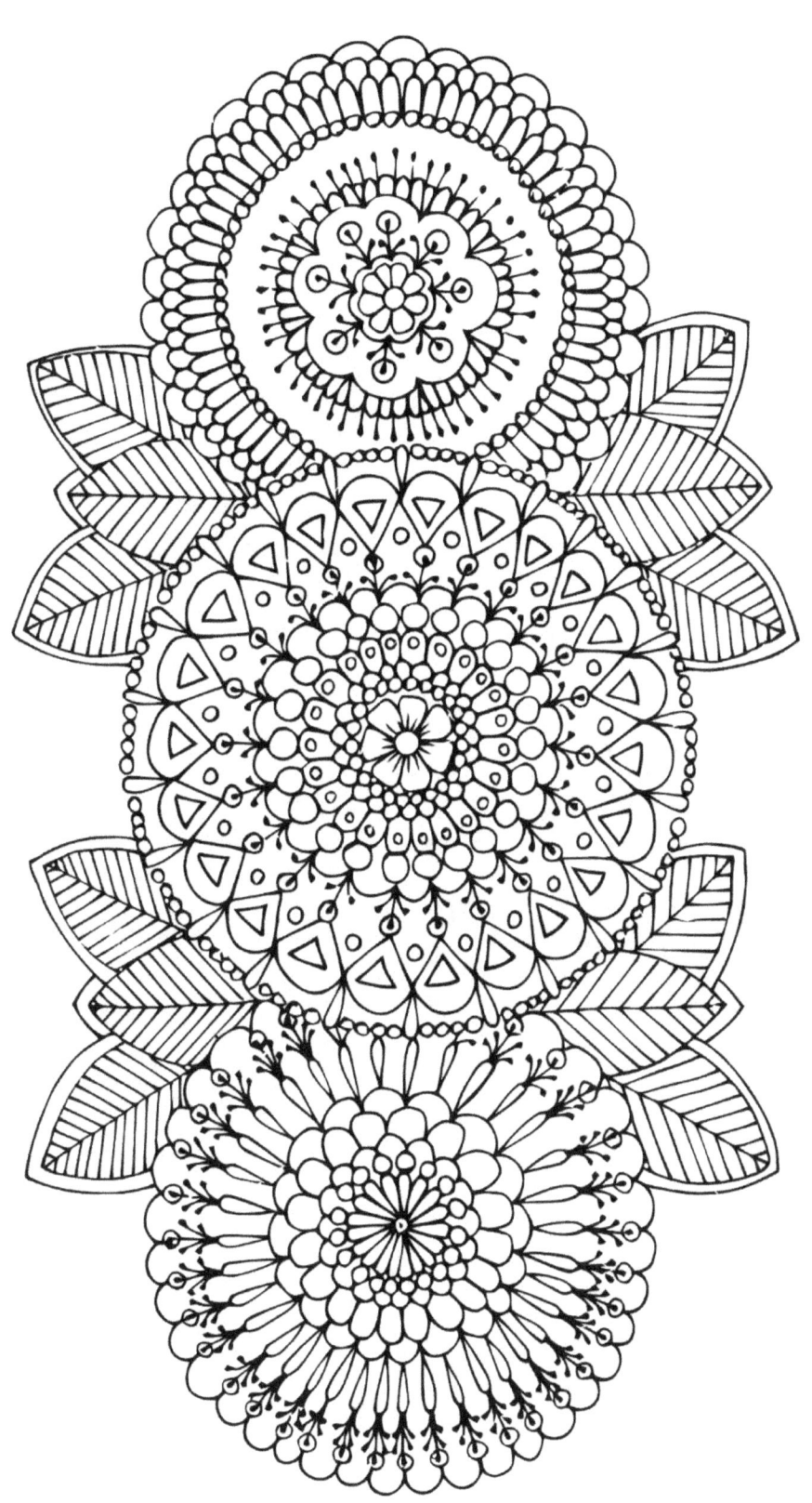

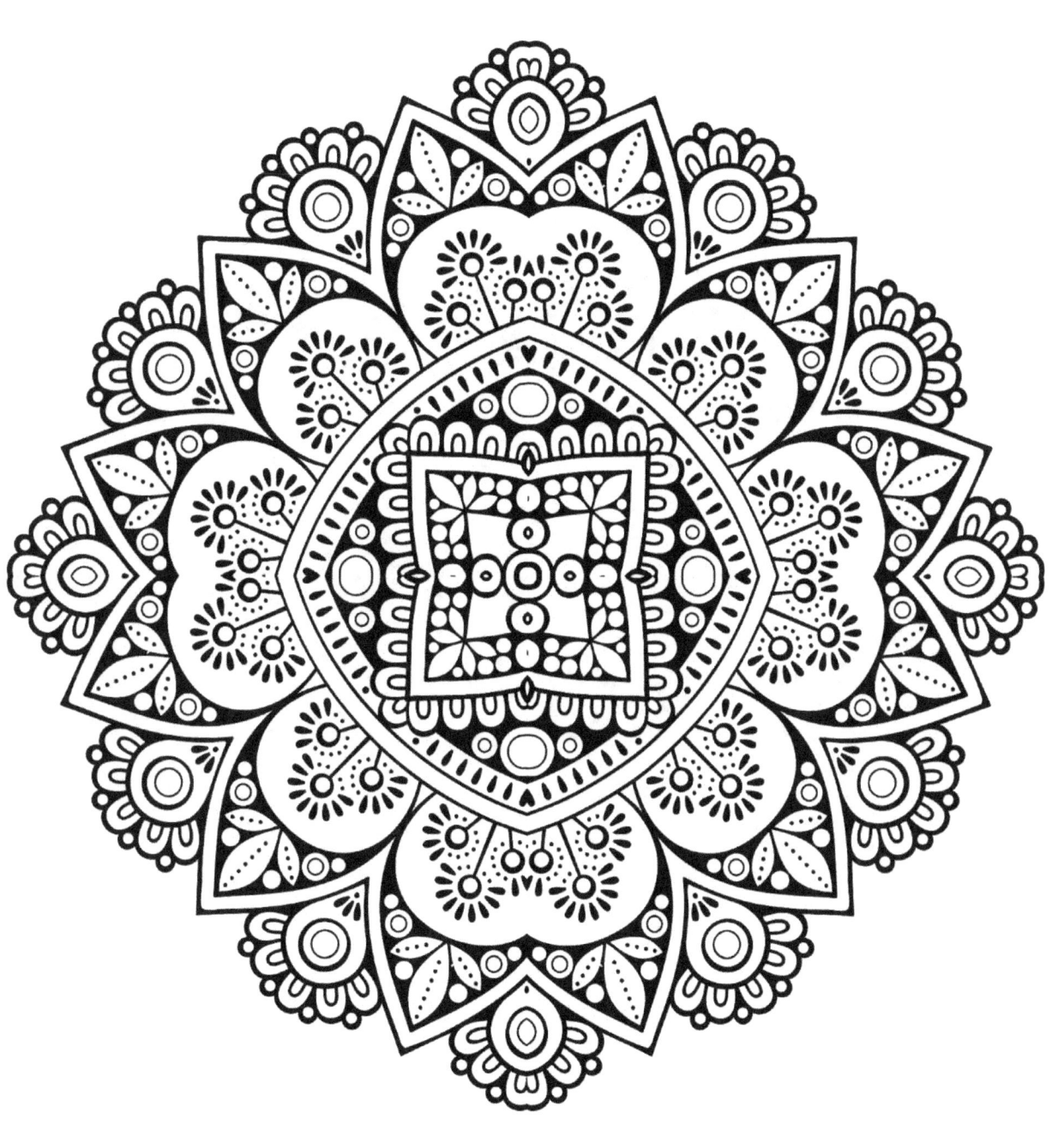

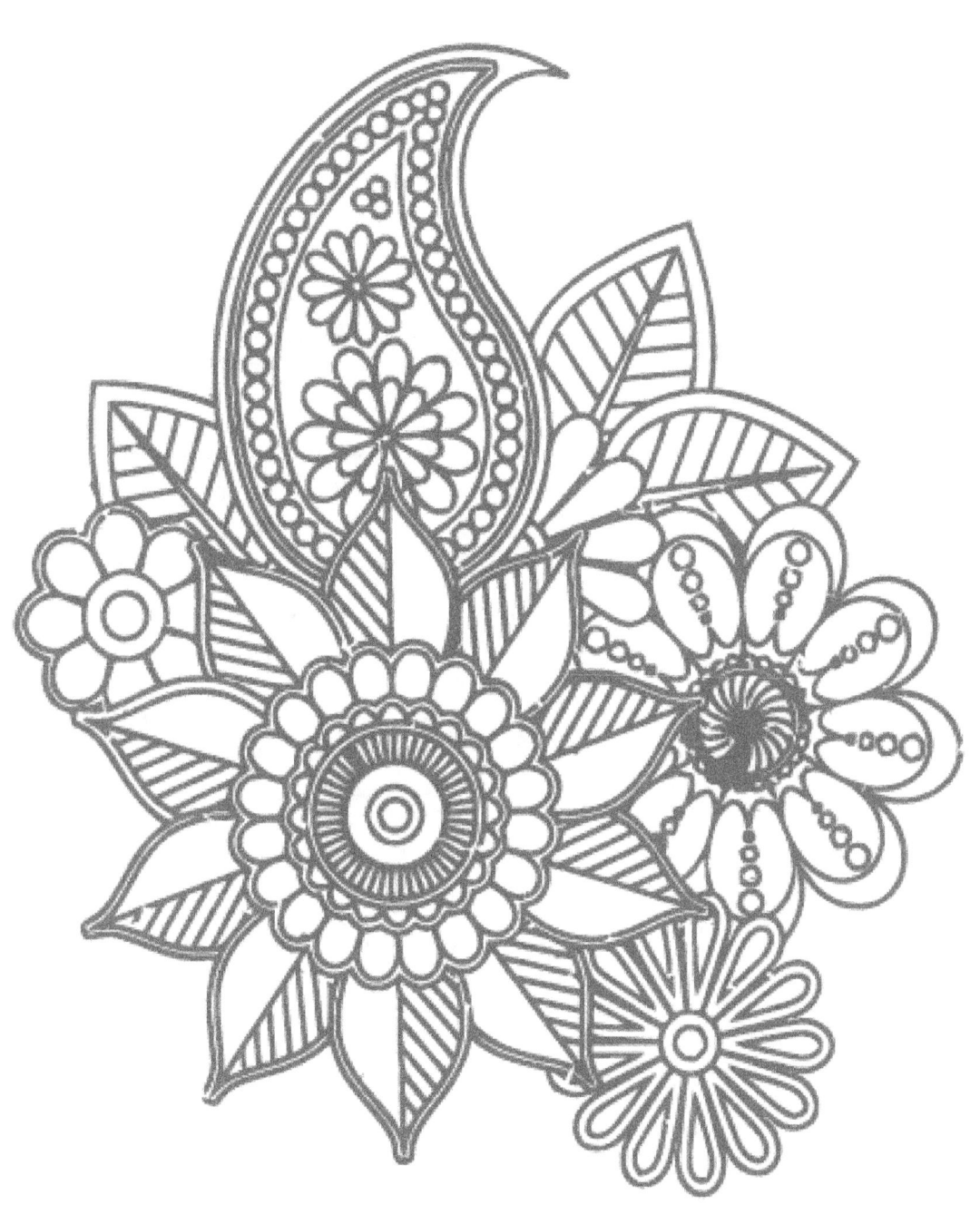

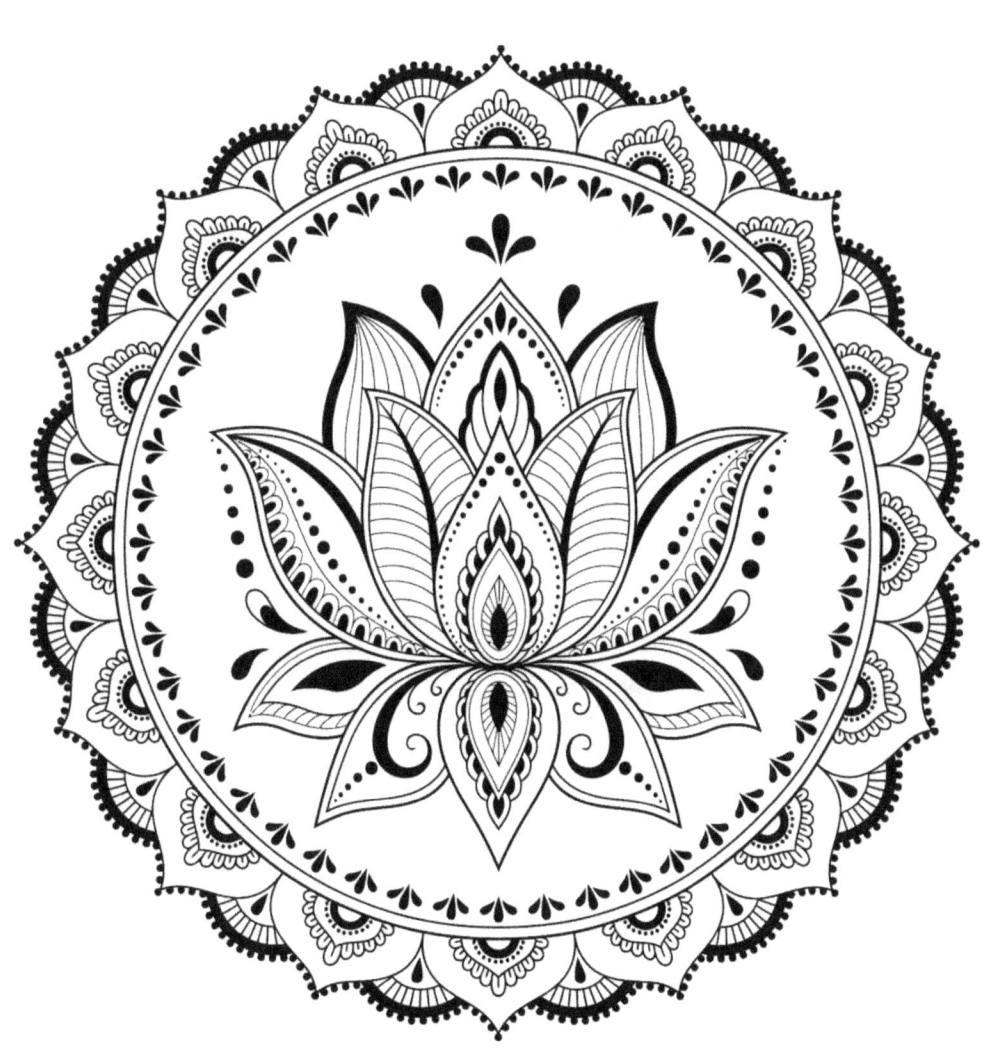

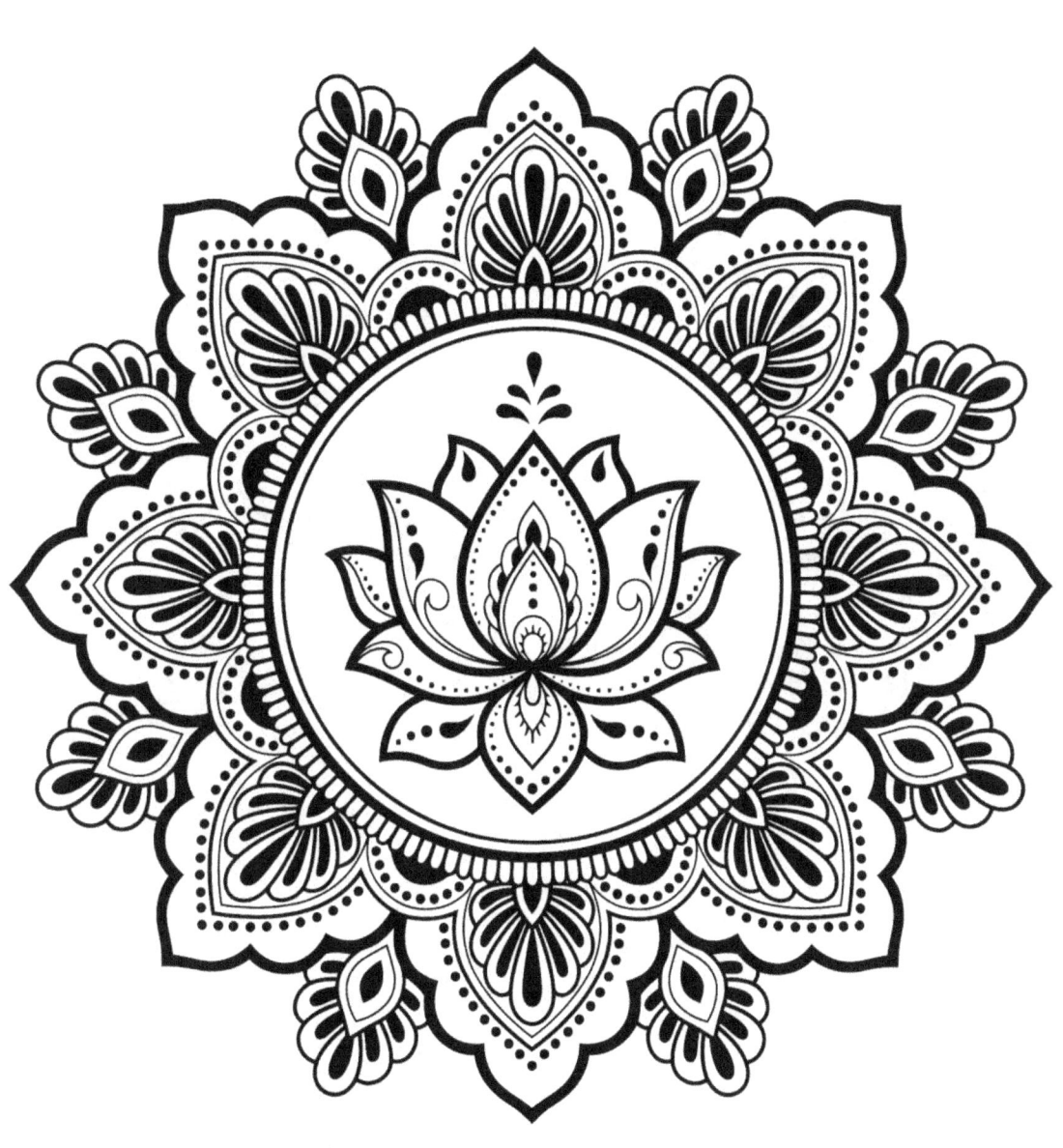

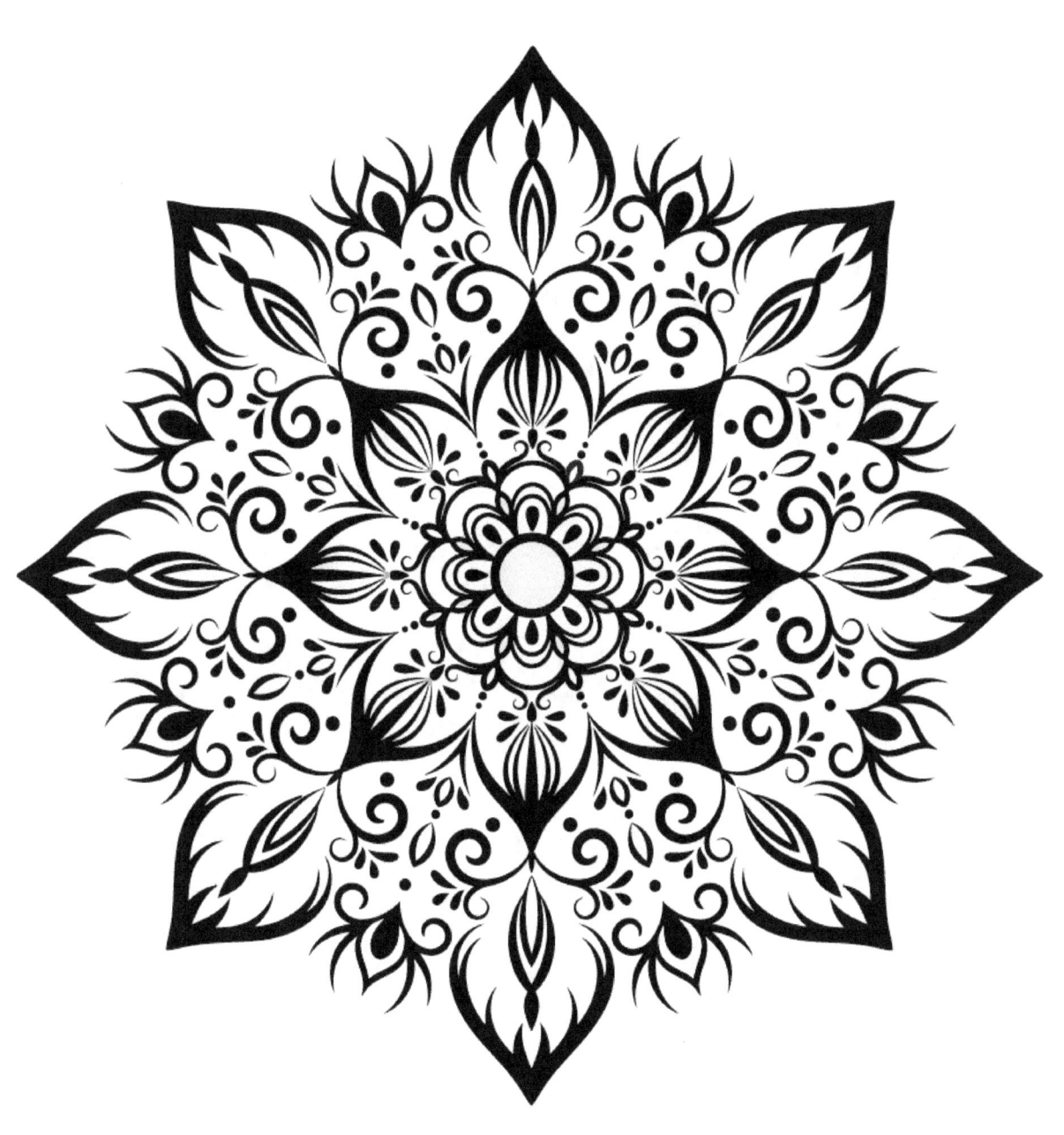

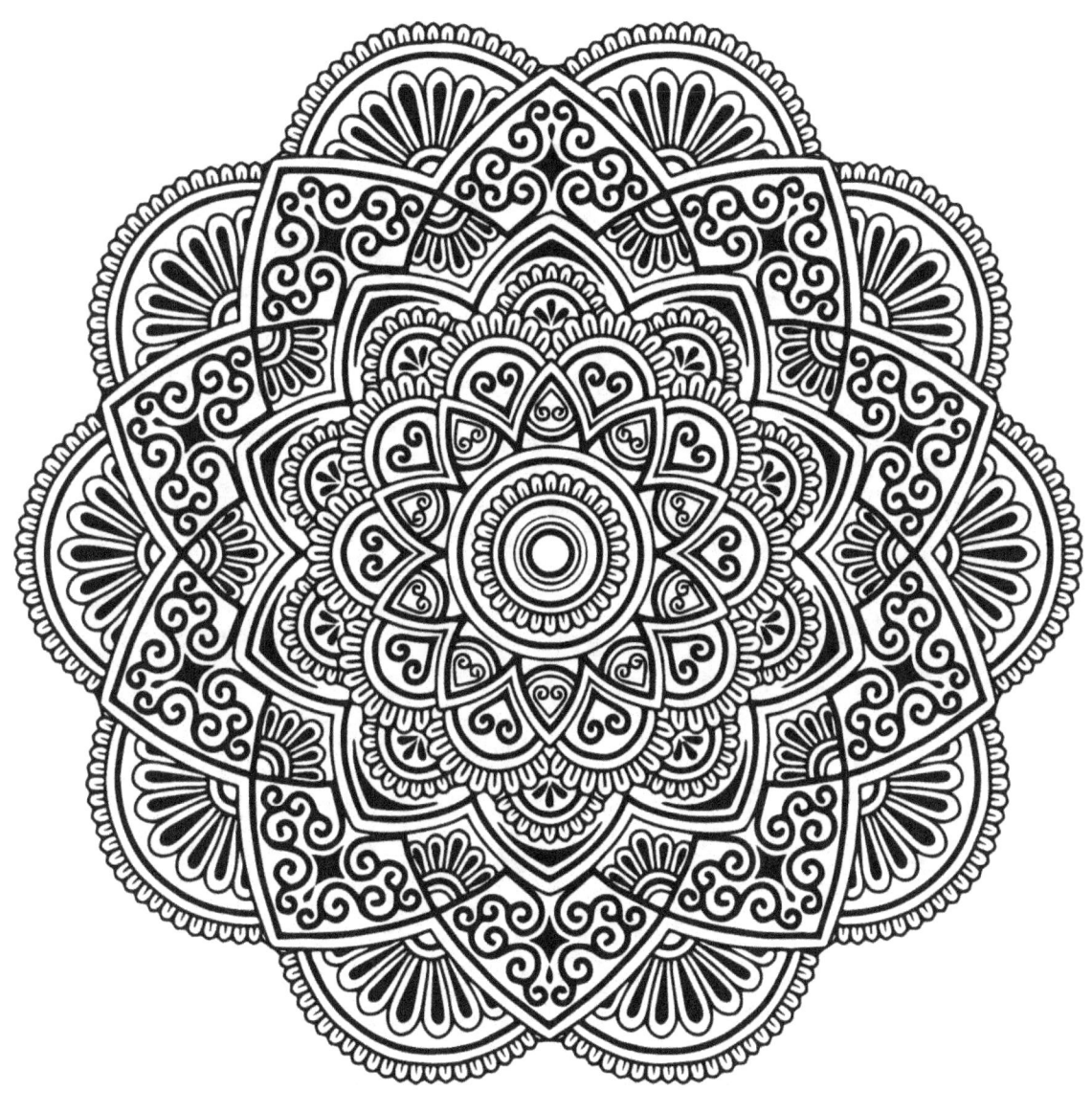

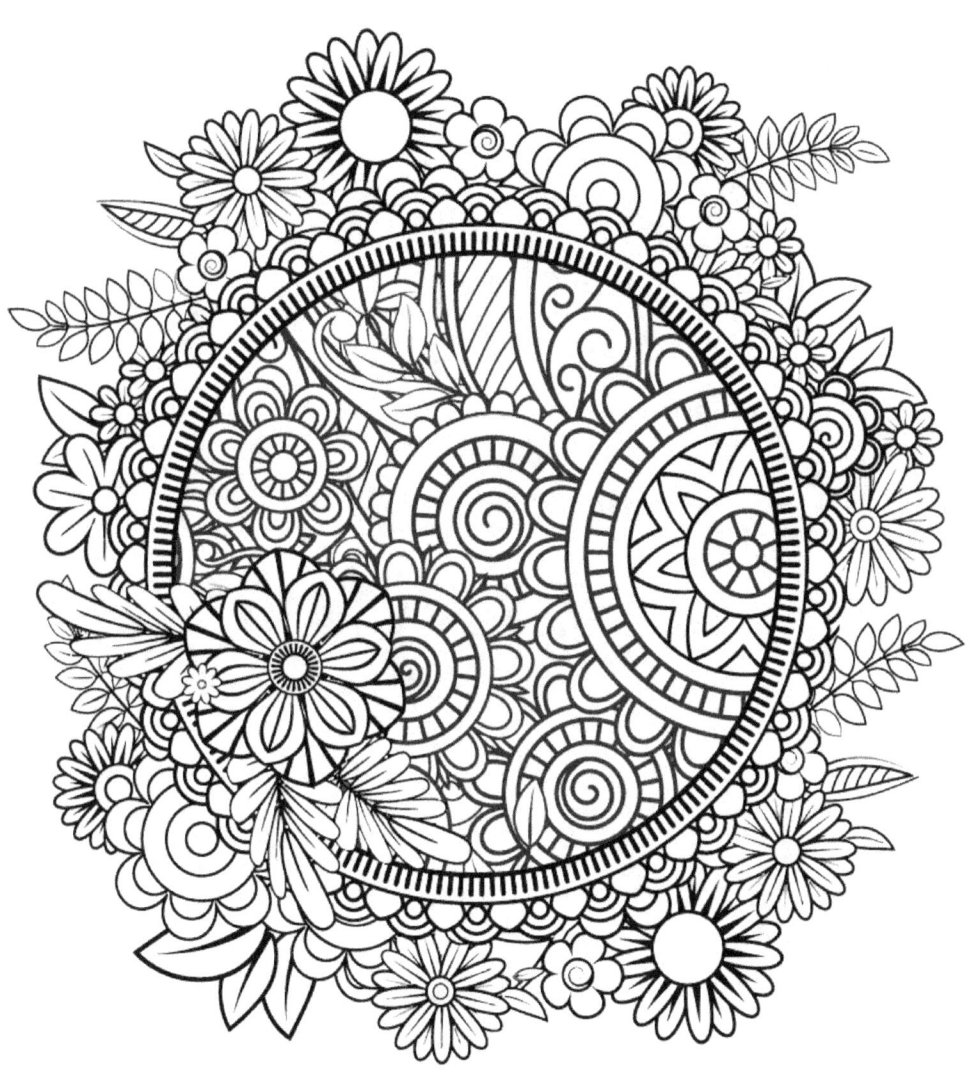

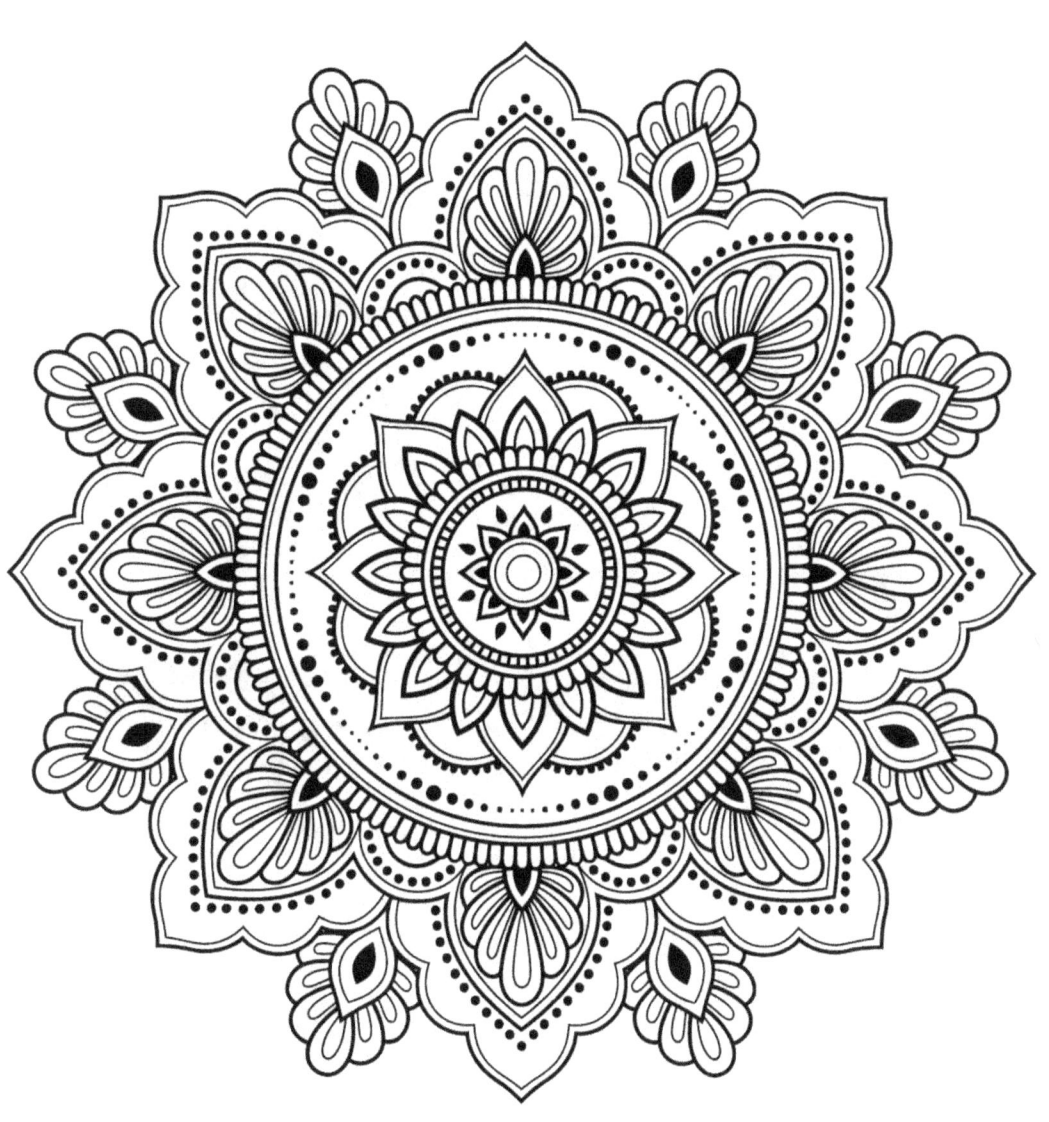

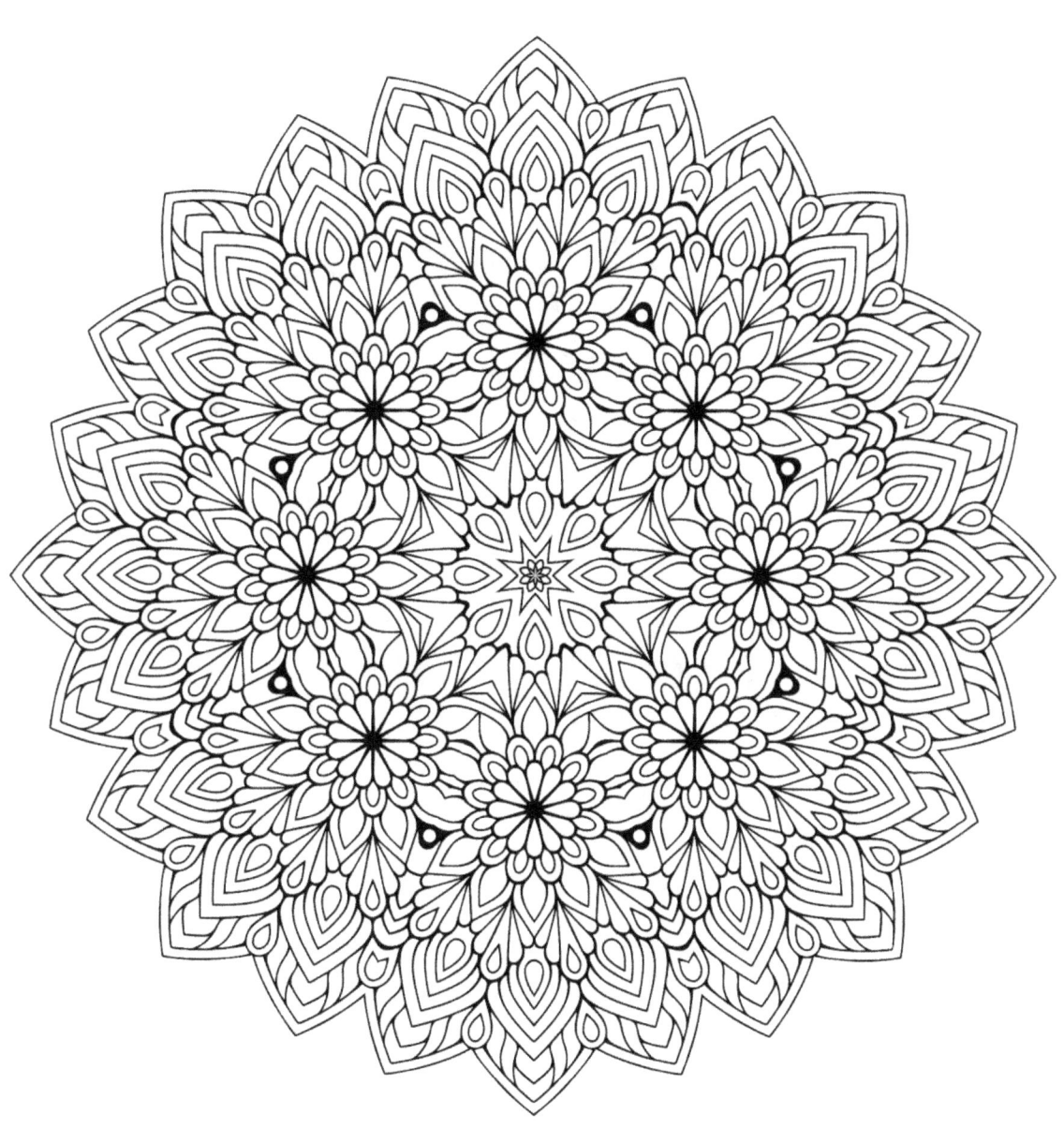

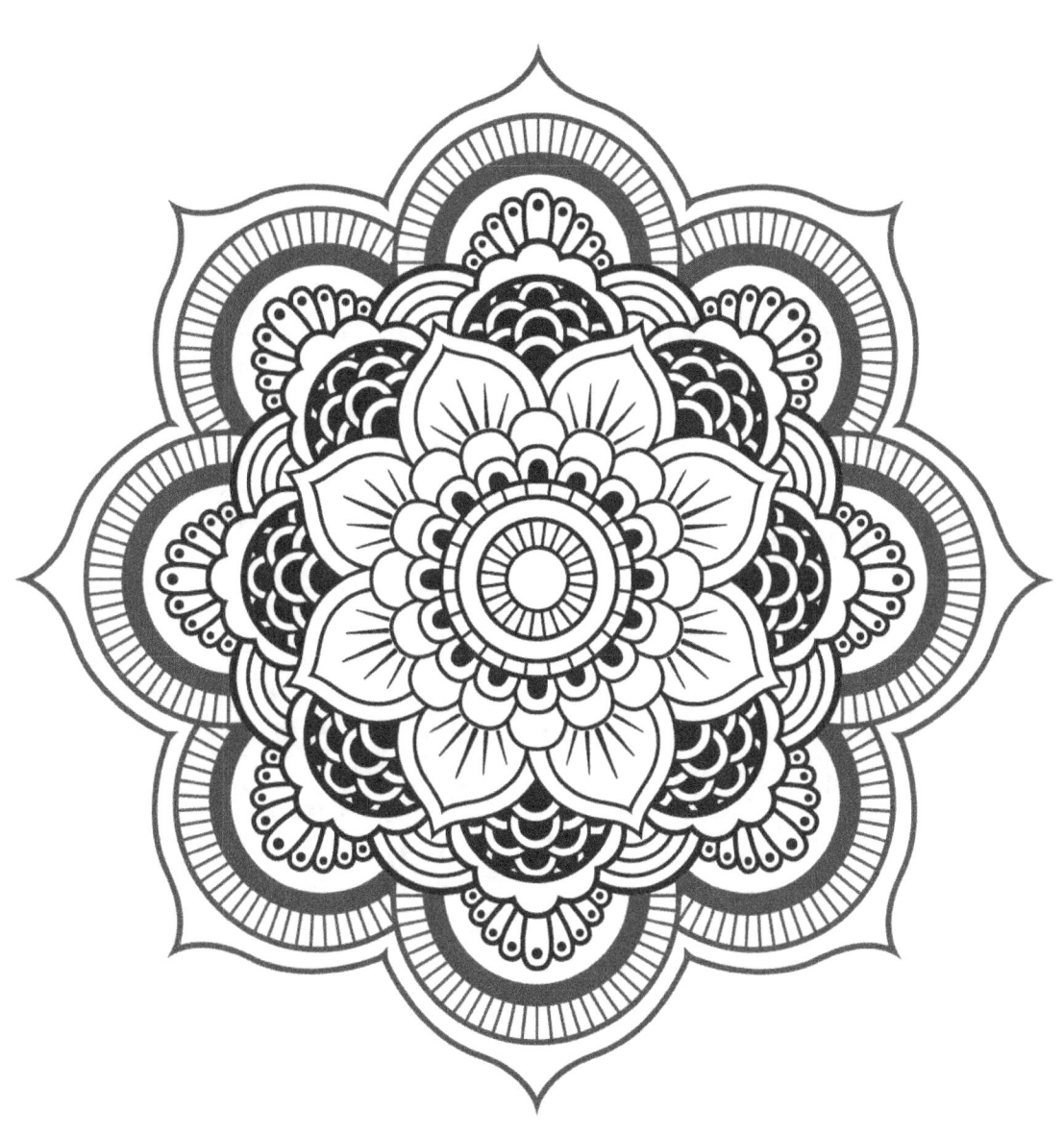

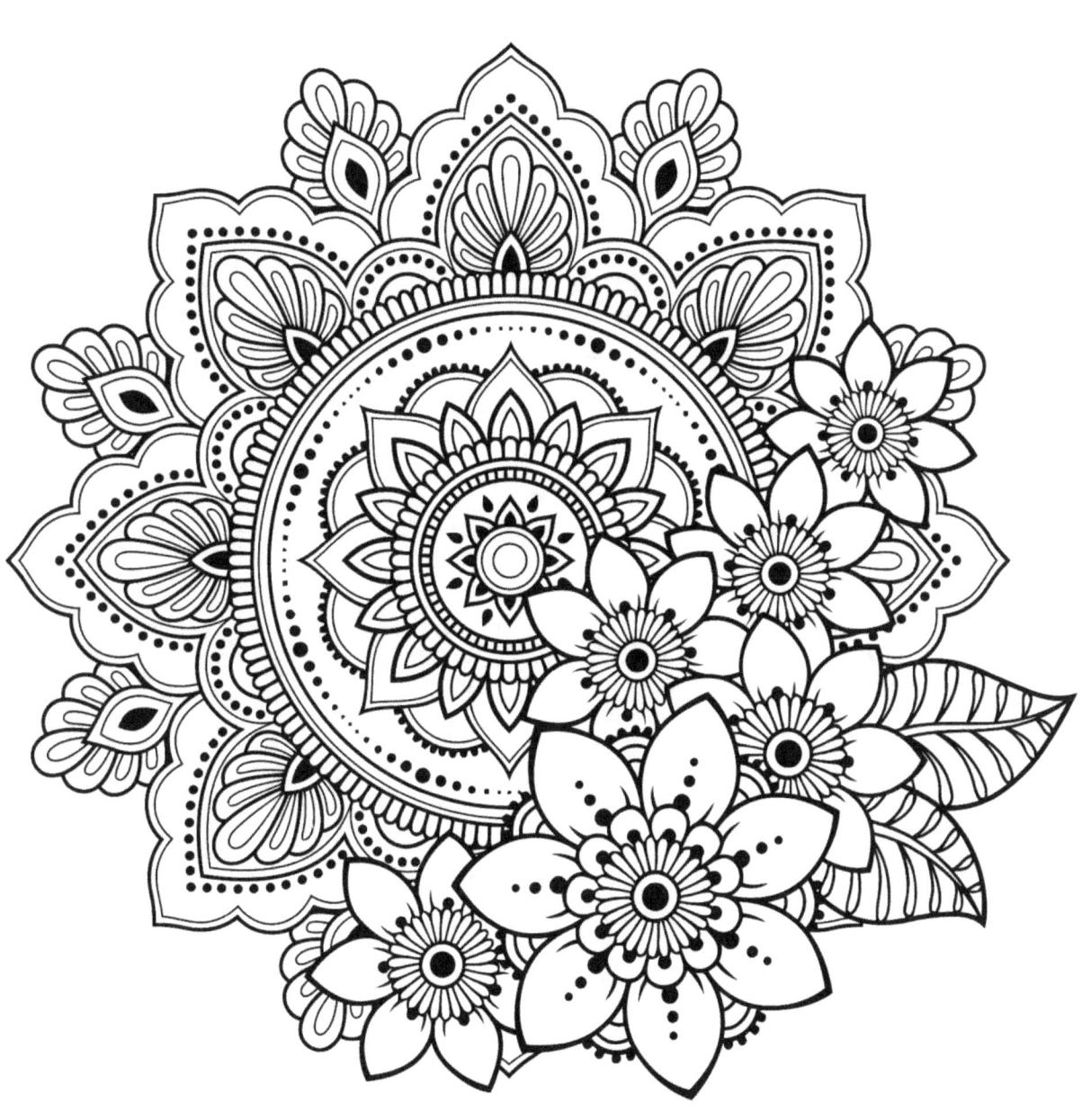

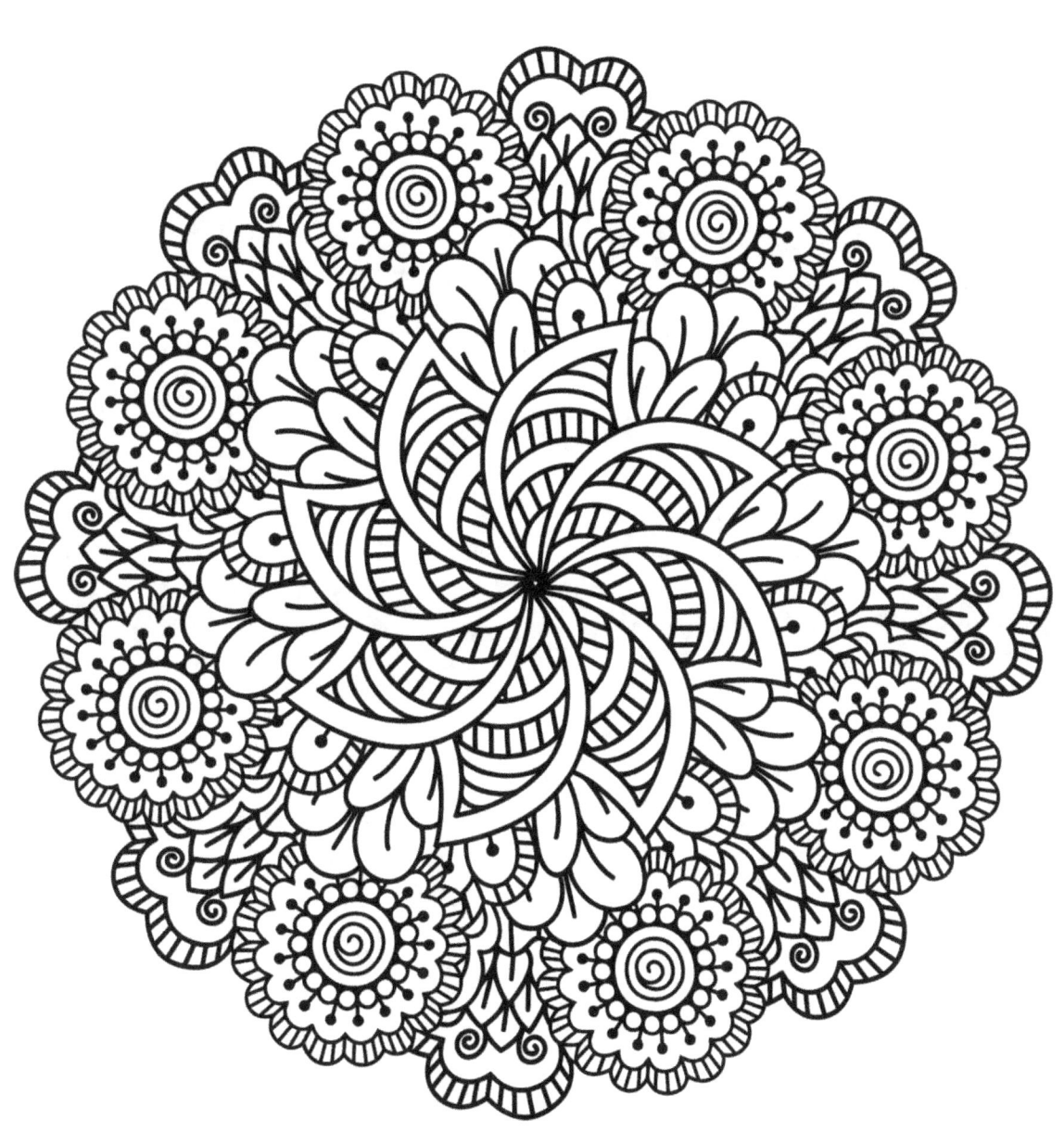

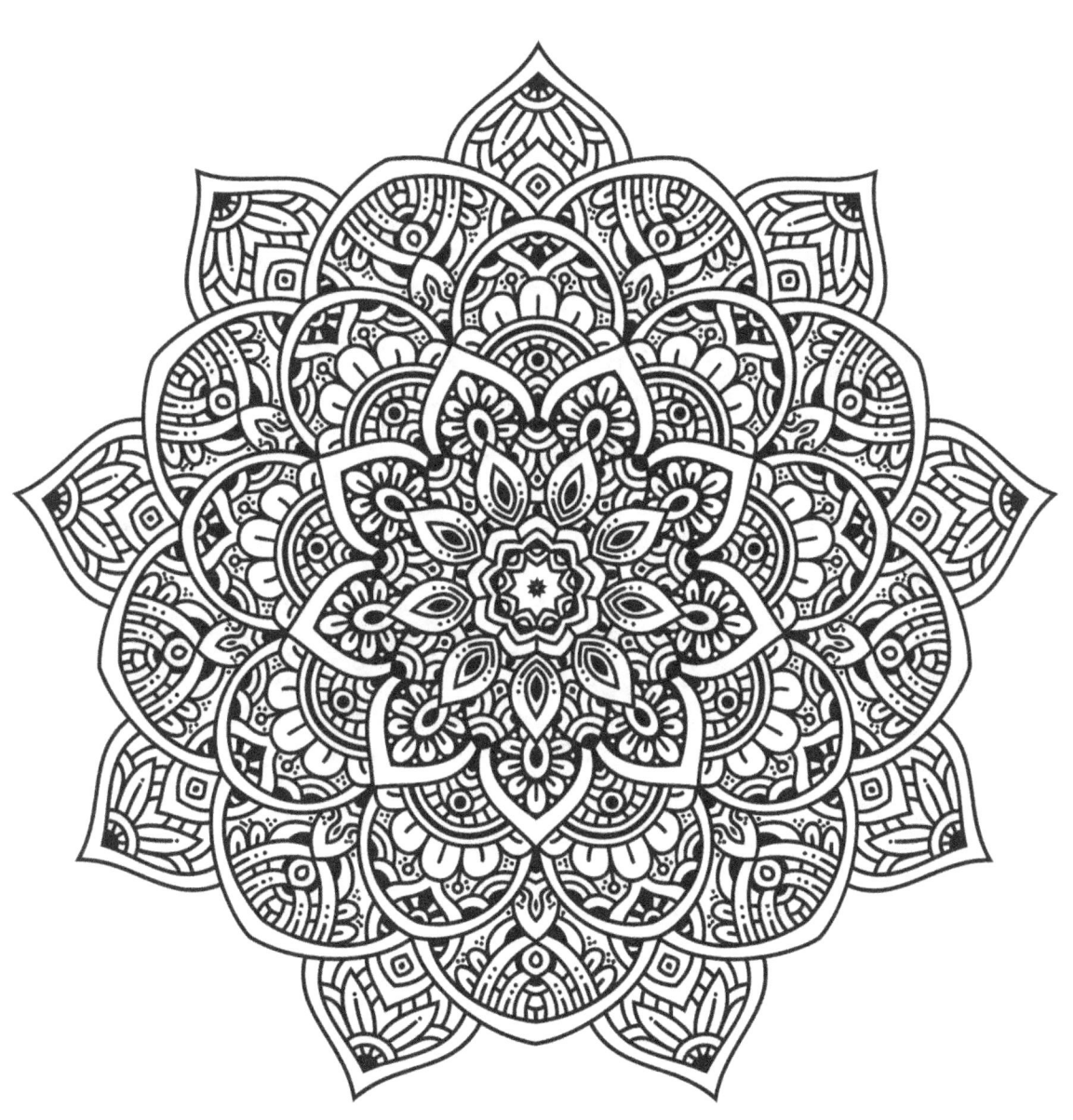

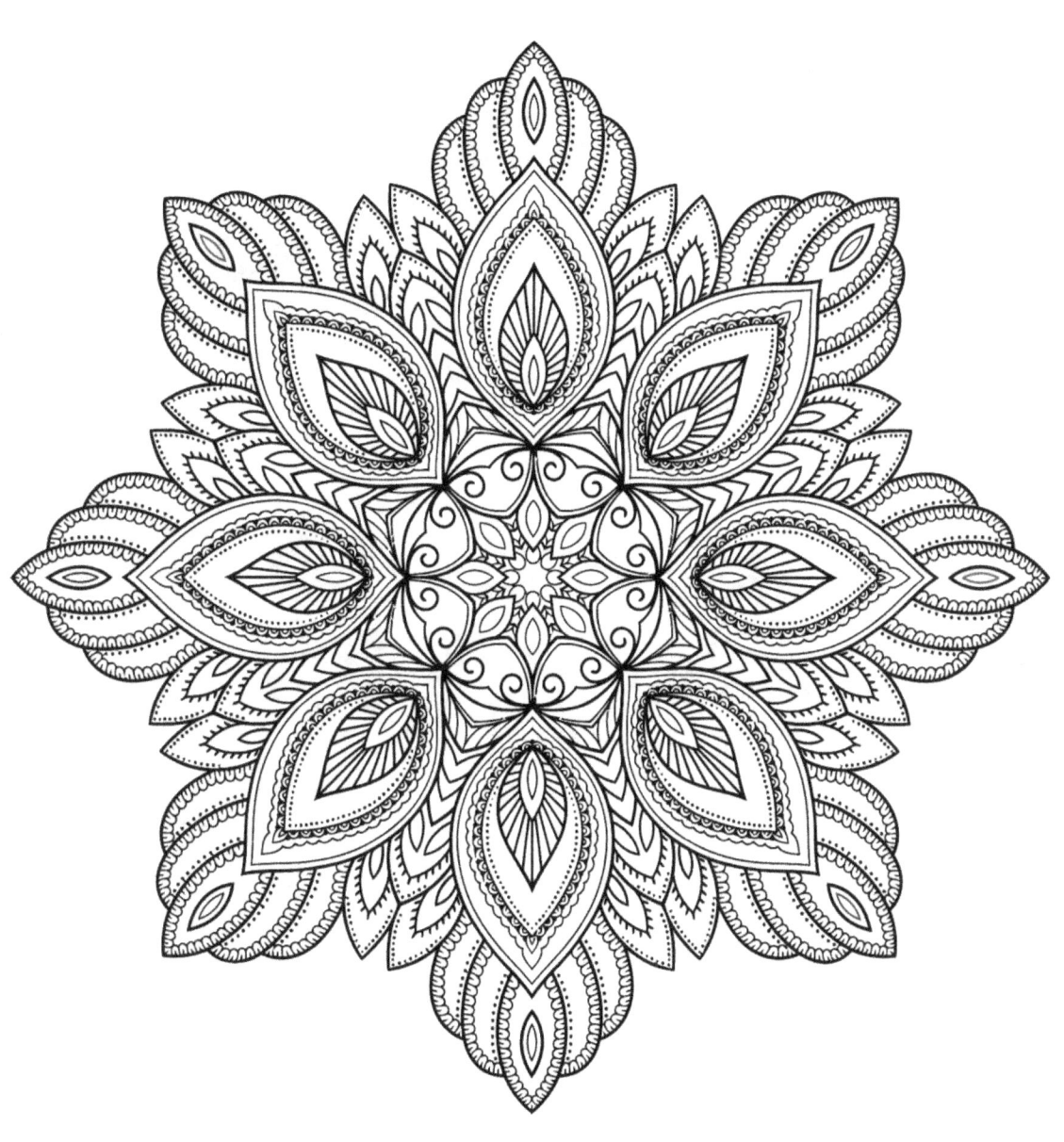

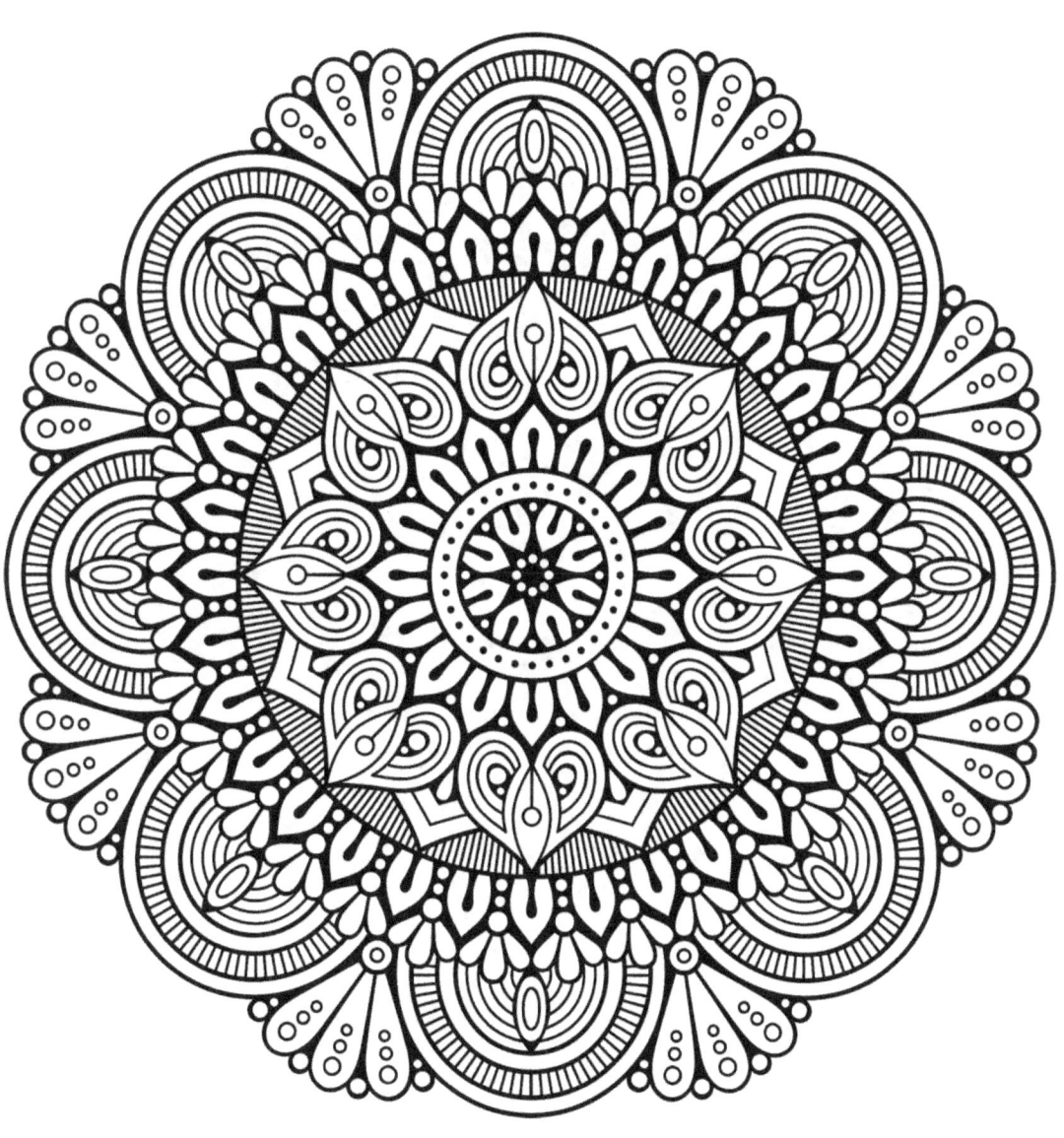

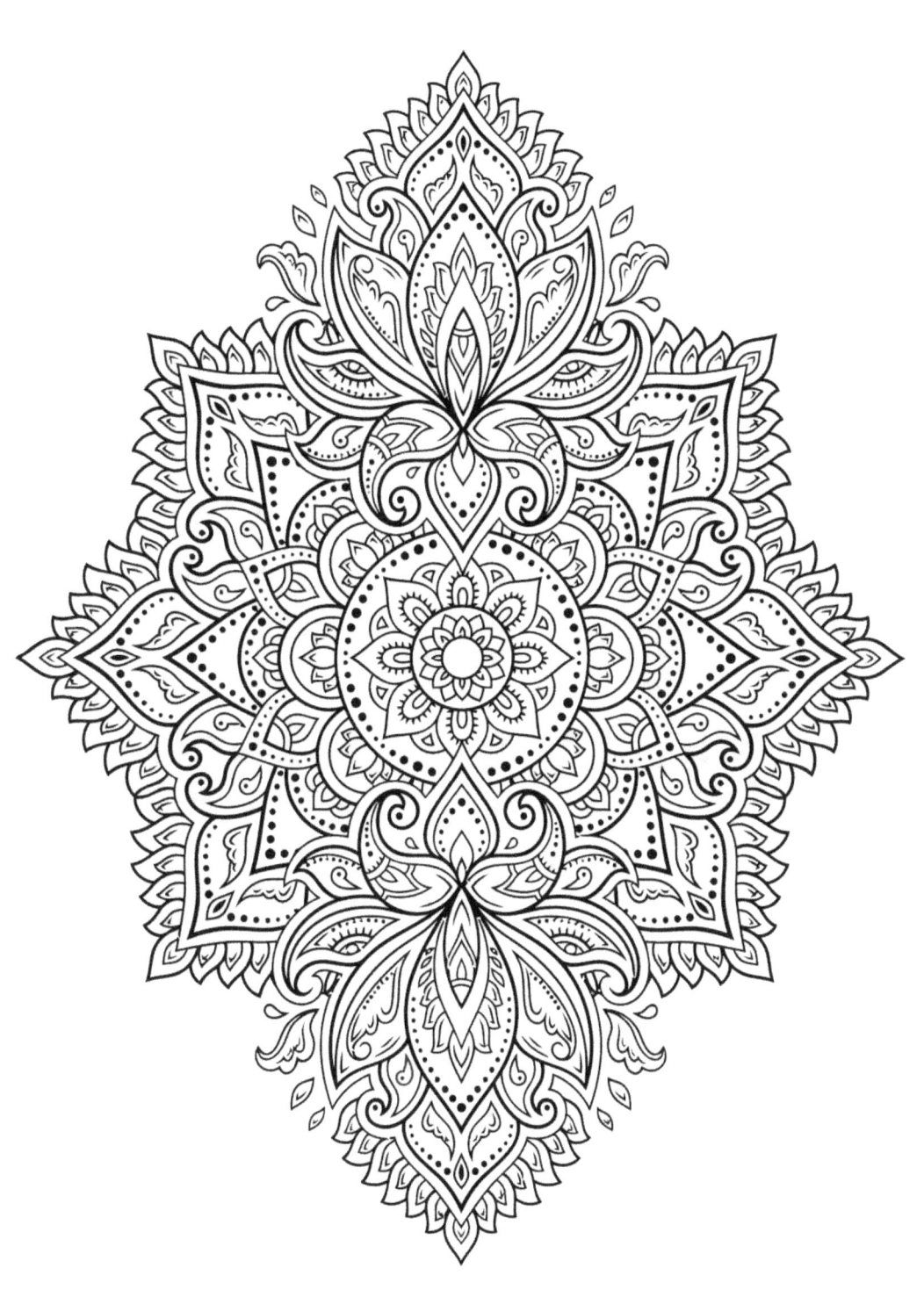

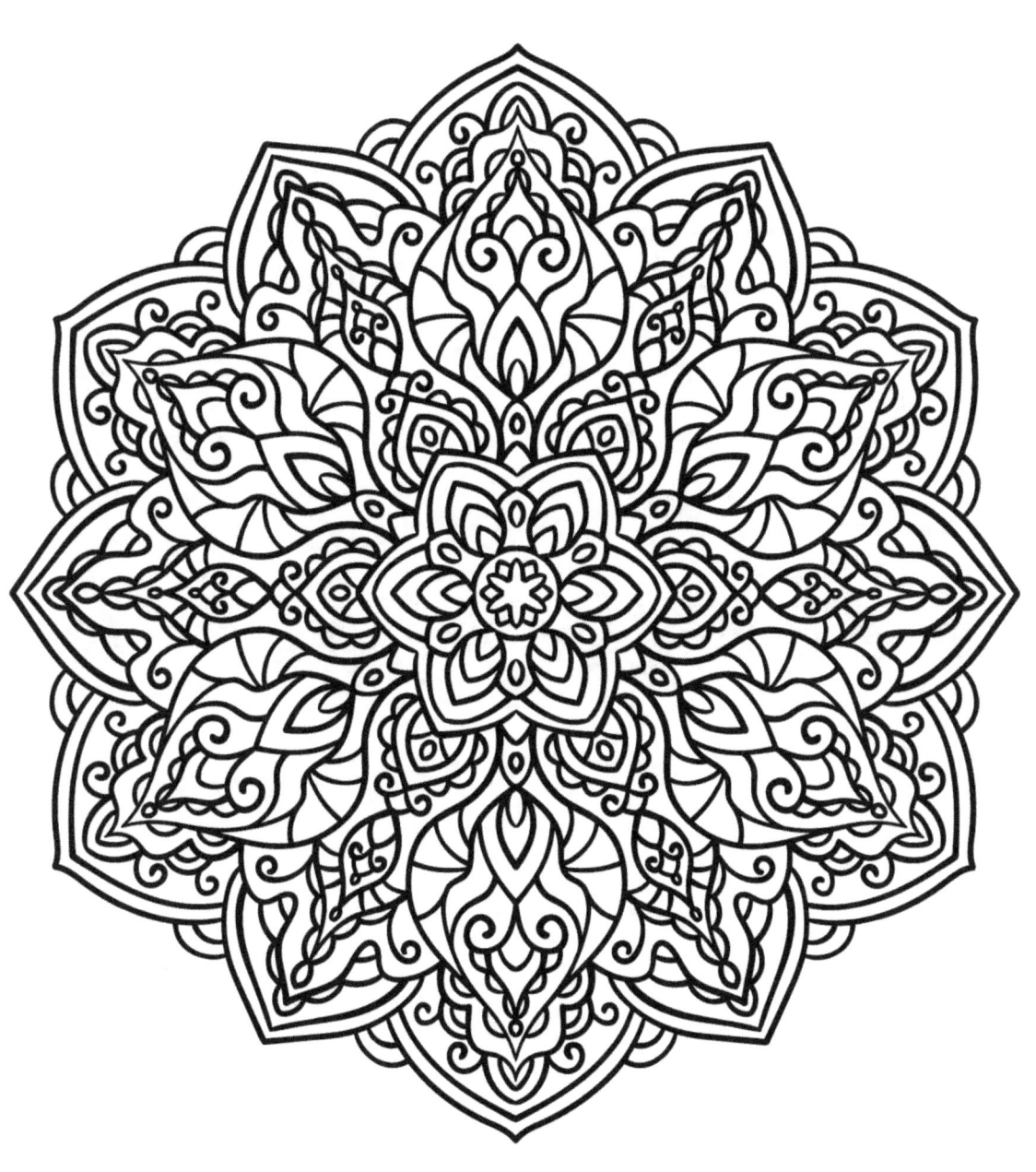

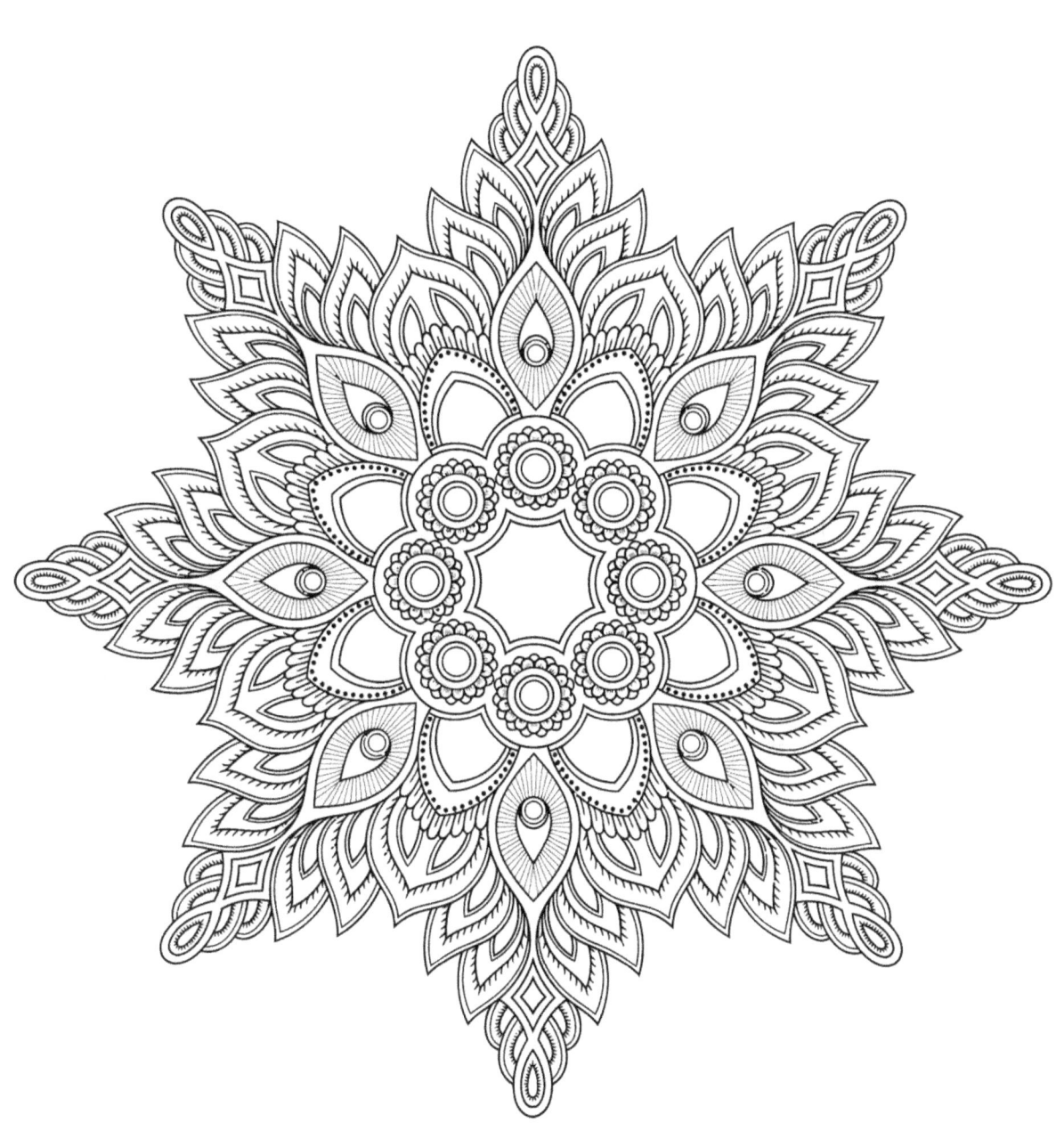

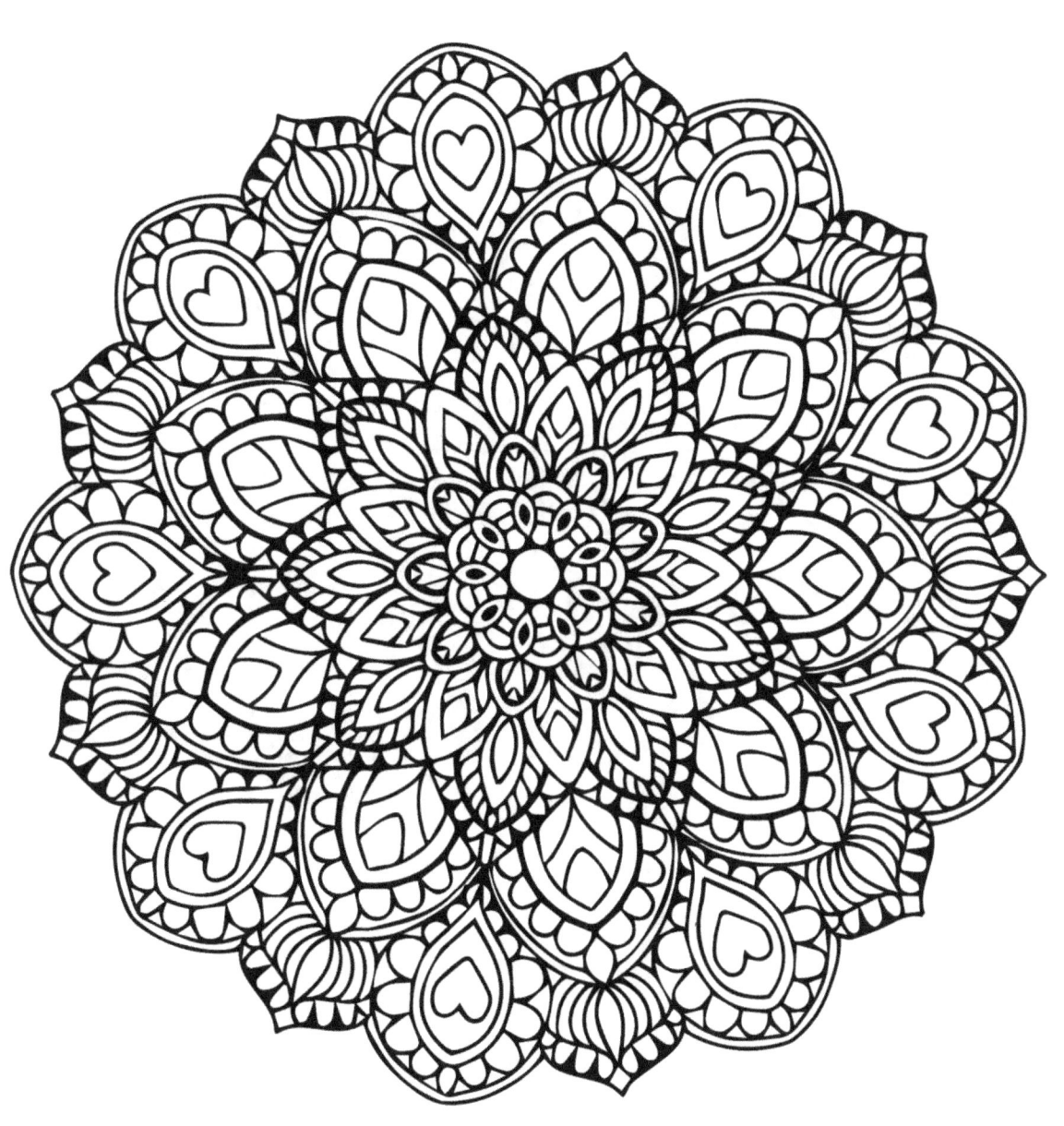

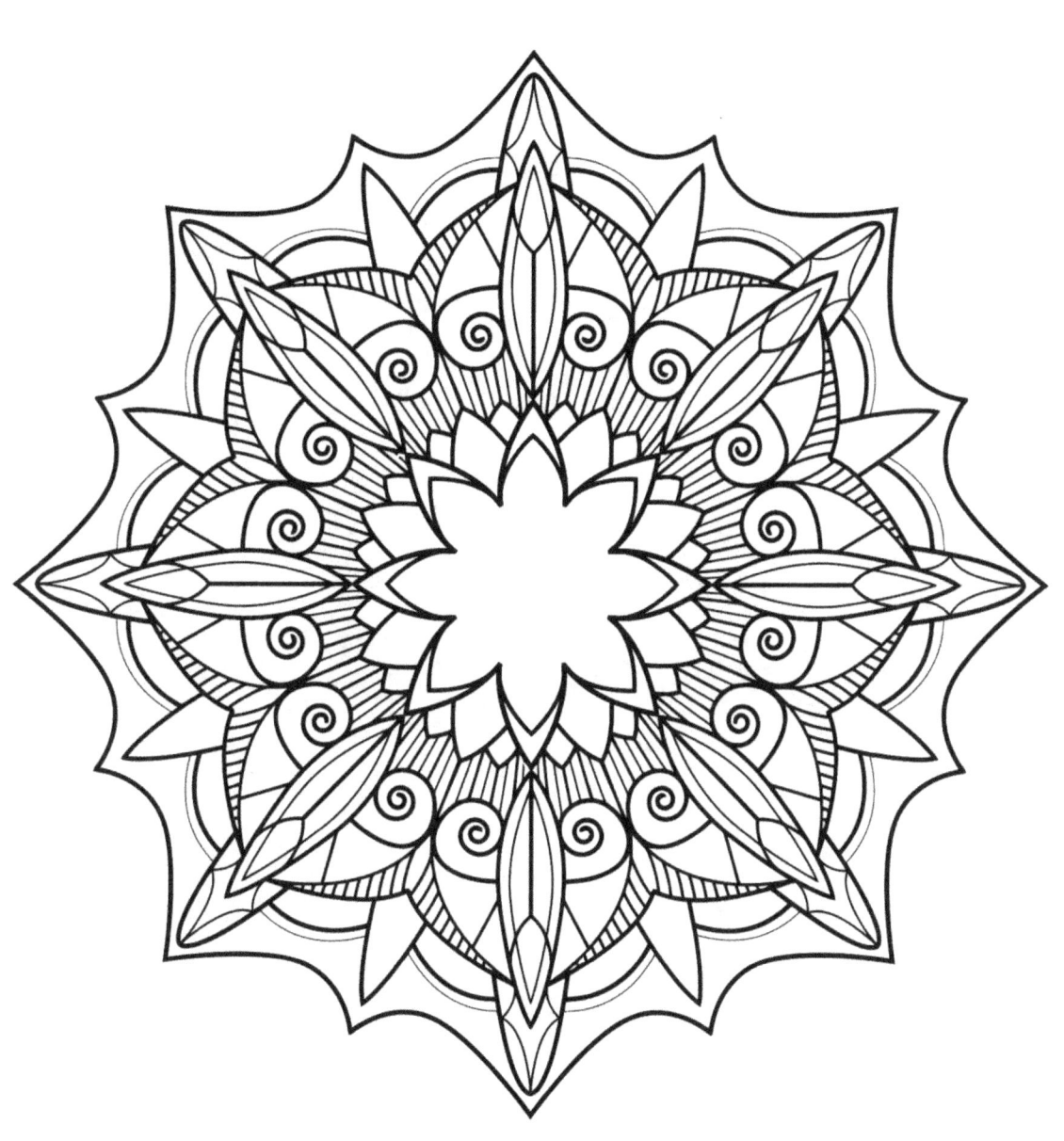

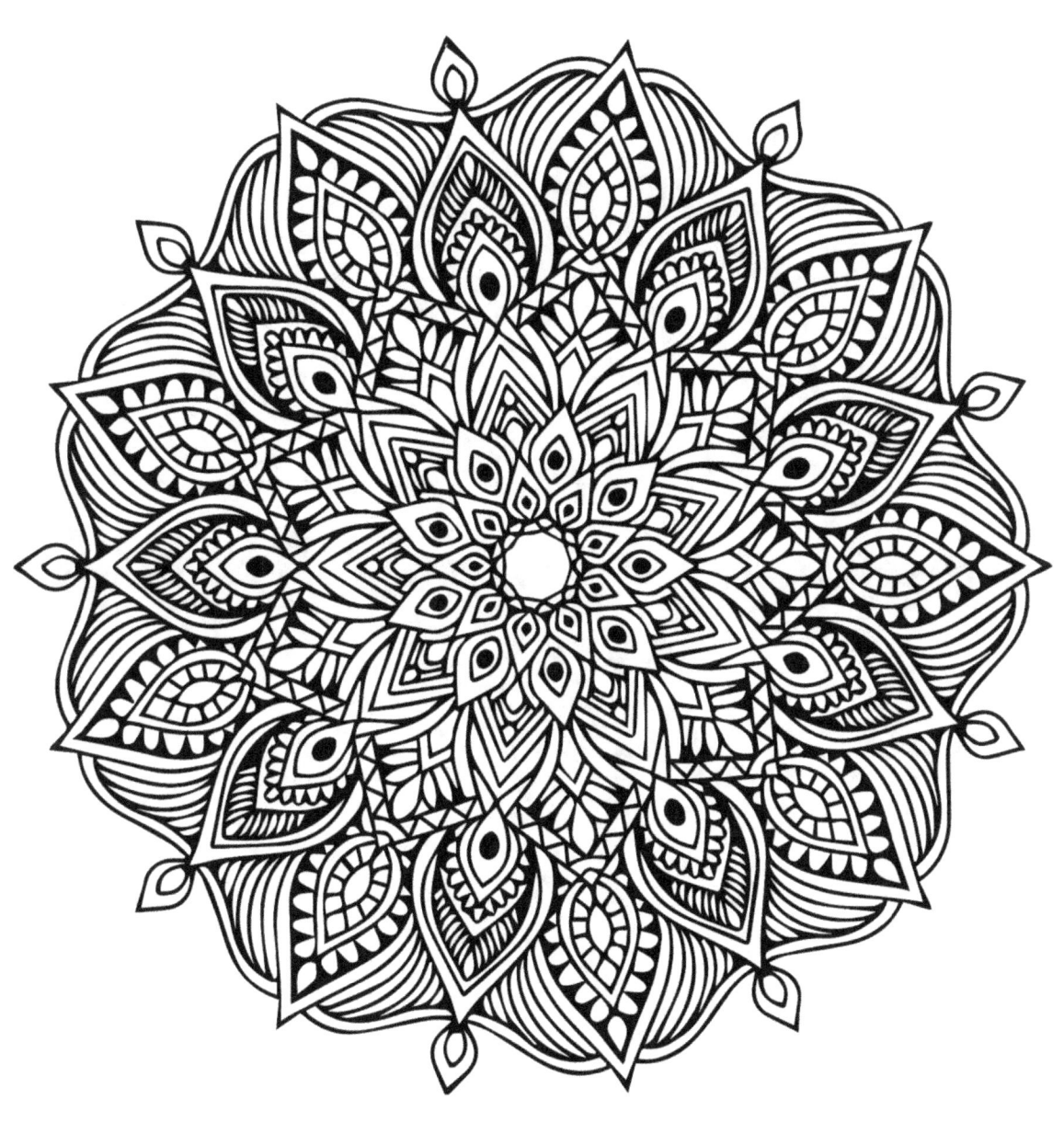

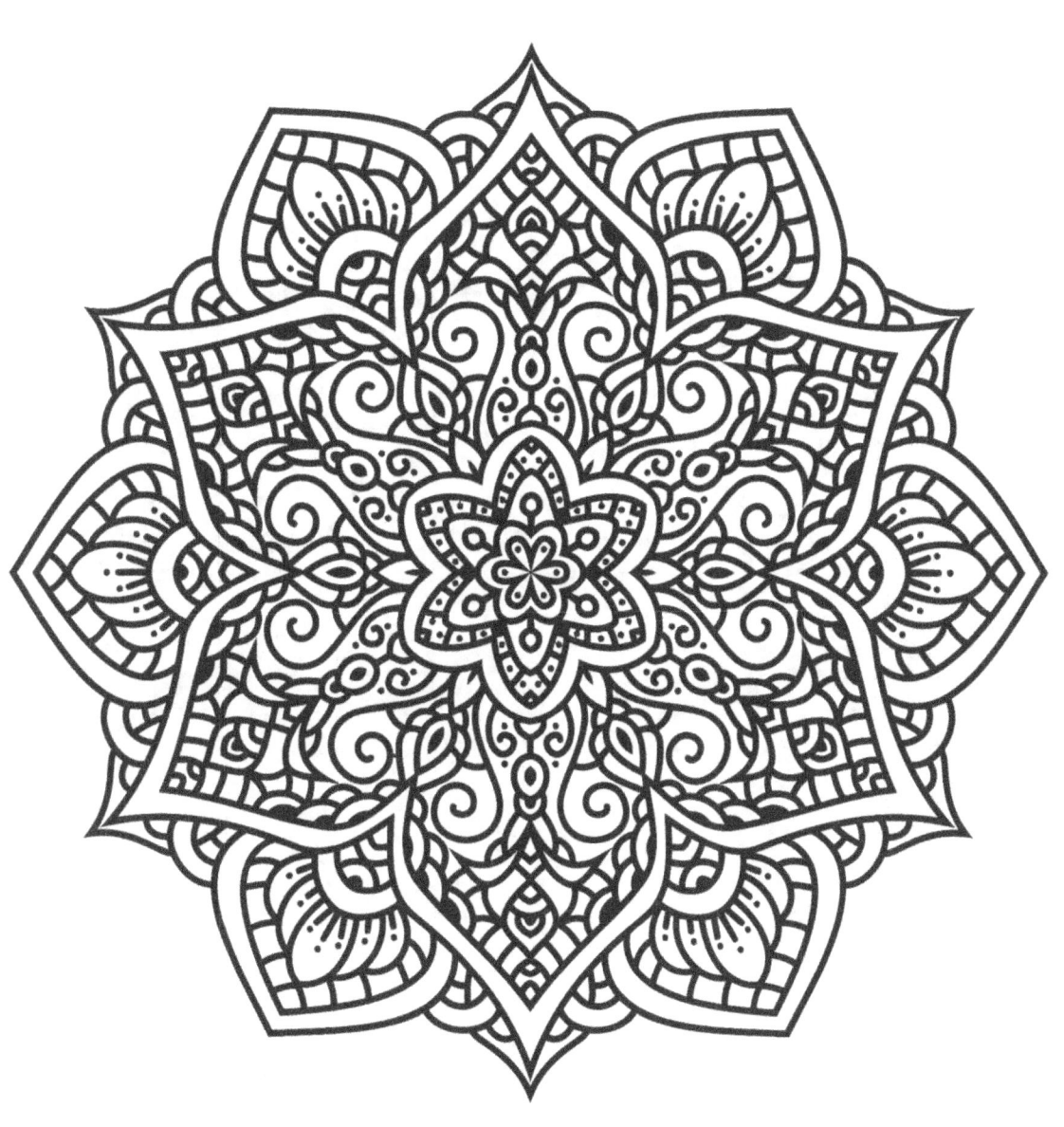

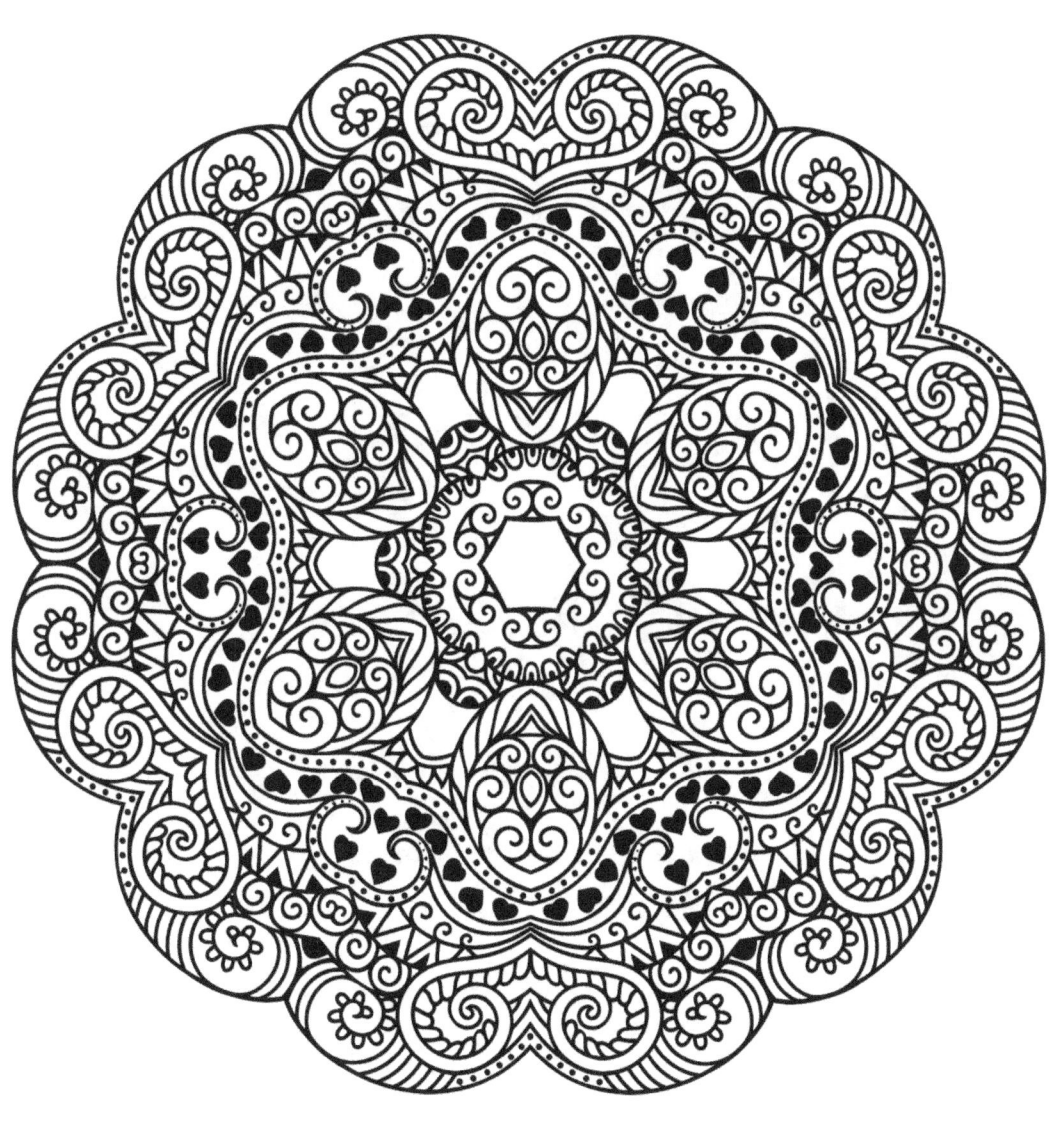

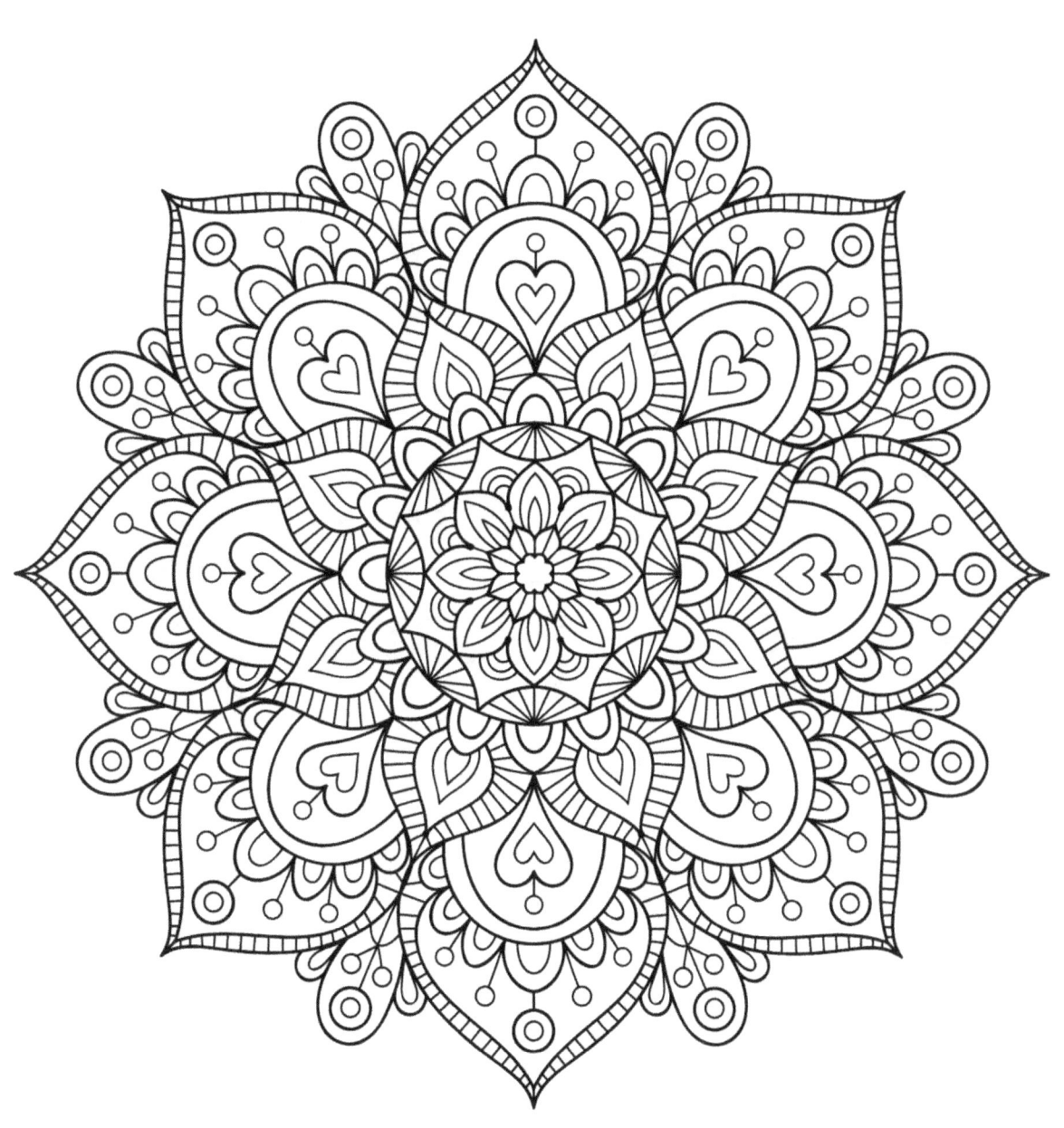

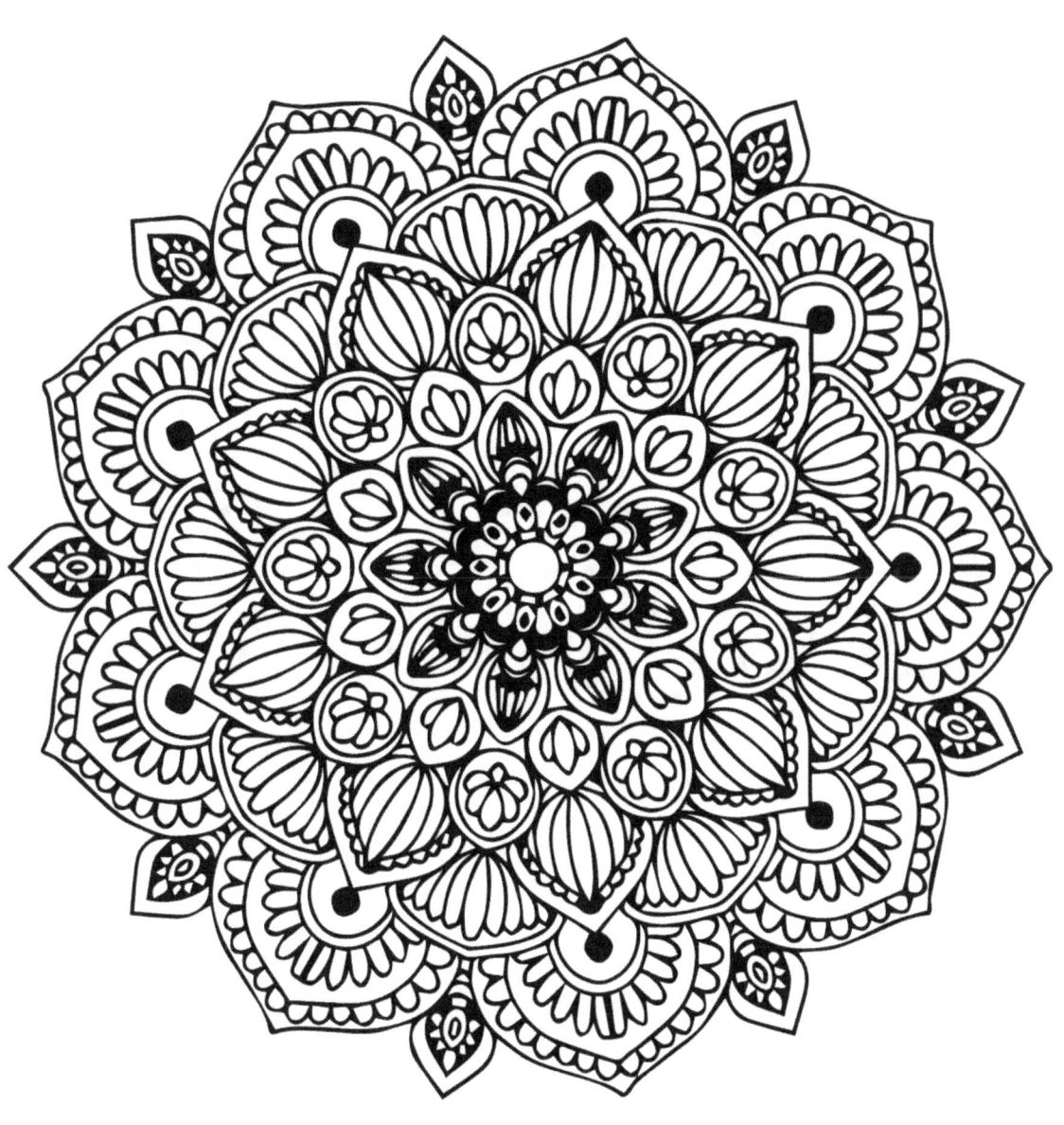

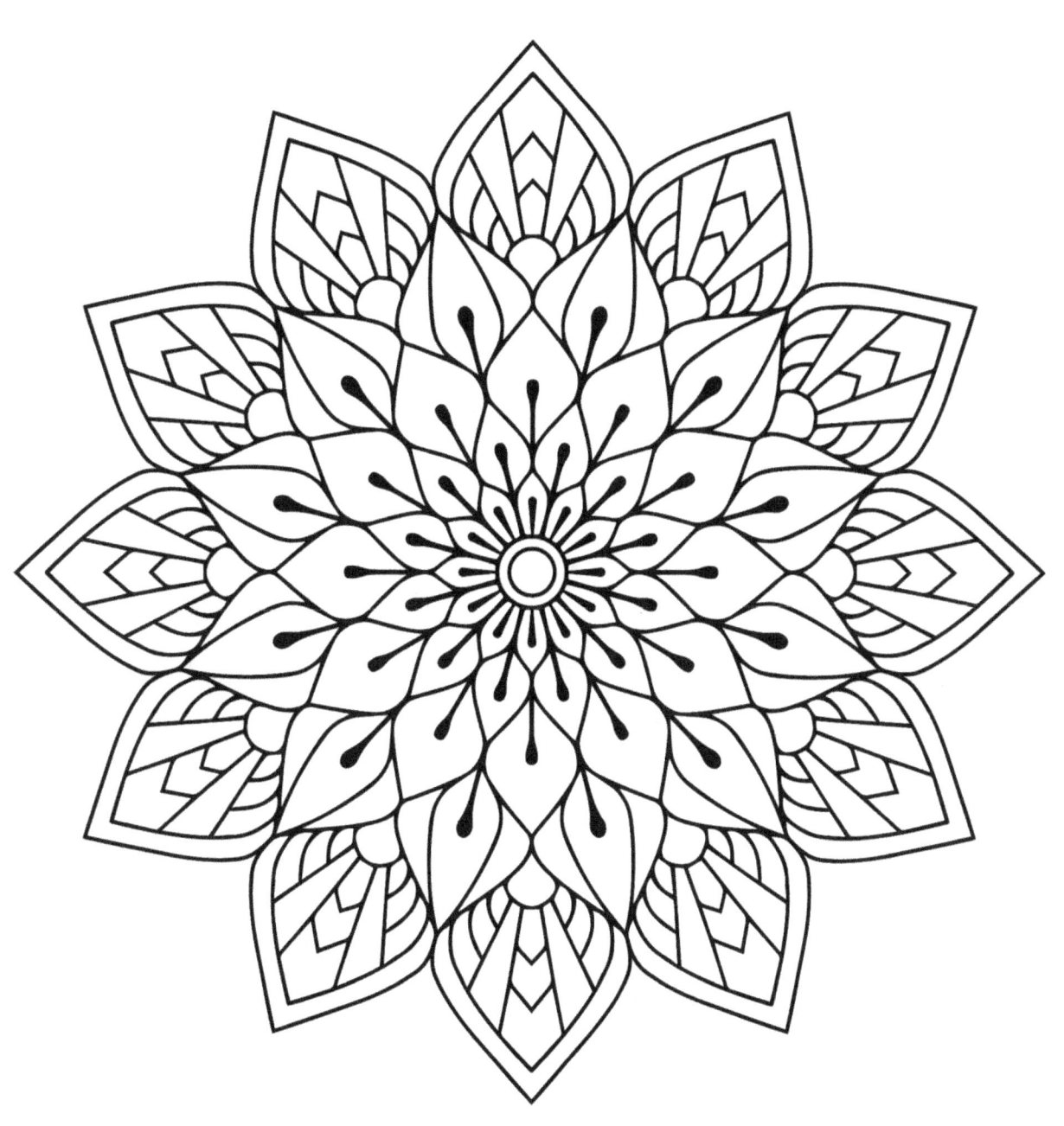

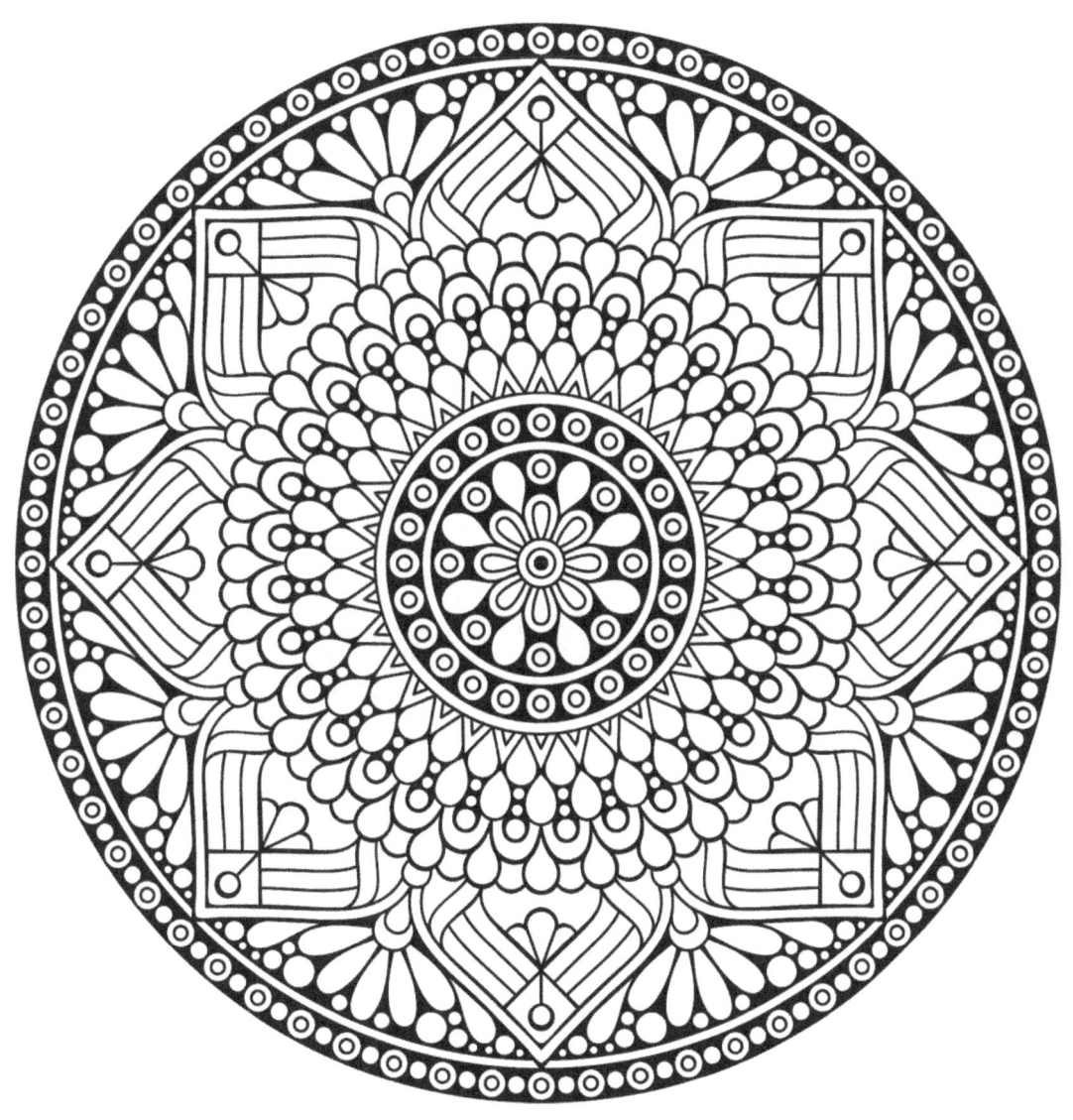

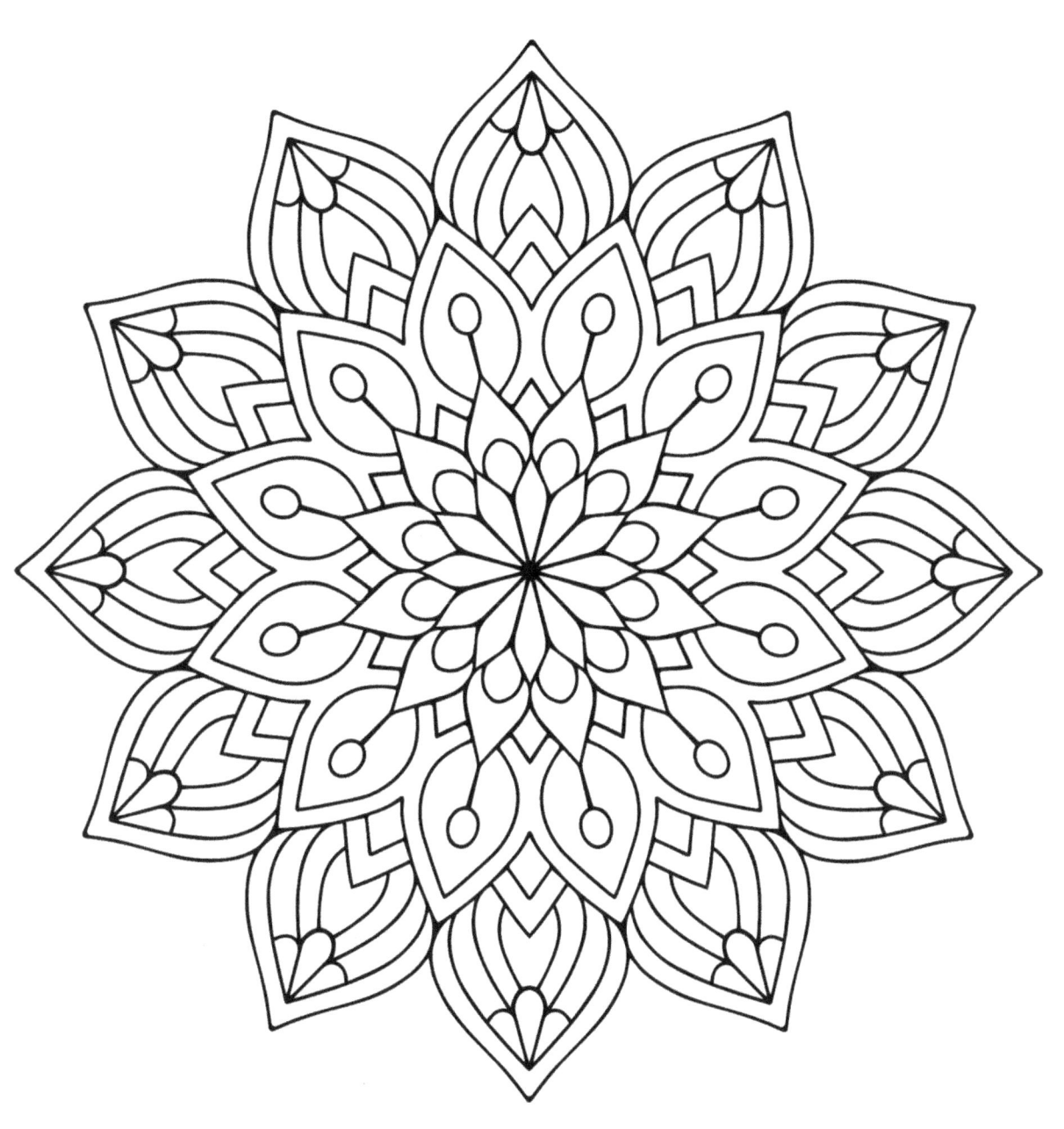

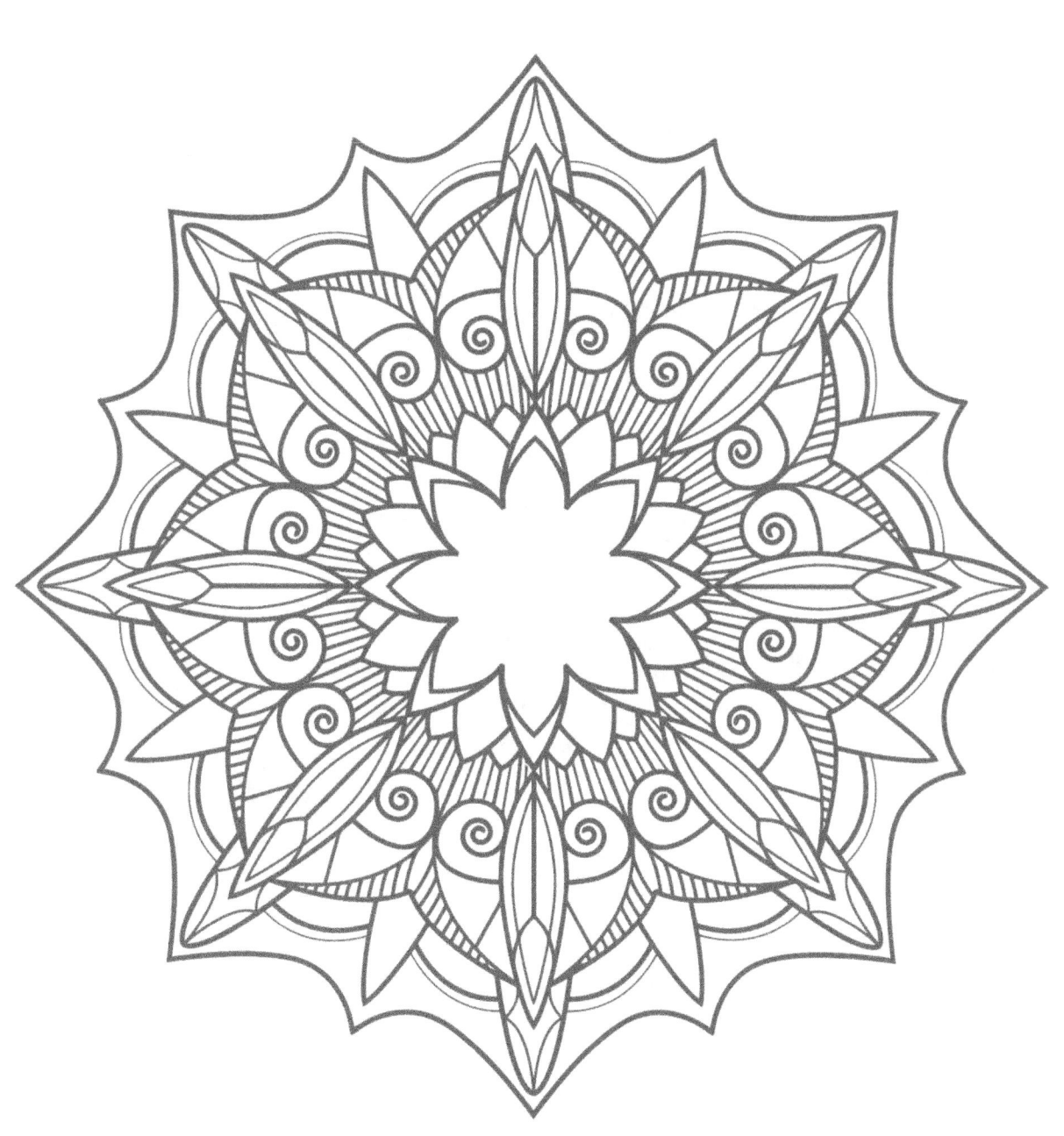

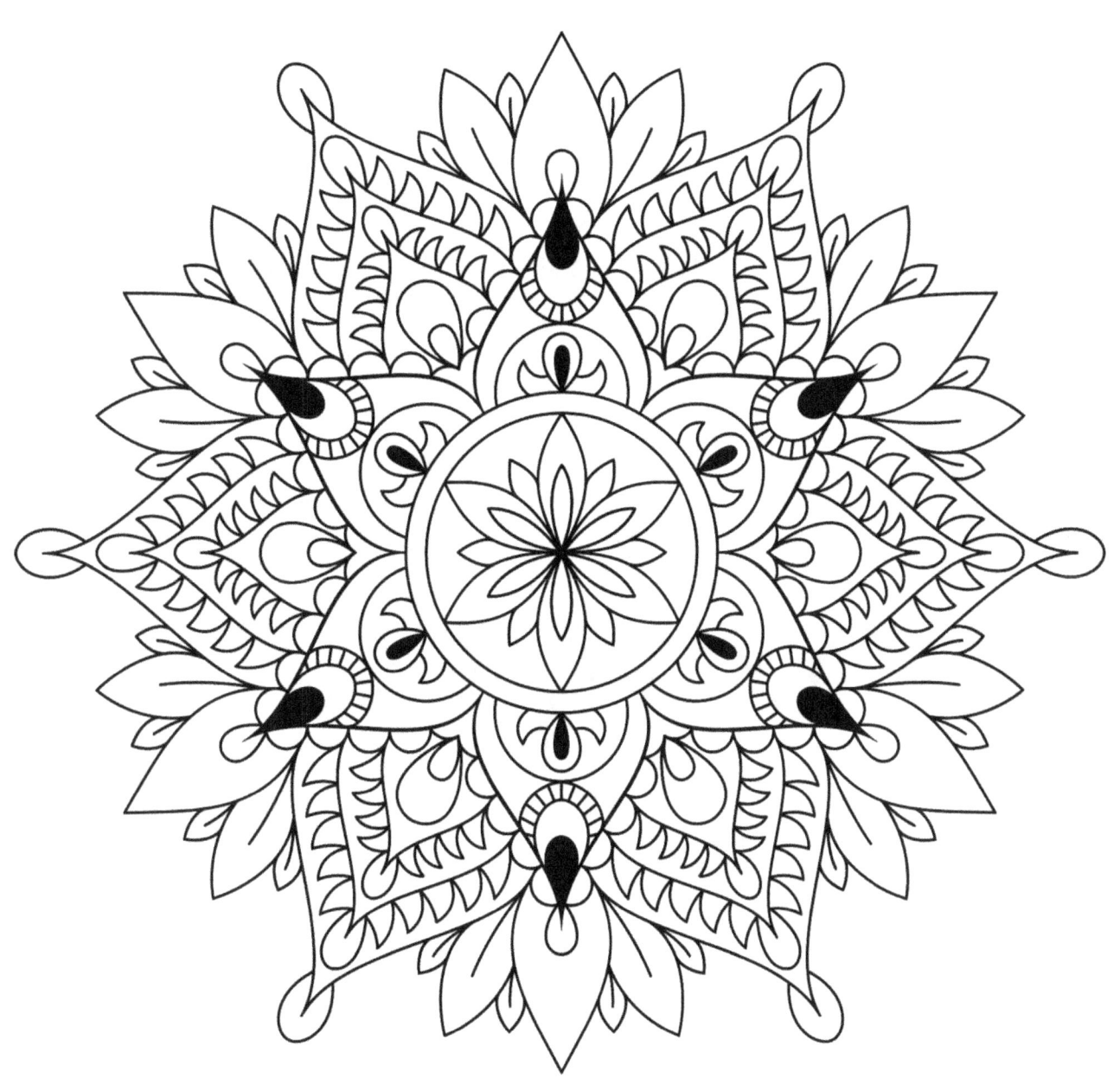

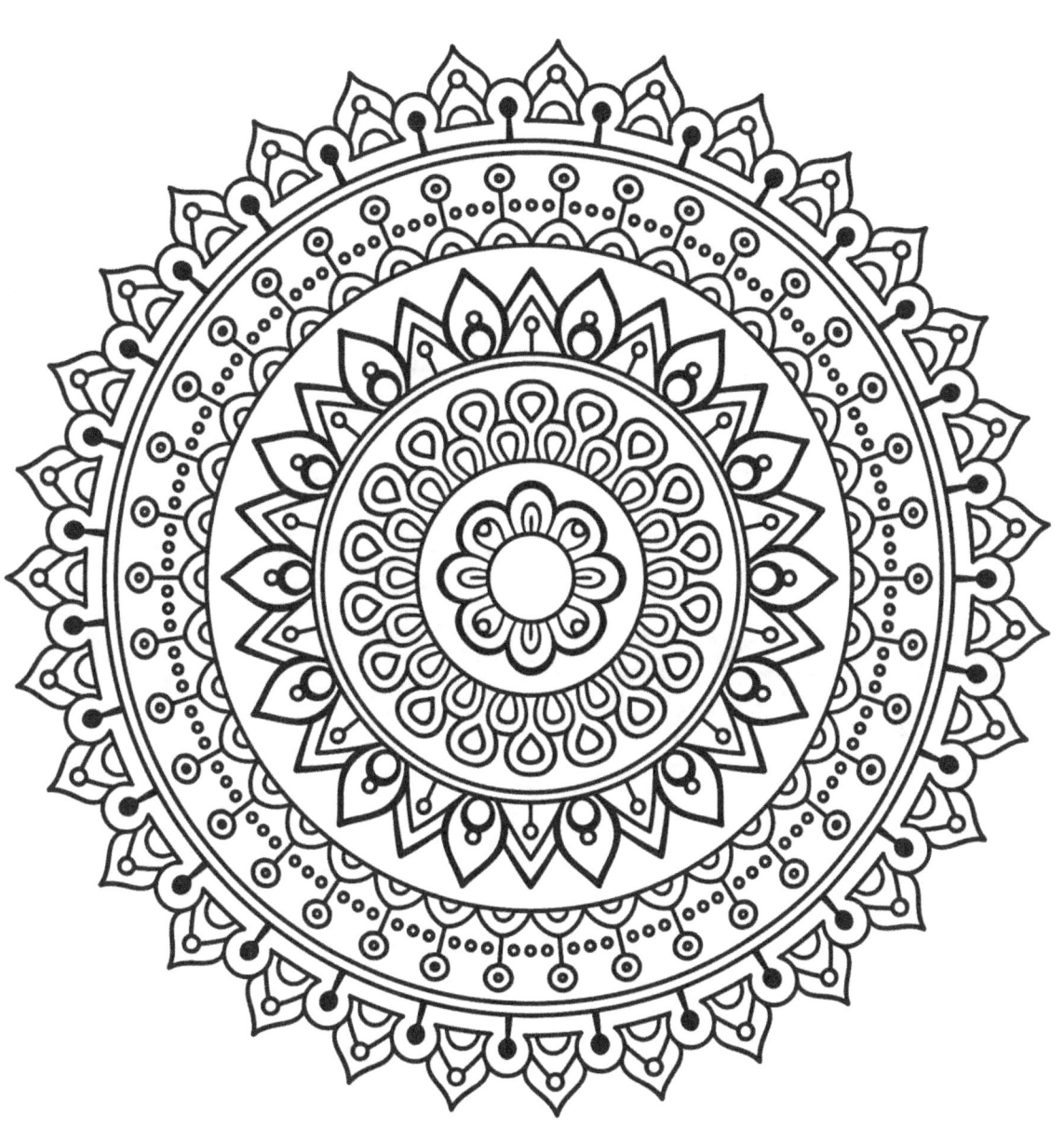

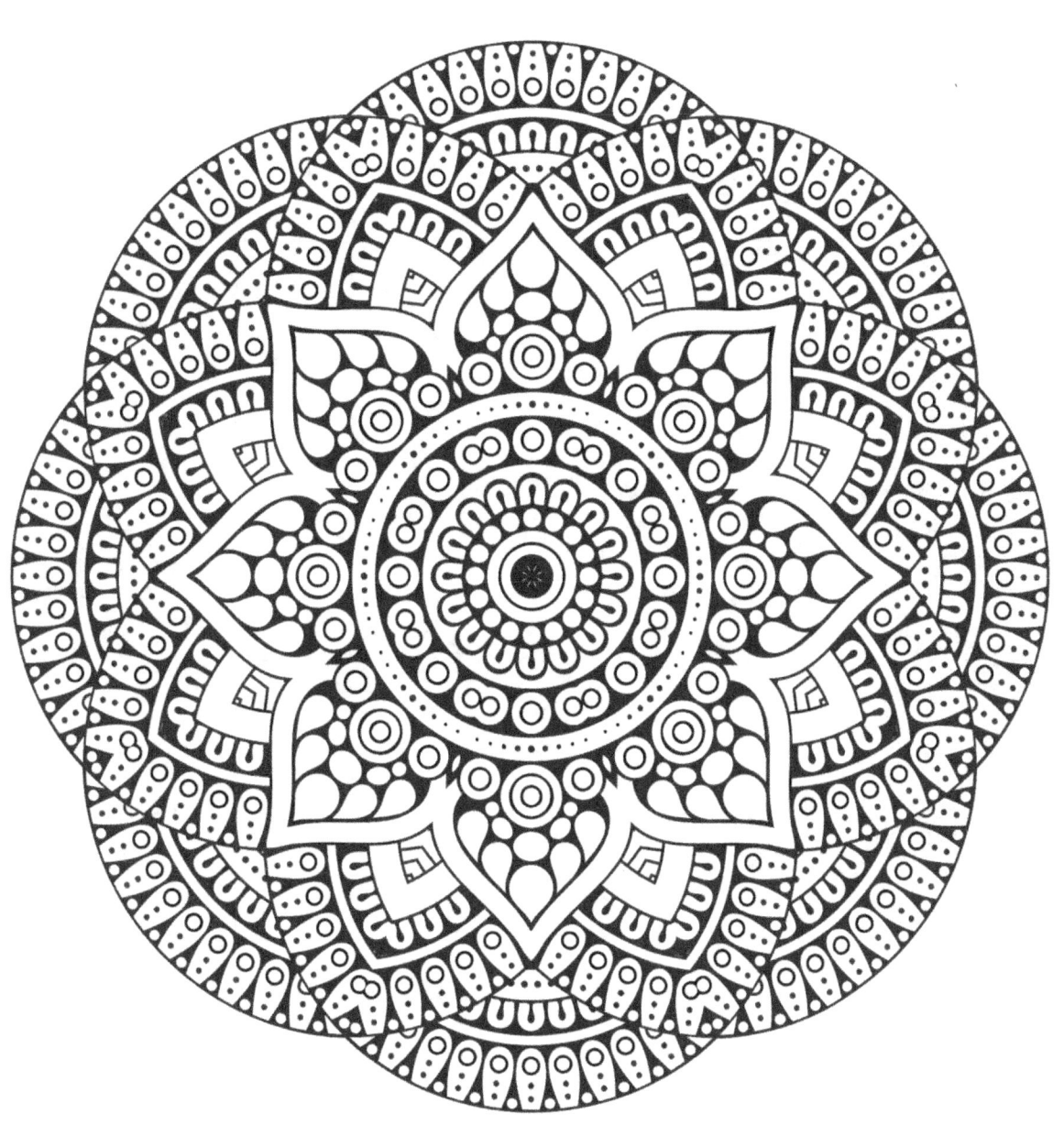

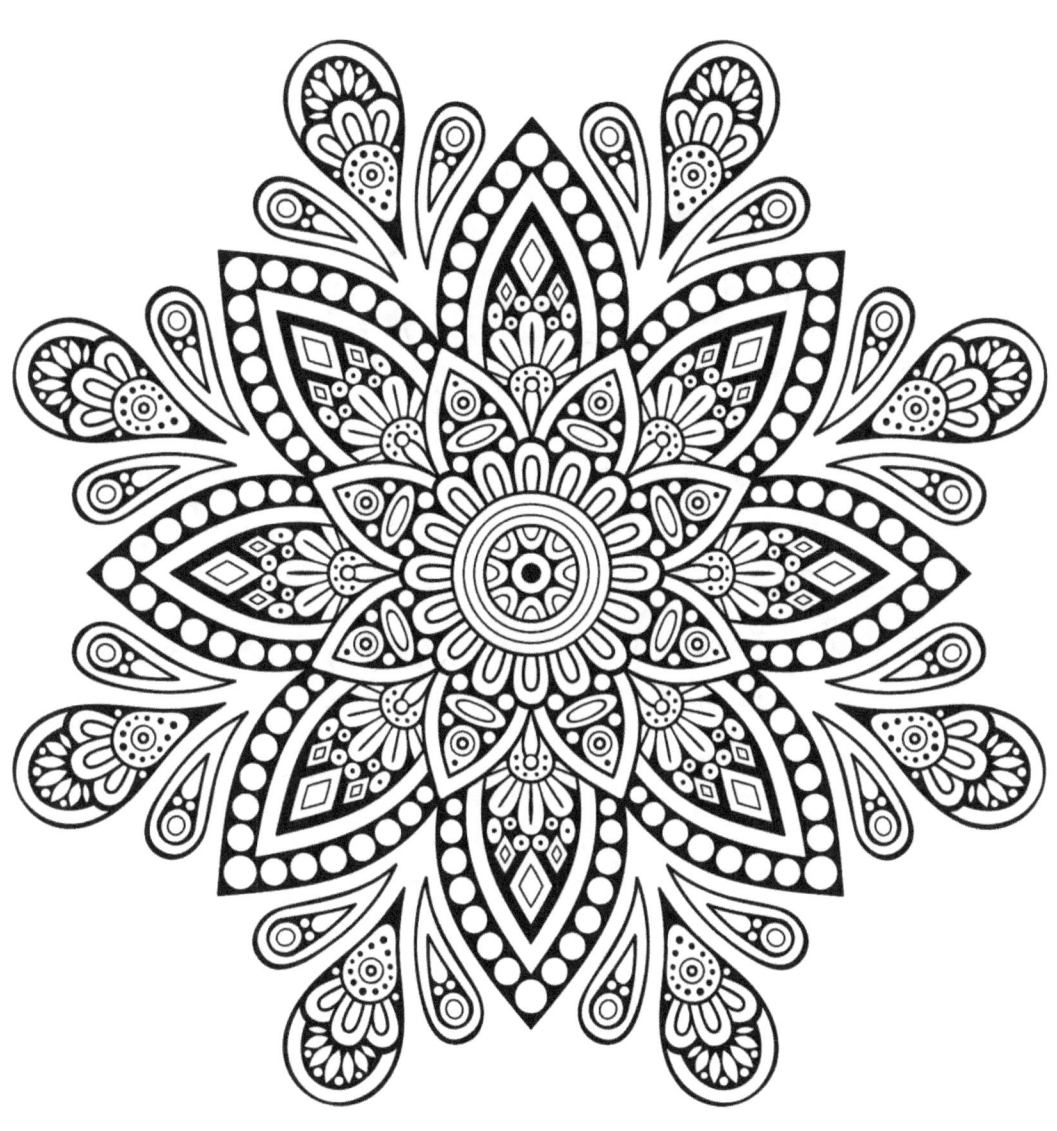

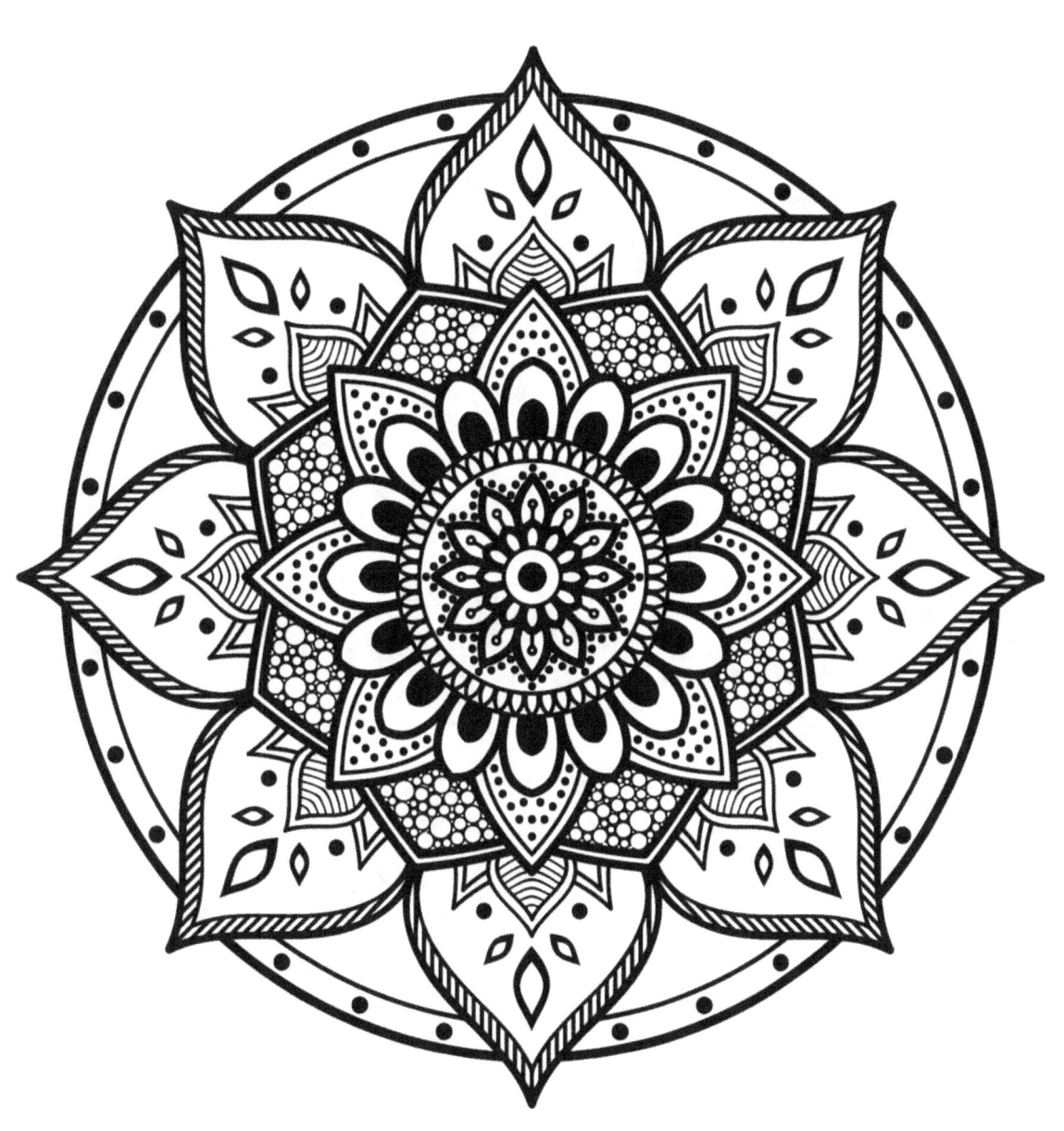

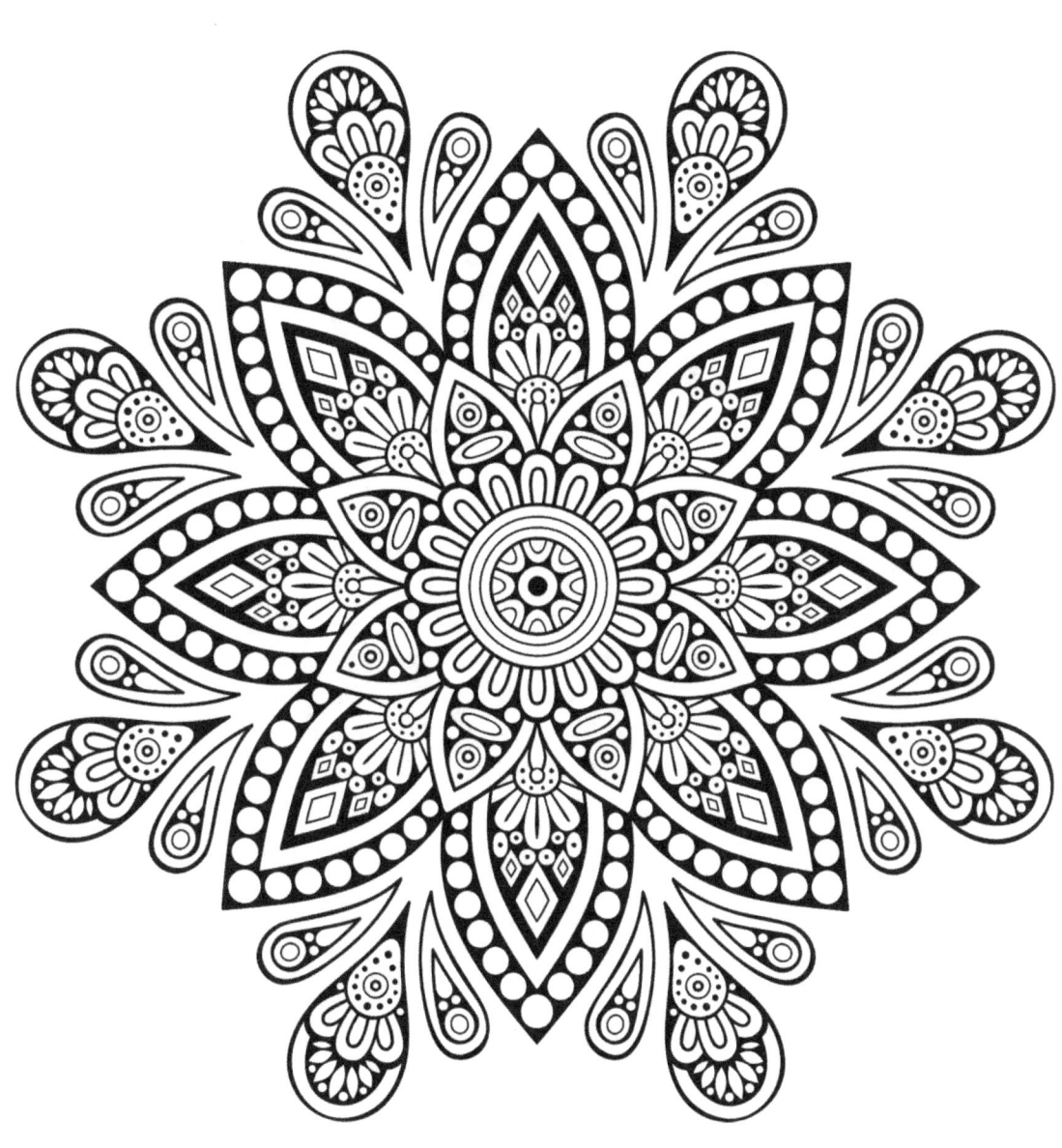

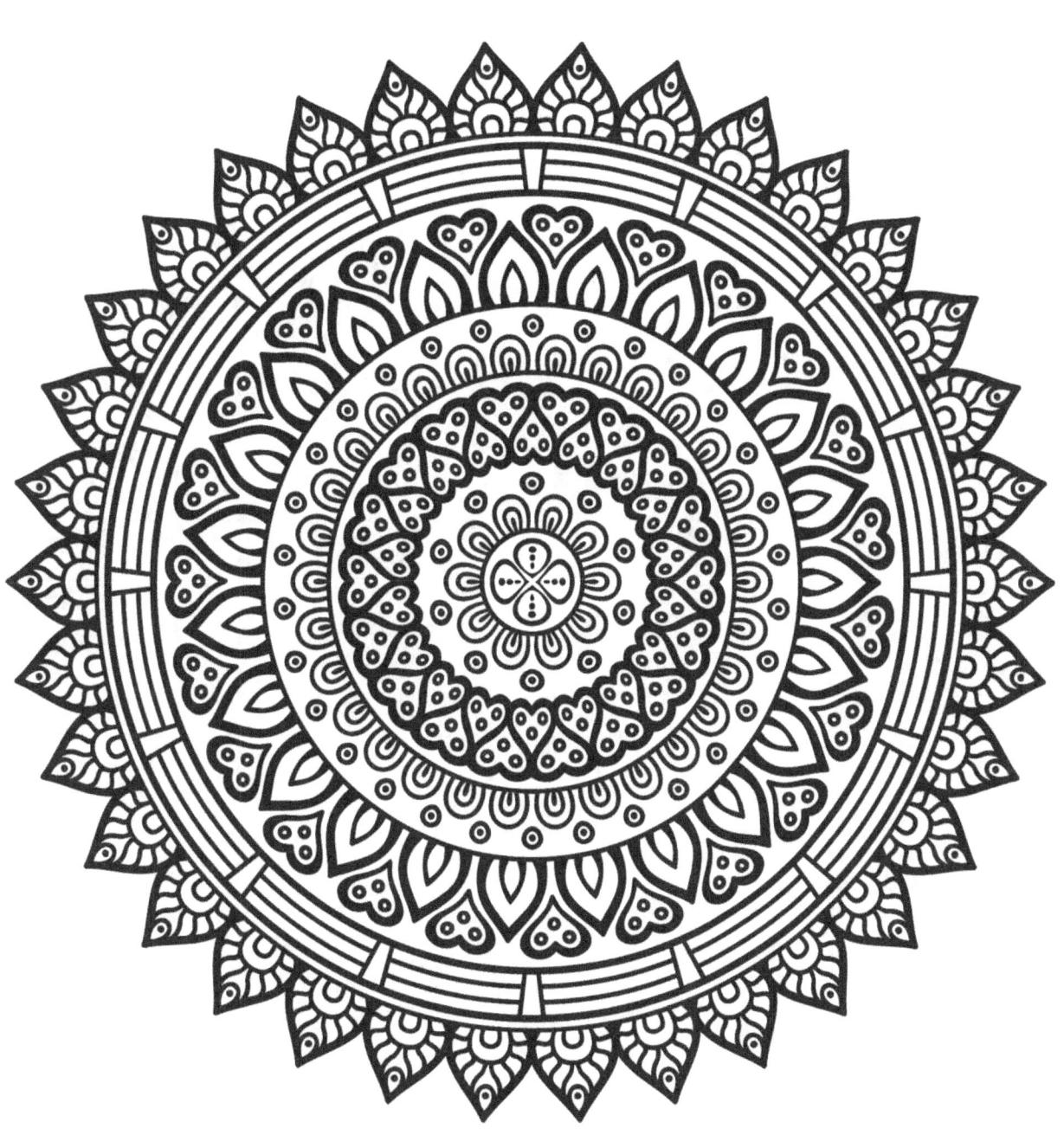

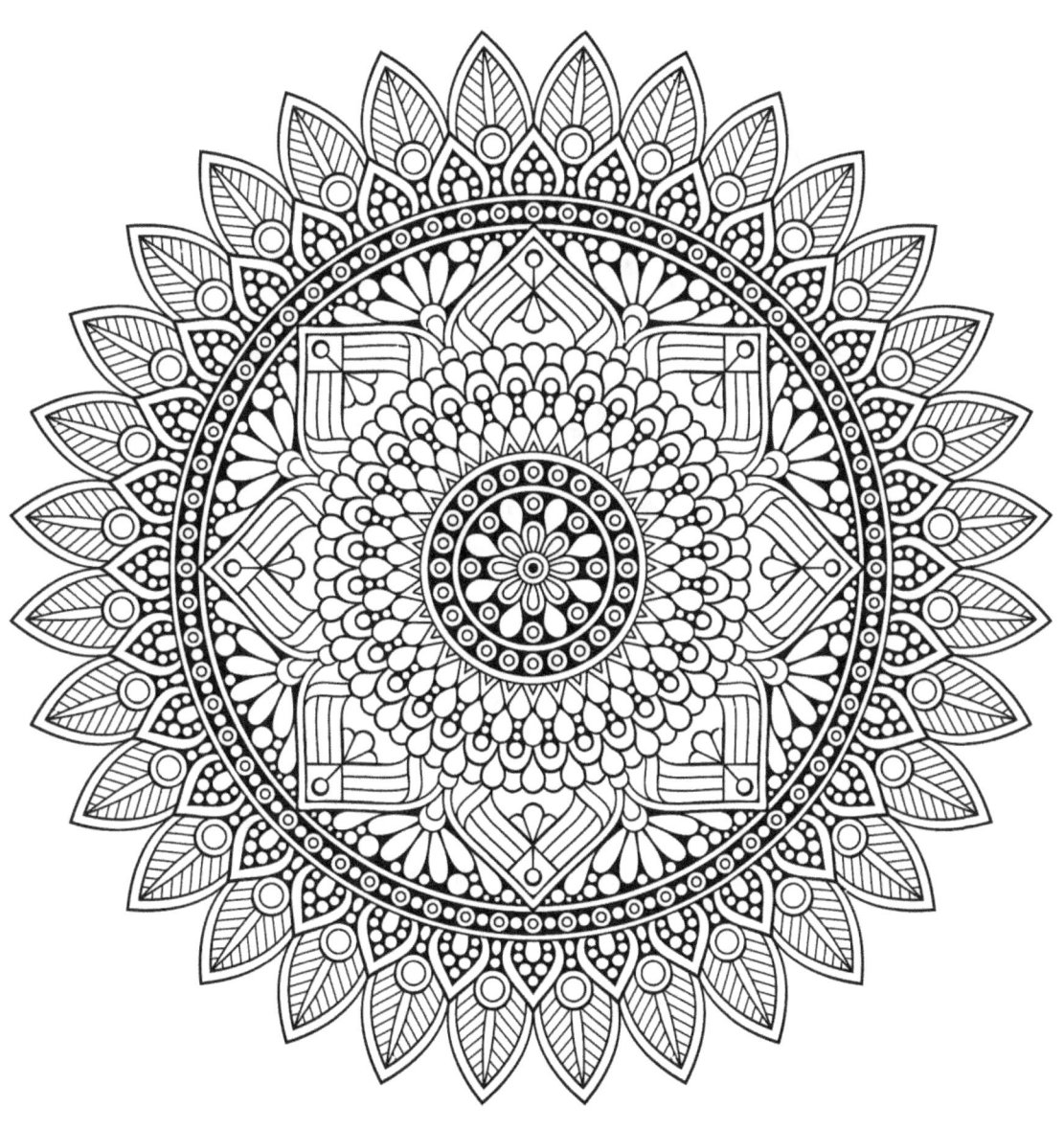

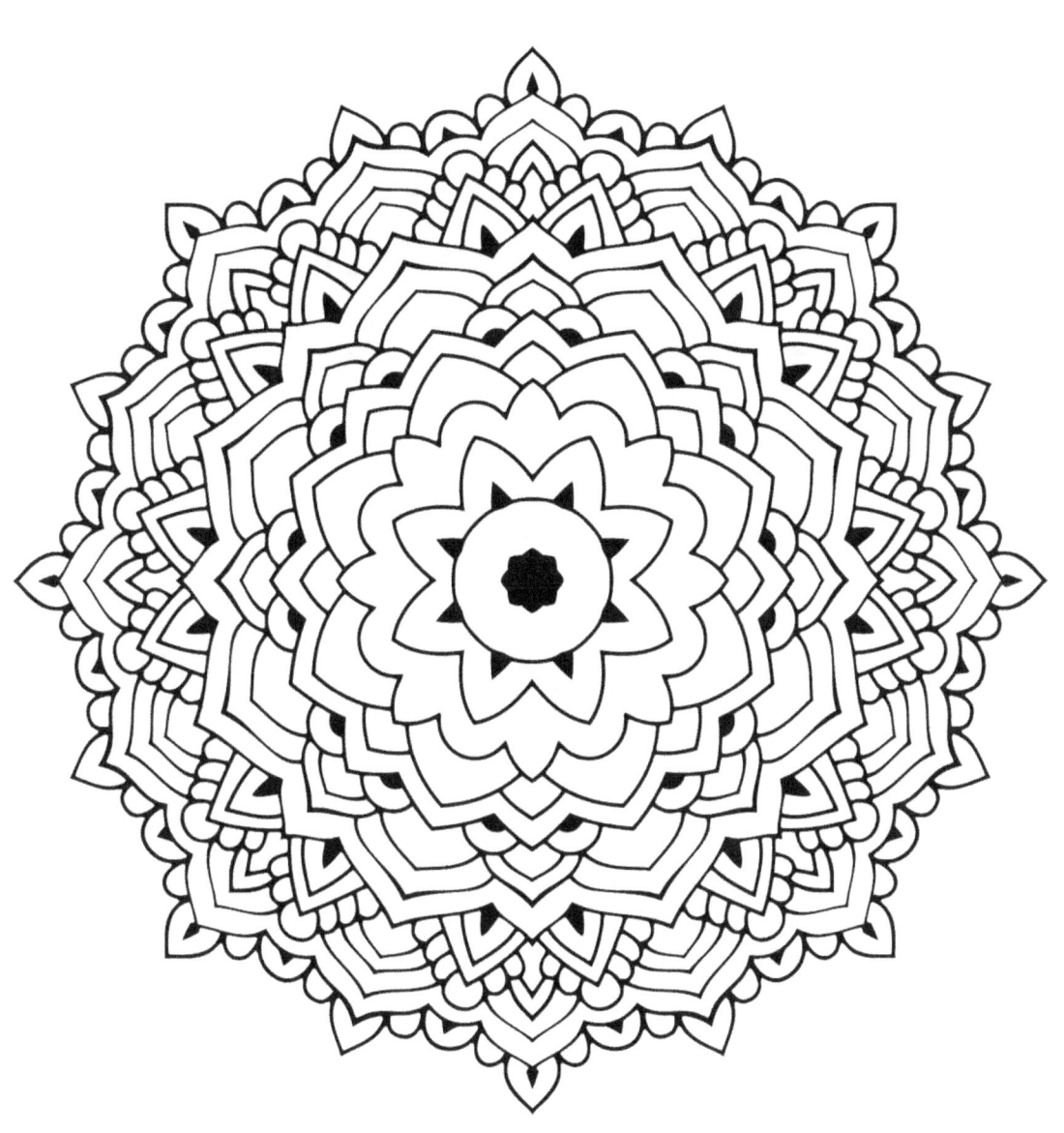

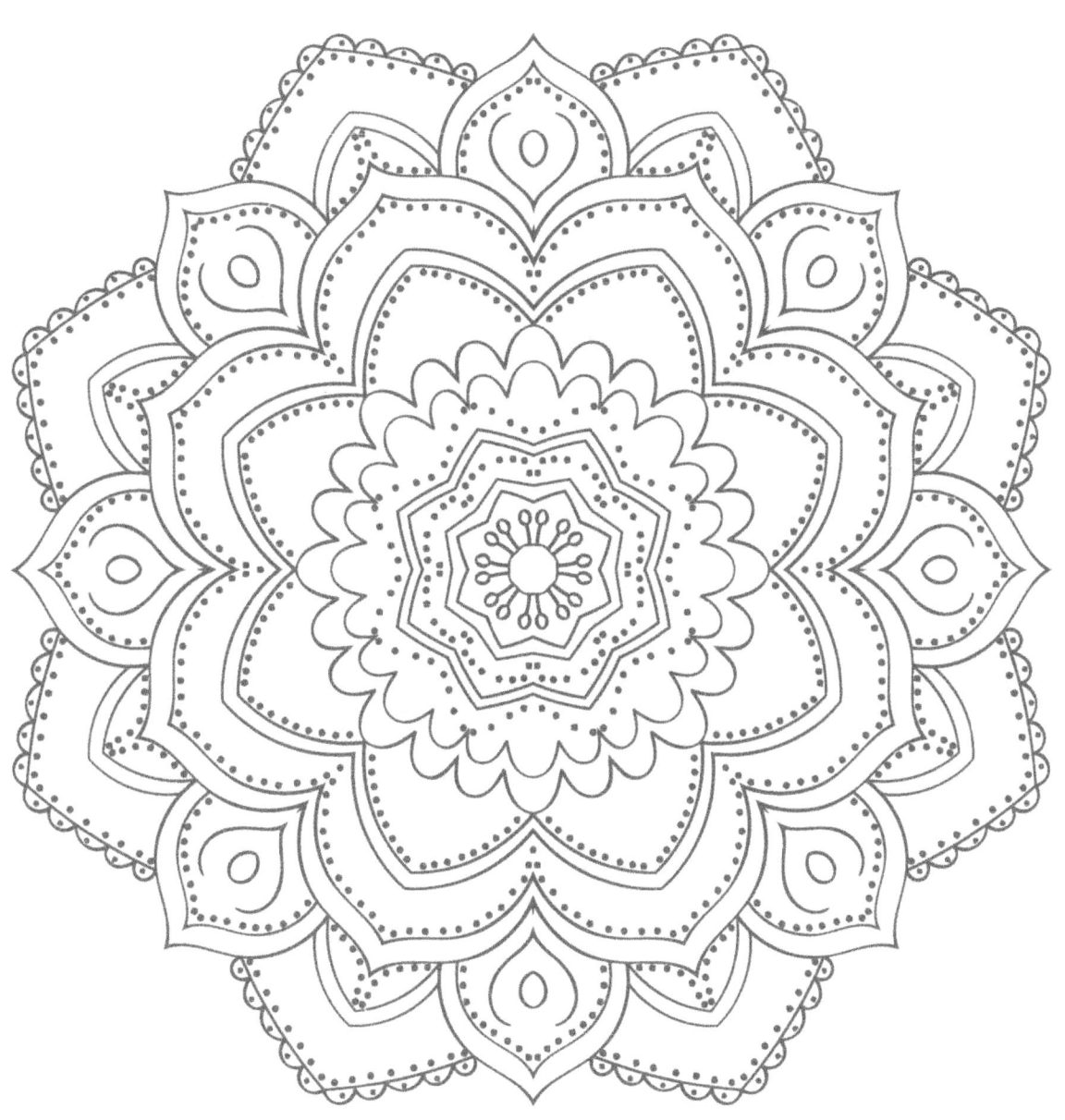

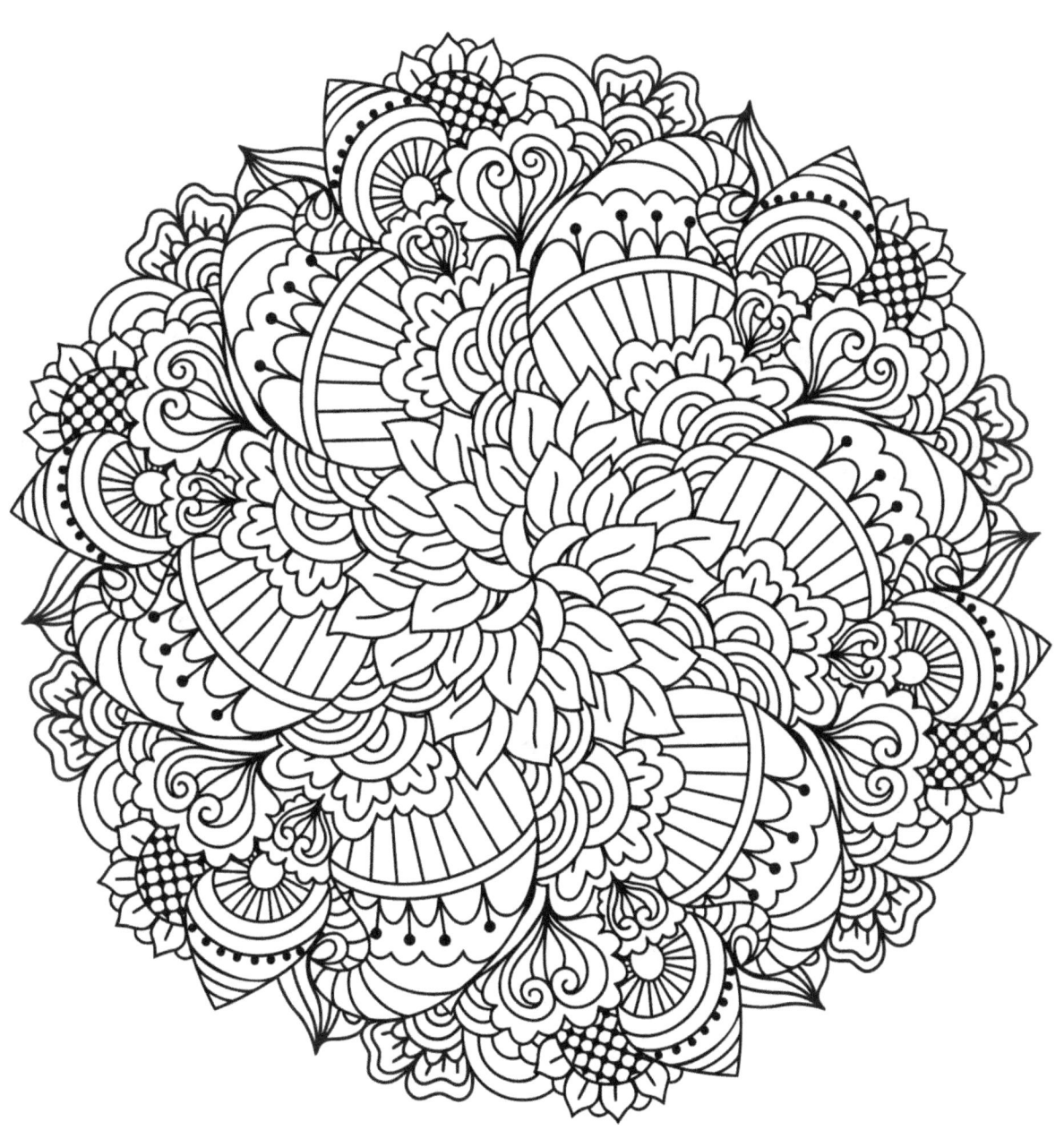

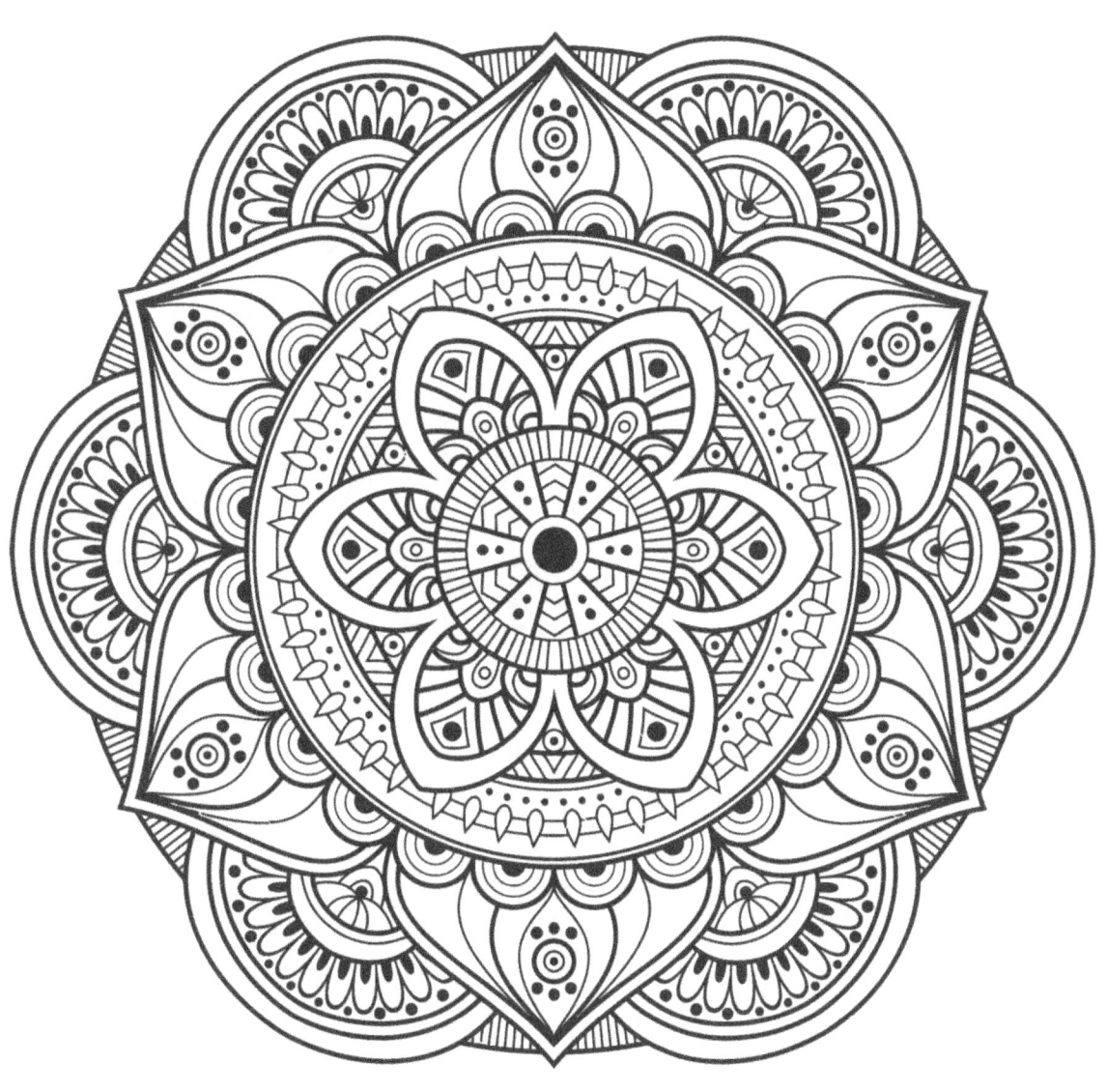

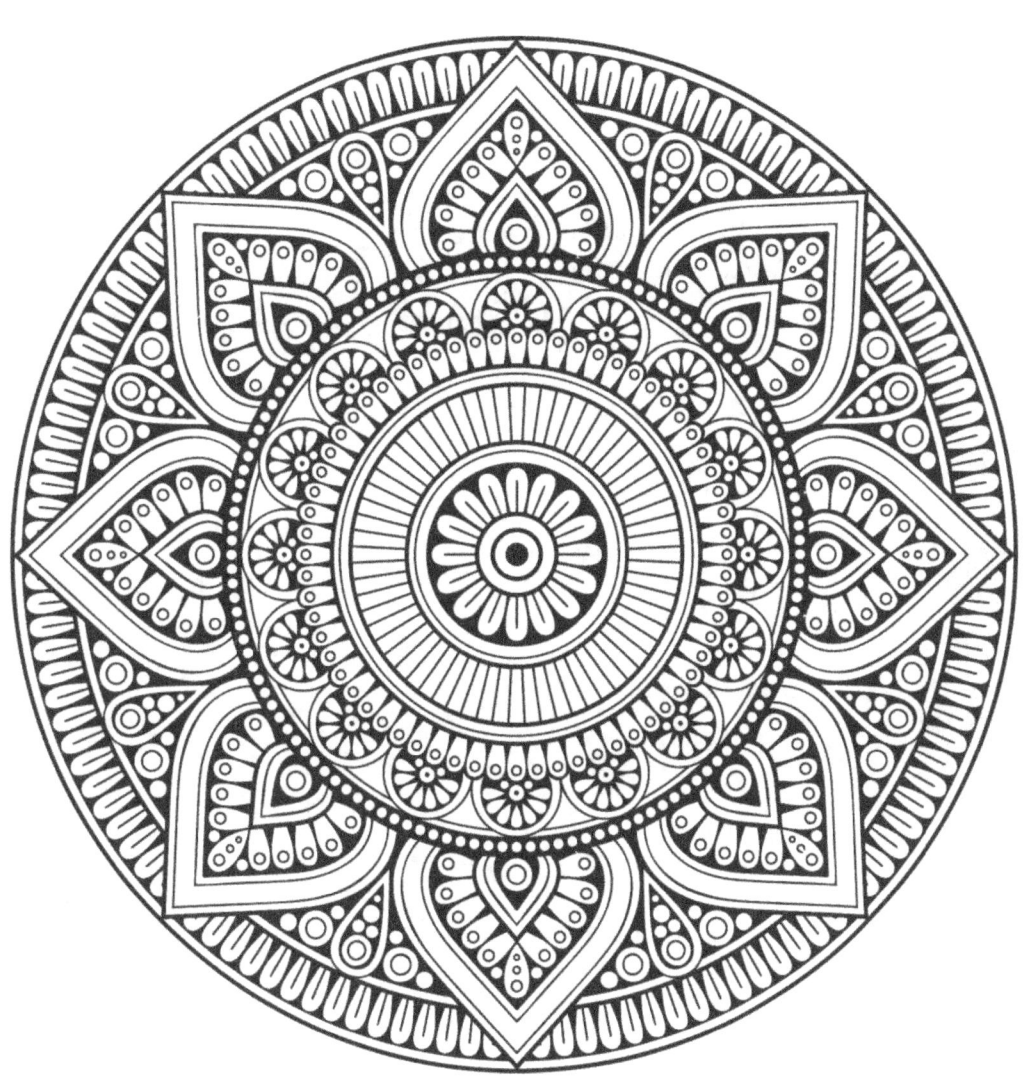

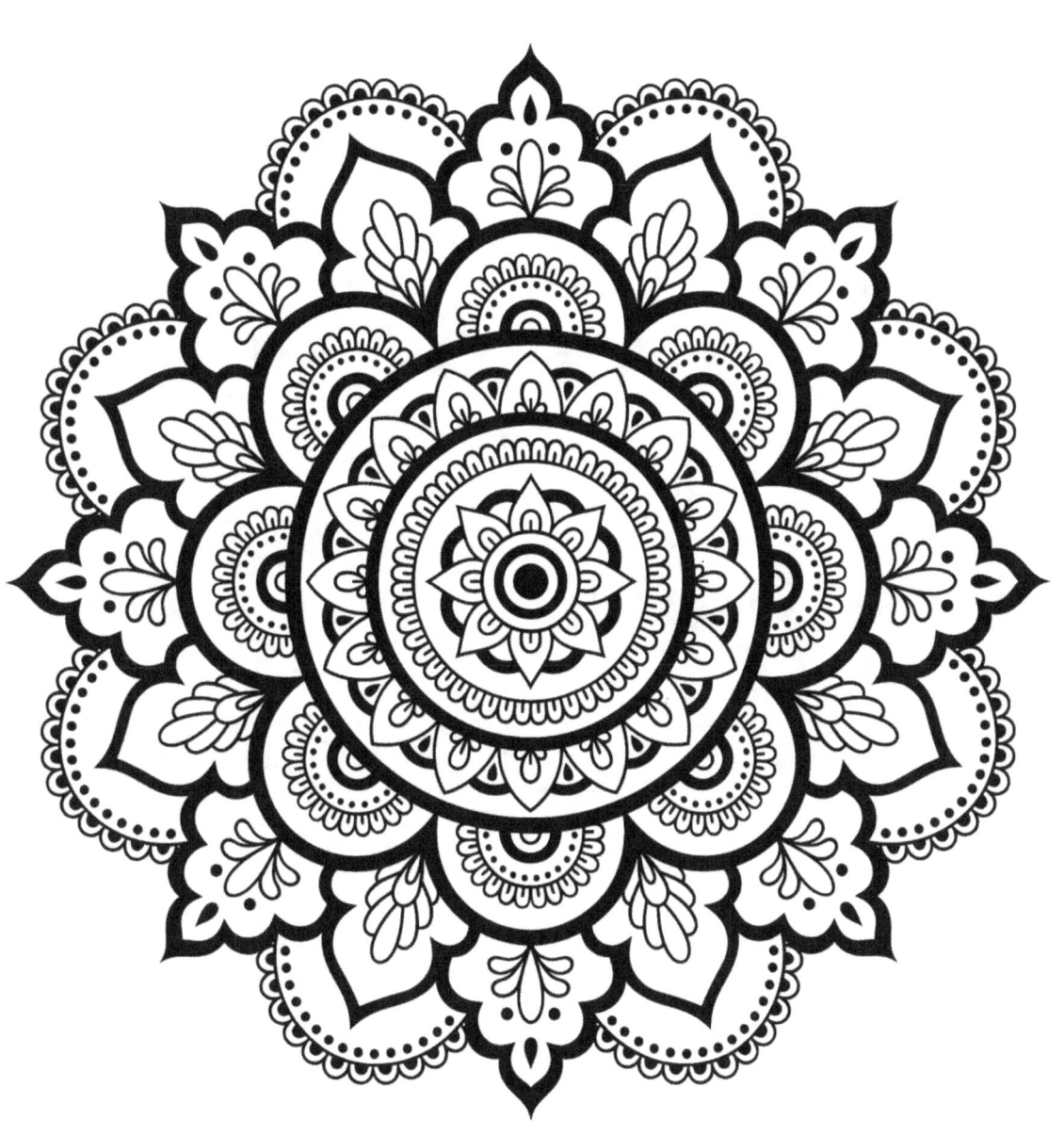

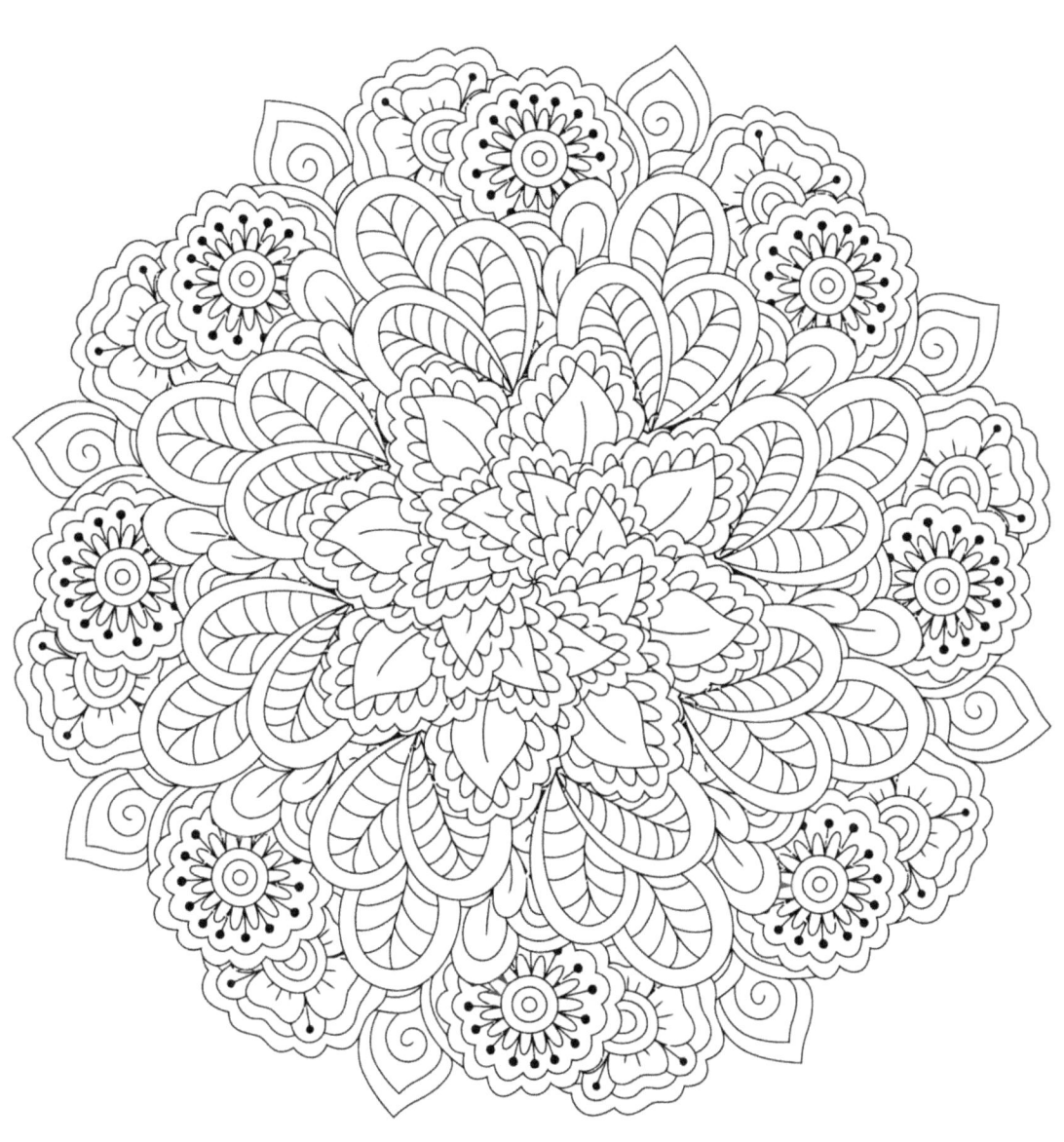

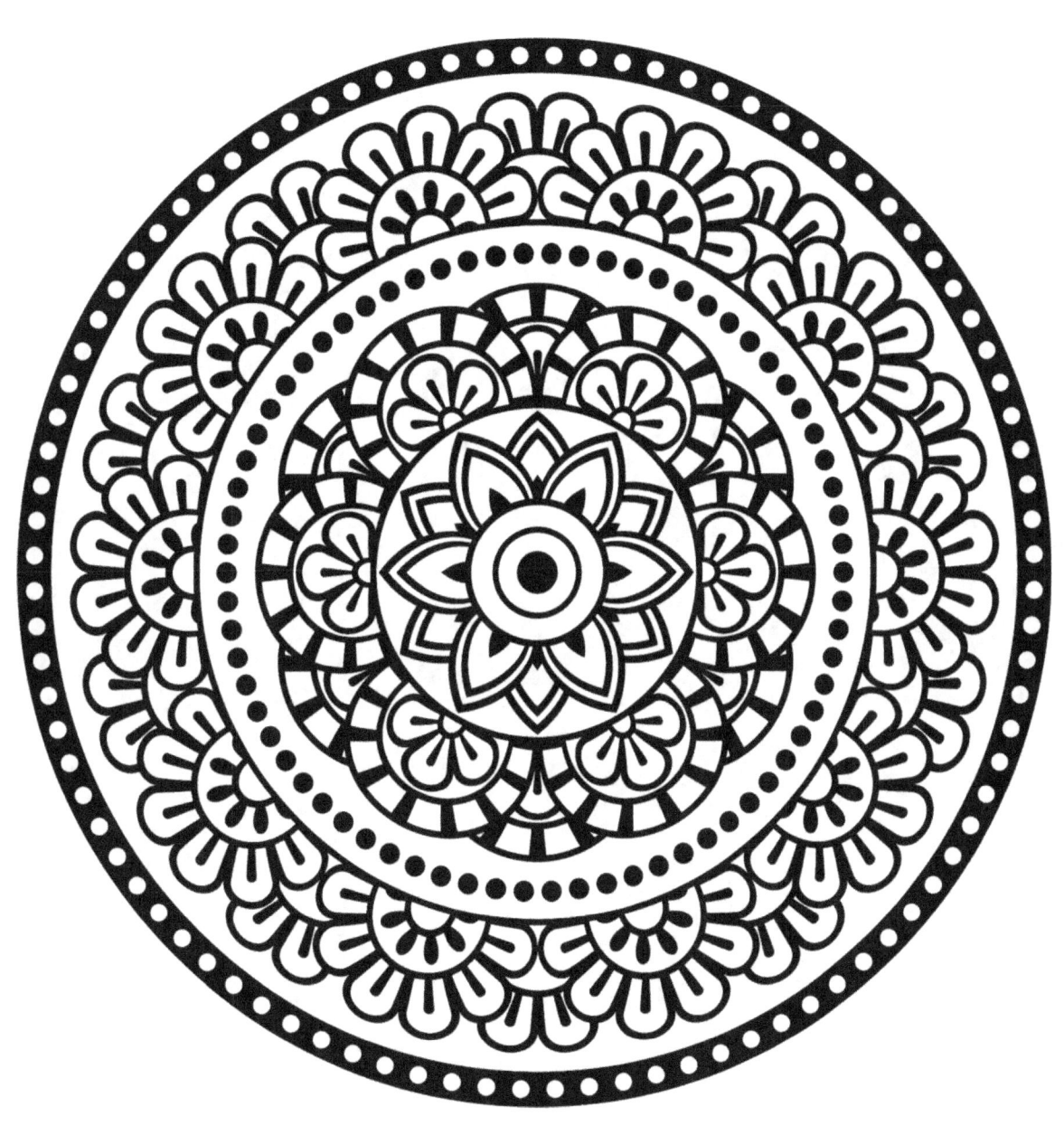

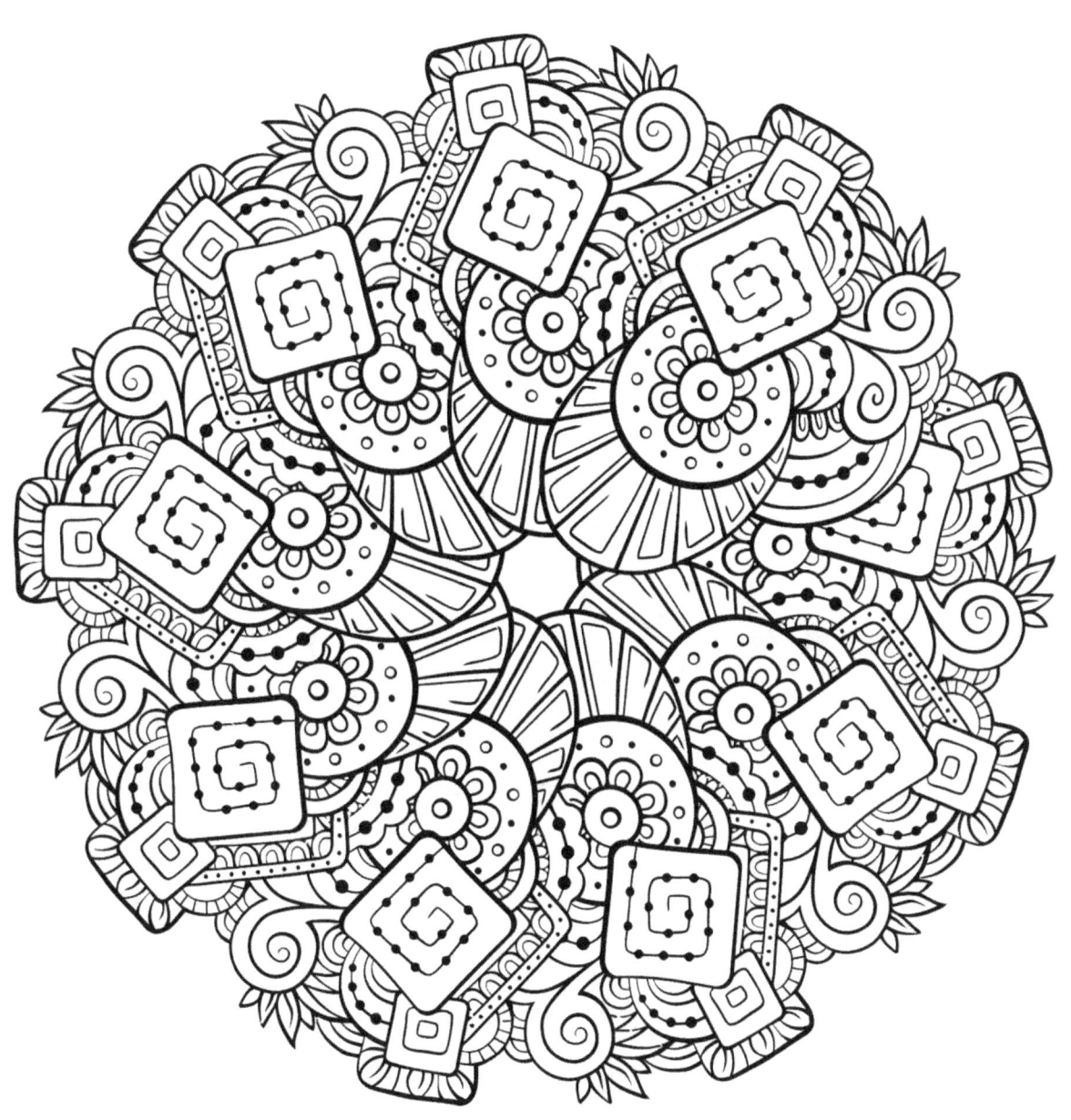

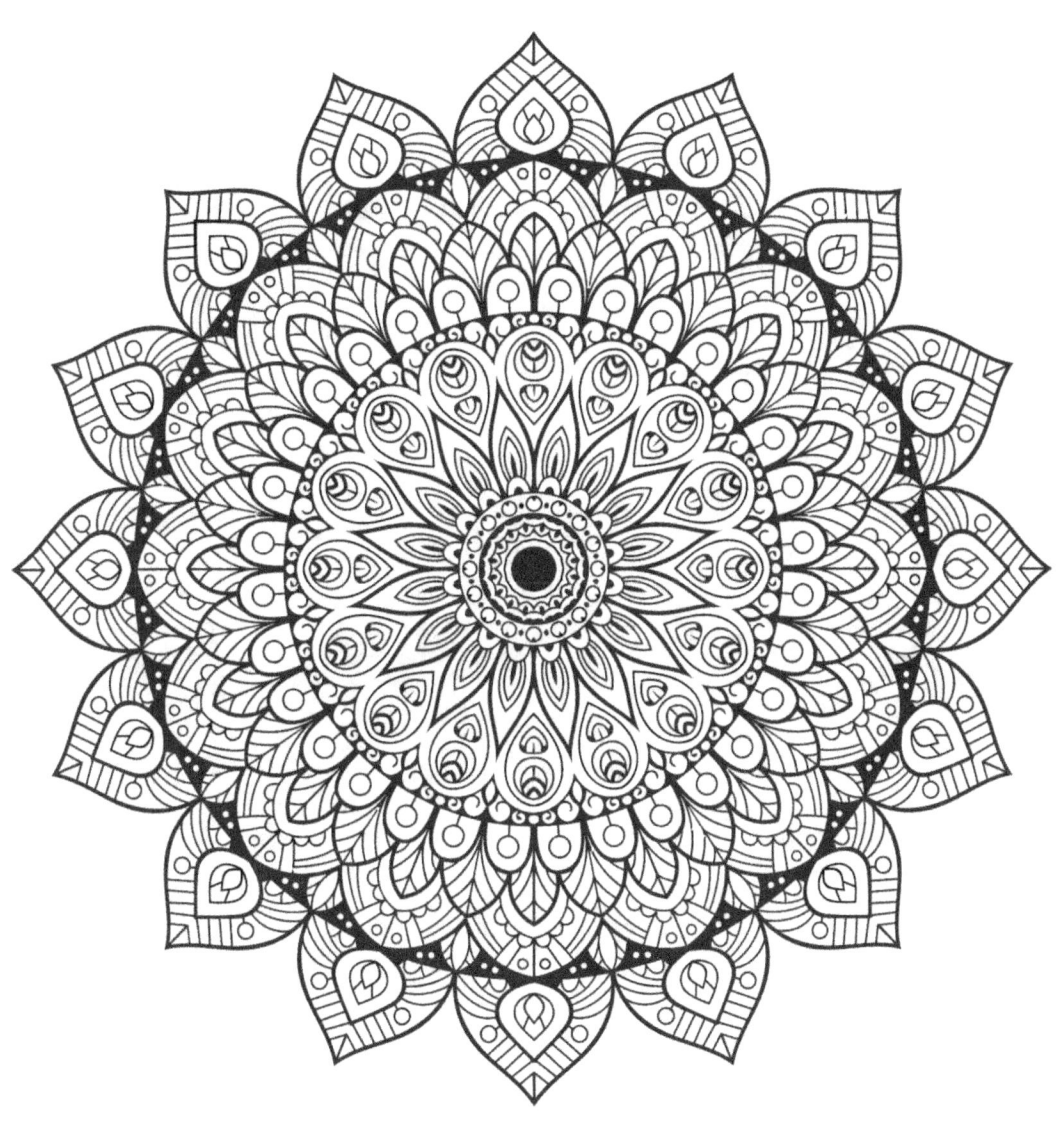

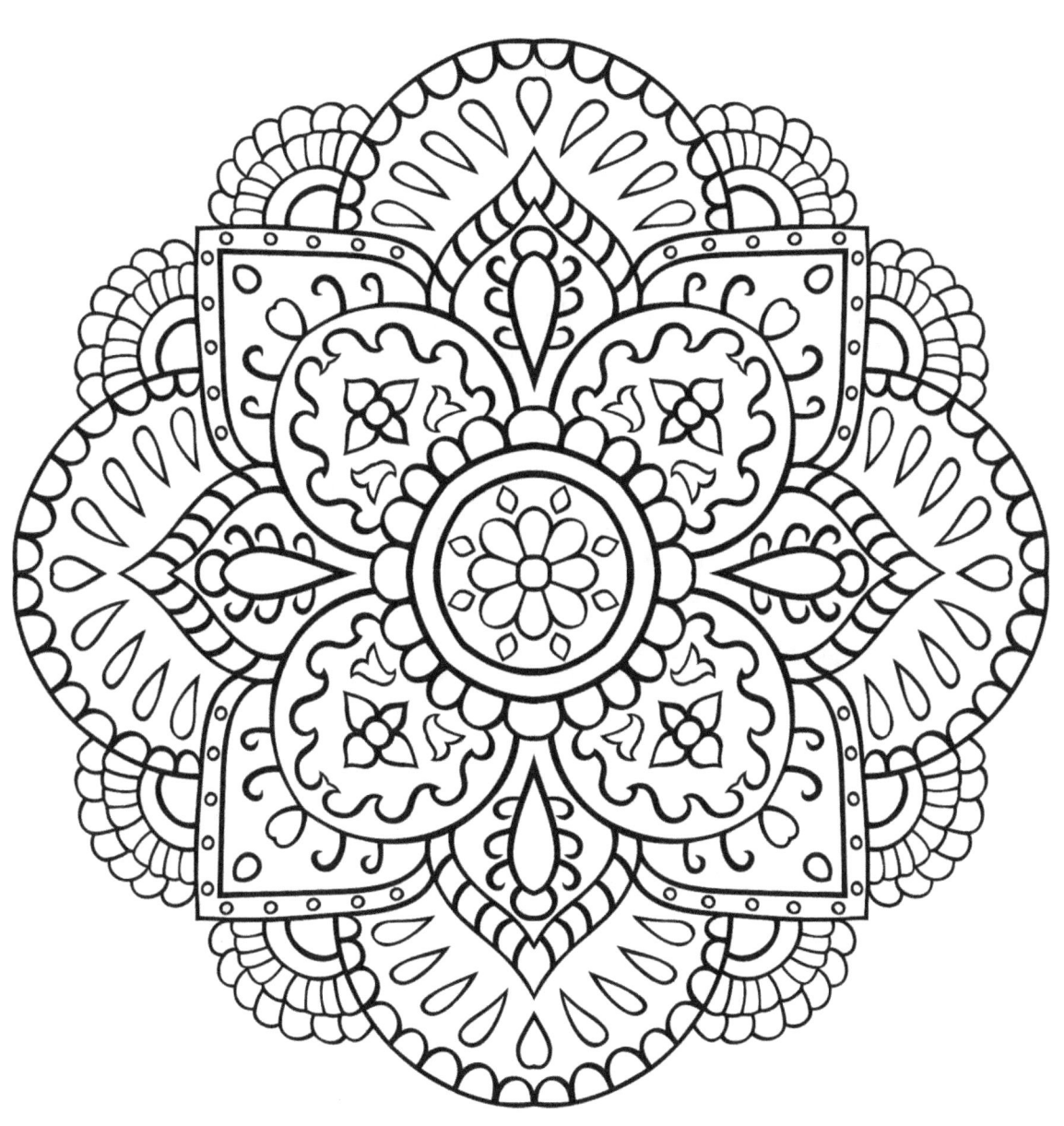

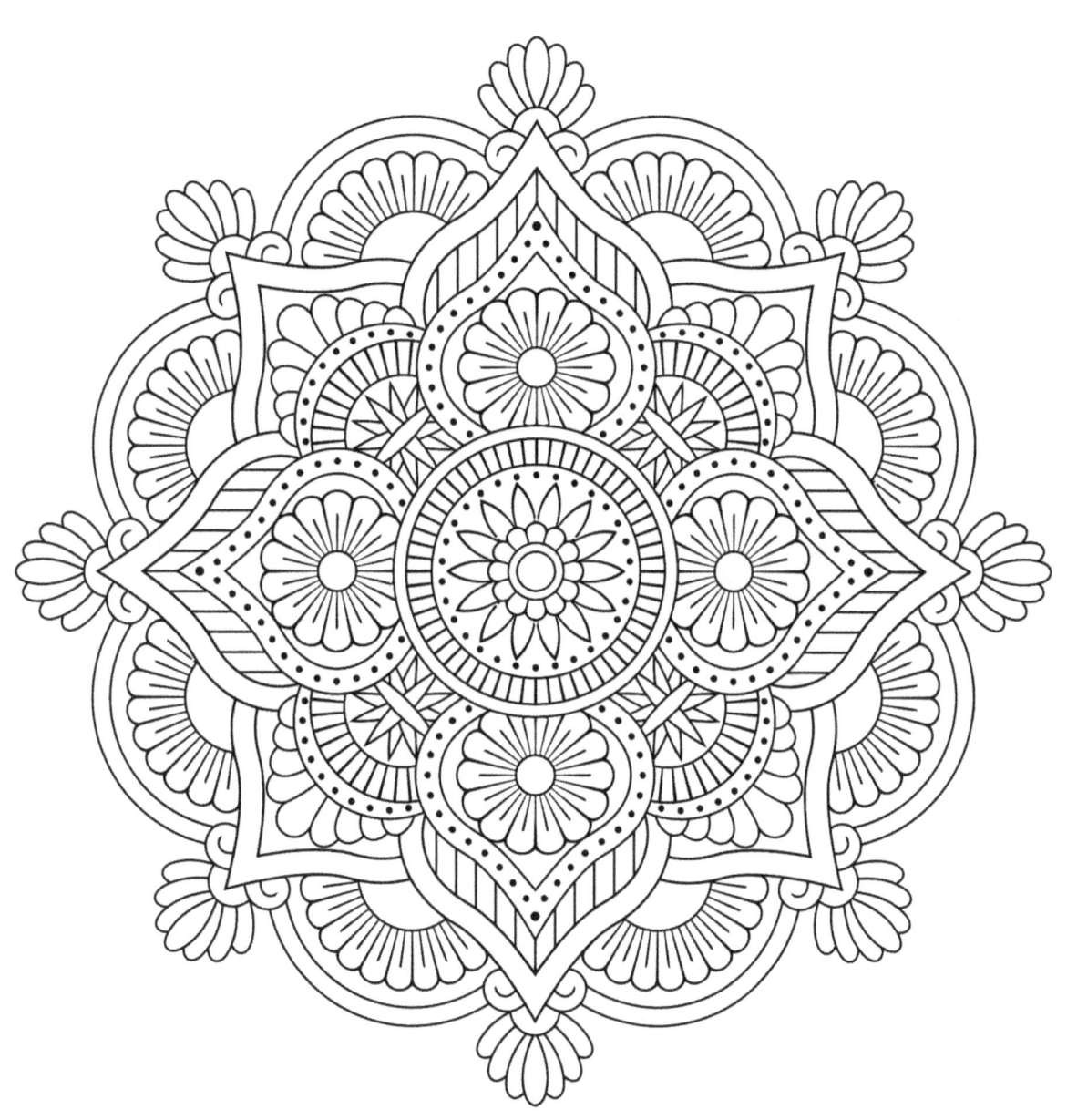